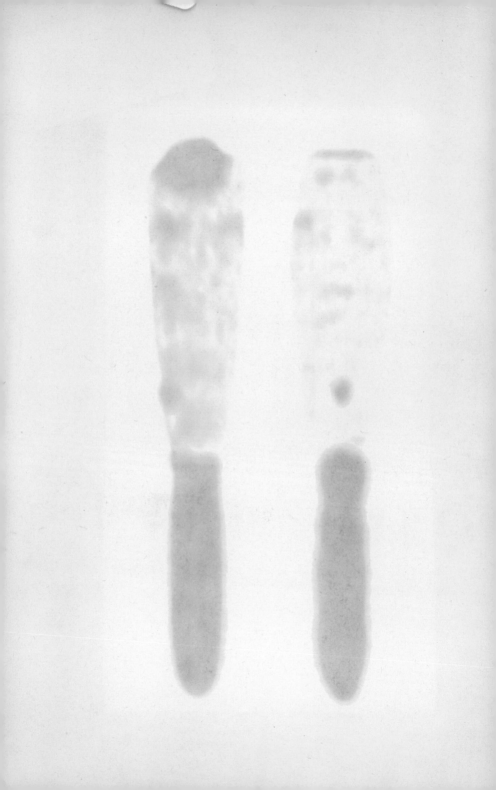

PHRASE AND PARAPHRASE
Some Innovative Uses of Language

Phrase and Paraphrase

Some Innovative Uses of Language

***

LILA R. GLEITMAN

EASTERN PENNSYLVANIA PSYCHIATRIC INSTITUTE
AND SWARTHMORE COLLEGE

HENRY GLEITMAN

UNIVERSITY OF PENNSYLVANIA

W · W · NORTON & COMPANY · INC ·  NEW YORK

To Abe and Eva, Eleanor and Claire

Contents

Tables and Figures

Preface

This monograph describes what happened when we asked a number of English speakers, representing different population groups, to paraphrase compound nouns. The answers they gave us were so systematic, so abstract, and so variously creative that we began to think we had perhaps hit upon a medium through which the speaker could show how he thinks about language. In pursuing the paraphrases our subjects devised we gained an enhanced appreciation of the power and scope of generative grammars; at the same time, we were led to revise some of our conceptions about how the study of formal grammars will ultimately fit into a psychological theory of language. The empirical step we have taken here is small and very tentative, but we hope it underlines the central role of paraphrasing in understanding the relations between speaker and linguistic system. These relations are our primary concern; for to us the goal of psycholinguistics is to show how the speaker's underlying knowledge is translated into verbal performance.

We have tried to put the experimental work into a context that will be accessible to both psychologists and linguists. To that end, we first present a brief sketch of the linguistic theory we have adapted in interpreting the results (essentially, the picture of generative grammar given by Noam Chomsky in 1965). Chapter 2 is a (highly selective) review of recent work in psycholinguistics that seems to be related to the transformational view. Chapter 3 presents an informal linguistic description of compound nouns; chapter 4 describes the series of experiments in paraphrasing; and chapter 5 is an attempt to give a coherent account of our results.

The experimental work evolved out of some pilot studies embarked upon as part of a dissertation (Gleitman, 1967). Thanks are due to Henry Hiz, who served as thesis adviser and offered valuable criticisms and suggestions about that work. Thanks are also due to Henry Hoenigswald for his generous help and support during that time. We are also indebted to Elizabeth Shipley and Carlota Smith for their help during the initial stages of this project in trying to understand the problem and devising possible ways to test the hypotheses.

We had the great benefit of critical readings of drafts of this manuscript by Dwight Bolinger, Jack Catlin, Julian Hochberg, Ulrich Neisser, Elizabeth Shipley, and David Williams. We are particularly indebted to Harris Savin, whose penetrating (and occasionally devastating) reviews of the manuscript led to extensive revision and clarification. Savin's substantive contributions to the grammatical description of chapter 3 are gratefully acknowledged.

Thanks are also due to Nicki Ollman and Rebecca Bernheim, who conducted the various experiments and contributed substantially to designing a system for scoring the responses. Mrs. Bernheim later collaborated with us in the design and analysis of the immediate-memory studies which are discussed in chapter 4 (Gleitman and Bernheim, 1968). We also thank Iris Patterson for her heroic labors in helping us put this manuscript together.

Financial support for the research was given by the National Institutes of Health under Grant #MH–07990 and by the Eastern Pennsylvania Psychiatric Institute. We wish to thank especially Richard Schultz of the Eastern Pennsylvania Psychiatric Institute for indispensable administrative support of the research reported here.

Phrase and Paraphrase
Some Innovative Uses of Language

1

Transformational Grammar: The Study of Linguistic Competence

In the short history of psycholinguistics, serious differences of opinion have arisen about what is meant when we say *language,* and thus about what the psychology of language is or ought to be. Very similar questions about the data for a theory of language have plagued linguists from time to time, even before their current associations with psychologists began. It is a historical curiosity that the battles among linguists concerning the philosophical propriety of data and method for studying language were concurrently enacted among psychologists studying learning and perception. The same issues have returned to harass the collaboration between linguists and psychologists. The aim of this joint effort, now called psycholinguistics, at first seemed eminently clear—linguists would inform psychologists concerning the nature of human language and psychologists would study the way it is learned and perceived and used. Ten years after the inception of the enterprise, these distinctions have become blurred indeed; for psychologists remain perplexed about the linguists' view of language, and linguists in turn have their own conception of what speakers know and how they know it.

Our purpose here is to try to find some meeting ground so

that the discourse between linguists and psychologists may become clearer and at least some superficial sources of misunderstanding laid to rest. To this general end, we briefly discuss in this chapter some of the fundamental empirical claims of the generative grammarians and some approaches to their experimental verification. In chapter 2, we review the recent psycholinguistic literature in the context of attempts to fit some facts and observations about behavior into the linguistic edifice. In subsequent chapters, we present some studies of language use that seem to us to suggest tentative directions for a reconciliation between language and its imperfect users.

Form of the Grammar

It is obvious that there are many ways to say the same thing. In fact, the ability "to say it in one's own words" is intuitively taken as an index of understanding. Certain kinds of paraphrase appear to be systematic in natural language. For example, so-called active and passive voice sentences of English convey essentially the same meaning, a fact known to grammarians of all persuasions. Zellig Harris (1957) and Noam Chomsky (1957) began the study of transformational grammars when they became aware that a basic inadequacy of traditional grammars was their failure to give a coherent account of such relationships among sentence types. It has been a continuing goal of modern linguistics to explain how people recognize and understand these relations.

Although parenthetical remarks in the appendices of traditional grammars acknowledged the existence of constructional paraphrase, it was rarely noted how pervasive, how characteristic of language, is the availability of alternative constructional types that keep meaning constant. Consider, for example, the following pairs:

The gate pinched the heiress.
The heiress was pinched by the gate.

Age is correlated with wisdom.
Age and wisdom correlate.

Marilyn is glorious to behold.
It is glorious to behold Marilyn.

In contrast, some sentences seem to be intrinsically ambiguous, and their ambiguity can be explicated by reference to other sentences which are paraphrases of the first but not paraphrases of each other; for example:

The heiress was pinched by the gate.
The gate pinched the heiress.
The heiress was pinched near the gate.

John ran down the block.
John ran the block down.
Down the block ran John.

Smoking volcanoes can be dangerous.
It can be dangerous to smoke volcanoes.
Volcanoes that smoke can be dangerous.

A basic goal of transformational grammars is to give an account of the constructional web that embodies these various relationships and to do so in a way that will support a description of the speaker-listener who deals with them every day in an effortless, scarcely conscious, fashion.[1]

The most serious constraints on the nature of such a grammar are imposed by the recognition that the use of language is productive and unlimited. In 1957, in *Syntactic Structures*, Chomsky pointed out that this self-evident truth—that speakers can produce and understand sentences that they never heard before—

[1] For ease of explication, we adopt the following terminological conventions: *utterance,* an act of speaking, or the object produced by such an act—a token, not a type; *sentence,* a sequence of words that is assigned at least one derivation by the grammar—a type, not a token; *ambiguity,* the case where more than one interpretation is available, the situation that results when more than one derivation is assigned to a sentence; *reading of a sentence,* one of these derivations or interpretations; *paraphrase,* a sentence with the same meaning as some other sentence, a sentence assigned the same deep structure as some other sentence.

must be the basis for any significant study of language structure. With this crucial insight the study of *projective* or *creative* aspects of language, long submerged in a stultifying behaviorist tradition, was renewed. The grammar is to describe not only what happens to have been said but must project whatever can be said in a language. The ability of speakers to form novel sentences and to understand how they fit into the web of constructional relations is taken as the basic phenomenon requiring descriptive counterpoint in a generative grammar. Chomsky set the problem this way in 1957:

> The fundamental aim in the linguistic analysis of a language L is to separate the *grammatical* sequences which are the sentences of L from the *ungrammatical* sequences which are not sentences of L and to study the structure of the grammatical sequences. . . . a grammar mirrors the behavior of the speaker who, on the basis of a finite and accidental experience with language, can produce or understand an indefinite number of new sentences. Indeed, any explication of the notion "grammatical in L" (i.e., any characterization of "grammatical in L" in terms of "observed utterance of L") can be thought of as offering an explanation for this fundamental aspect of linguistic behavior. (Pp. 13, 14)

The immediate task for linguistics, according to this view, is to develop a set of explicit rules (*a generative grammar*) that will describe the infinite set of sentences in some revealing way, imposing a description upon them that will explicate such concepts as ambiguity and paraphrase.

To account for the endless ways in which sentences are formed and are embedded within each other, Chomsky and his colleagues (*see* particularly, Chomsky, 1964*a*; 1965; Katz and Postal, 1964) have proposed grammars that consist of three components: a *syntactic* component, a *semantic* component, and a *phonological* component. Speaking very roughly, the structure generated within the syntactic component is "referred to" the semantic component for meaningful interpretation and to the phonological component for actual pronunciation. It will be relevant for our discussion to give a brief sketch of the form of the syntactic component, essentially as described by Chomsky in 1965.

The syntactic component of the grammar is said to contain

(1) *a base component* (a set of rewrite rules) that generates an indefinite number of *deep-structure* representations of sentences (*bases*); and (2) *a transformational component* (a set of transformational rules) that relates the bases to various *surface-structure* representations of sentences. The deep-structure representations are relevant to the semantic component (i.e., the deep-structure representations embody all meaningful relations in the sentence) and the surface-structure representations are relevant to the phonological component (they reflect the actual ordered set of formatives that are the basis for pronunciation).

Base-structure rules look familiar enough to anyone who has had the painful experience of parsing sentences. Strictures like those of traditional grammar (*Every sentence is composed of a subject and a predicate*) are reflected in rewrite rules of a comparably simple sort; for example:

[i] S → NP VP (read: *Sentence* can be rewritten as *Noun Phrase* followed by *Verb Phrase*)

[ii] NP → (T) N (*Noun Phrase* can be rewritten as *Article* (optionally) followed by *Noun*)

Bases for the infinite set of sentences are provided by building recursive devices into the rules. For example:

[iii] NP → (T) N (S)

By this rule, the symbol *S* (which also appears in rule [i]) may (optionally) be introduced again, that is, it is asserted that sentences may be embedded in noun phrases. Thus, indefinitely complex sentences are provided with a basis. A sequence such as *He who steals my purse steals trash* would require a complex basis since, as we shall see, *who steals my purse* is to be regarded as a sentence embedded in a noun phrase.

The deep-structure description, or derivation, can be shown as a tree diagram (*see* fig. 1a). Surface-structure descriptions, derived from the basis through the transformational rules, can be similarly displayed (*see* fig. 1b). The transformational rule can be conceived as an operation on the deep-structure tree that has the effect of producing the surface-structure tree.

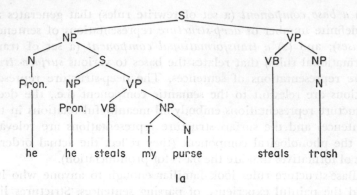

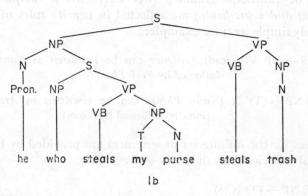

FIGURE 1. PARTIAL DEEP-STRUCTURE (*1a*) AND SURFACE-STRUCTURE (*1b*) REPRESENTATIONS OF THE SENTENCE *He who steals my purse steals trash.*

An abstract representation of all sentences can be derived with base rules, once recursive devices are employed. The transformational rules provide an apparatus for describing aspects of ambiguity and paraphrase in a natural way. For a single abstract sentential meaning (e.g., *boy* [actor] *bite* [action] *dog* [object]), there is a single deep-structure representation. The transformational rules applicable to this deep structure, however, may alternatively assign various surface structures (e.g., *The boy bites the dog; The dog is bitten by the boy*). Constructional paraphrases are, then, pairs of sentences with identical deep structures and different surface structures. The speaker, in some sense, should be aware that the sentences are different in structure, but alike in meaning. (*See* note 1, p. 14.)

Similarly, two different deep structures may eventuate in the same surface structure, thus creating an ambiguity. The sentence *Volcanoes smoke* can be embedded in the sentence (*Something*) *can be dangerous* in such a way that the output surface structure will be *Smoking volcanoes can be dangerous*. But the output surface structure is identical for certain embeddings of (*Someone*) *smokes volcanoes* in (*Something*) *can be dangerous*. The speaker is at least on occasion aware that there are two readings available (he laughs; he groans) for the single word sequence.

In short, generative grammars describe well-formed word sequences in the language, but they also describe an underlying "abstract" organization of sentences that is in no direct way given in the utterance itself, or in the corpus of all utterances. On this issue—the existence of a level of organization not directly reflected in the spoken forms of language—the generative grammarians departed from the views of their immediate empiricist forebears. The empiricist school (often called *structural linguistics*) under the leadership of Leonard Bloomfield had assumed on the contrary that regularities in utterances (i.e., distributional constraints on the occurrence of sounds, words, etc.) could form a sufficient basis for the study of language structure. Sharply reacting against this approach, Chomsky and other generative grammarians have shown that language organization is only remotely reflected in the actual forms of the spoken language (Chomsky, 1965). (*See* note 2, p. 15.)

Primary Empirical Claims

Generative grammar is designed to describe and illuminate certain basic features of language organization; primarily, the ability to classify sentences (i.e., separate the infinite set of well-formed sentences from the infinite set of nonsentences in the language), the ability to perceive paraphrase, and the ability to perceive constructional ambiguity. There can be little question of the elegance and intuitive appeal of the accounts that transformationalists have given of these abilities. On the basis of this considerable explanatory accomplishment, linguists can confidently assert that these grammars in some way reflect an underlying mental reality, an organization of language that impinges on the individual when he speaks and comprehends his native tongue.

It would seem at first glance that generative grammars constitute a set of empirical hypotheses about "language behavior" and that these hypotheses ought to be verifiable in some fairly direct ways by studying such behavior—after all, though the grammar gives no direct account of actual utterances, it appears to provide a direct account of the sources of various linguistic judgments. Is it the case, then, that we can ask people to exercise their abilities to classify, paraphrase, and discover ambiguities, thus determining the validity these concepts may have? It would be a fundamental misreading of the Chomskians' position to suppose that they believe the theoretical picture could be validated or invalidated by such simple tests. Though ultimately the theory must be adequate to describe the speaker's intuitions, these intuitions may not be uniformly accessible and may be reflected only very remotely in observable behavior. Thus, obtained judgments may provide no more reliable a basis for determining linguistic organization than do obtained utterances. For concreteness, let us consider a hypothetical test of the ability to classify.

Suppose we were to ask the average taxi driver, "Is the following a grammatical sentence in your dialect: *Colorless green ideas sleep furiously?*" We hesitate to set down his probable reply, but it surely will throw no light on his linguistic intuition. Worse, suppose we ask the average literary critic the same question. As a matter of historical fact, A. A. Hill (1961) did ask educated people this question, and it was not unusual for the respondent to rush off vowing to incorporate this sentence in his next poem. For various reasons, some less idiotic than others, we obviously cannot accept all aspects of the individual's performance in some putatively linguistic task as indications of his underlying organization of the matter of language. This problem seems superficial at first: even the lowly rat, full-well knowing the convolutions of his maze, may choose not to run. Some tact is obviously expected of the experimenter in distinguishing between "could not" and "would not." But the problem of determining the "empirical validity" of transformational grammars runs deeper, for these grammars have not generally been put forth as direct descriptions of any overt activity of any individual speaker at all. Chomsky (1965) writes:

> Linguistic theory is concerned primarily with an ideal speaker-listener, in a completely homogeneous speech-community, who knows its language perfectly and is unaffected by such grammatically irrelevant conditions as memory limitations, distractions, shifts of attention and interest, and errors (random or characteristic) in applying his knowledge of the language in actual performance. . . . To study actual linguistic performance, we must consider the interaction of a variety of factors, of which the underlying competence of the speaker-hearer is only one. . . . We thus make a fundamental distinction between *competence* (the speaker-hearer's knowledge of his language) and *performance* (the actual use of language in concrete situations). (P. 3)

The distinction between performance and competence must be recognized if any headway is to be made in understanding language structure. The structural (that is, empiricist) linguists were forced by doctrinaire considerations to accept every slip of the tongue as a legitimate linguistic datum: if utterances are to be studied directly, then the fact of having been uttered is the definition of grammaticalness. On the contrary, Chomsky assumes that there are obvious status differences among the word sequences that occur in speech; that what is actually said is only in part a consequence of strictly linguistic constraint. Thus the most cursory glance at a transformational grammar reveals *systematic* differences between the set of sentences described there and the set of spoken and written expressions. On the one hand, some sentences occur in the grammar but not in the spoken language. Some of these are too long or complex to be managed by the speaker; in principle these are unutterable. Others are too foolish or farfetched ever to gain any currency anywhere, anytime; in practice these are unspeakable. On the other hand there are many observed utterances that are not described in the grammar. Through inattention, interference, interruption, and so forth, the speaker produces utterances that the linguist has reason to exclude. Presumably, if we could strip away various contaminating factors in behavior, we might see the grammar bare. In sum, the grammar is not intended as a direct description of speech, nor of the various linguistic performances of an individual.

Given this viewpoint, it makes sense that transformational linguists have restricted their empirical inquiries to a few topics (the nature of linguistic judgments pertaining to classification, paraphrase, and ambiguity) and that they make such inquiries only of sophisticated informants—ignoring those who have a tin ear and those to whom the word *grammatical* may be obscure or provocative. These rarified aspects of performance easily provide the evidence necessary for describing the generalized linguistic homunculus, the Ideal Grammarian. In fact, the evidence cannot be collected in any other way. No confused informant can give the linguist the evidence he needs. No more can this bemused individual, by speech or act, convince the linguist that his apparent incompetence should be reflected as laws of language. By this account, the only incontrovertible empirical evidence for the psychological reality of generative grammar is the linguist's own performance in creating grammatical descriptions.

We thus begin with the notion of competence as a description of the ideal speaker-listener. In this sense, we understand the concept to refer to properties of the language, without prejudice to the ways these may be embodied in the speaker. Insofar as it is asserted only that grammars are descriptions of Language, that historical (though ever-changing) monument embodied in the literature and the rhetoric of the culture, there is no relevancy in submitting the grammars to further empirical review. Certainly school grammarians took this view of their enterprise, and if some misguided individual could be shown to disagree with these authorities, they changed the individual, not the rules of grammar. Indeed only the very weakest links are forged by the Chomskians between speaker and grammar: nowhere is it claimed that the speaker is aware of the rules, or that he can under all circumstances make judgments consonant with such rules, or that the rules directly explain how sentences are actually produced. It is claimed only that a generative and transformational grammar somehow impinges on various kinds of linguistic performance. Implicitly, it seems to be claimed in addition that a particular aspect of performance—the linguist's own act of making linguistic judgments—has special relevance to underlying competence and is singularly free from contaminating behavioral factors.

Secondary Claims and Some Methodological Questions

The linguistic description of the ideal speaker-listener is not sensibly subject to validation by "operational tests" of the speaker's behavior, for this behavior will be neither ideal nor purely linguistic. However, an extended definition of competence sometimes proposed does seem to be fair game for empirical review: competence is often equated with the tacit linguistic knowledge of the (actual, concrete) speaker-listener. At this point, the selection biases of the linguists—both in topics investigated and in subjects queried—have caused some dismay among critics (usually psychologists) more sensitive to matters of sampling who could not help asking what the population was to which the sample results were to apply; and in what way.[2] It seems obvious that linguists are making some further empirical claims when they impute the grammar to the individual speaker.

Only the most sophisticated speakers can supply the exquisite judgments required for writing a grammar. Most speakers fail to understand the question that is being asked and fail to give

2 Psychologists themselves, to be sure, have approached the study of language by means so bizarre that their relevance to any subject matter is seriously in question. Though we find them rigorously sampling large populations randomly, we find that they have traditionally asked subjects to do things—such as memorizing nonsense syllables—that have no discernible connection with fundamental problems in the psychology of language. Linguists have often laughed off psychologists' objections by referring to this dismal history of objective empirical testing; but this is no more than polemics.

stable responses to questions about syntactic structure. What measure of the competence of the Ideal Grammarian shall we grant to these individuals? The question is difficult: after all, the taxi driver, the poet, a man with laryngitis, may have more severe *performance* problems than the rest of us, and this may not bear at all on their *competence*.

Seizing this bull by the horns, the transformational linguists propose a simple solution: they grant all of the grammar to all individuals. They make the rather puzzling assertion that competence (knowledge, intuition about the language) is identical for all speakers. This summary endowment immediately resolves the problem of representative sampling, but it seems to us that this further claim, the claim of *equal competence among speakers,* lacks the stamp of intuitive authority that marks the primary conceptualizations of generative grammar.

Chomsky writes (1964*a*): "On the basis of a limited experience with the data of speech, each normal human has developed for himself a thorough competence in his native language." In this context, competence should be understood to refer to the speaker's capacity for acquiring (any) natural language under reasonable circumstances and also to the product of that learning, the "internalized generative grammar" in terms of which the adult speaks and understands his language. Katz (1964) claims that "variation in performance with intelligence [in nonlinguistic tasks] . . . contrasts with the performance of speakers with respect to some purely linguistic skill, where no significant individual differences are found."

This claim for equal competence is very strong indeed and requires from the believer a certain act of faith. Our difficulty in understanding this apparently tangential claim is intensified when we read that, at least for some of the Chomskian linguists, the issue has been reduced to one of definition. Katz (*ibid.*) writes, "a necessary condition for something to be part of the subject matter of a linguistic theory is that each speaker be able to perform in that regard much as every other does." If when individual differences are found we are to be told, by virtue of this very finding, that the tasks for which we found them must therefore be extralinguistic, then the hypothesis of equal competence is doomed to invulnerability.

Of course we can ask no one for a direct display of competence, but it would certainly appear that we have some obligation to ask whether all speakers can provide the hints (the judgments and the utterances) that led us to concede the grammar to elite populations. Otherwise, we are locked in an irresolvable paradox: any failure can be called a failure of performance, every success a reflection of competence. It is of primary interest to know in what sense the concept of competence refers to a universal human ability. Obviously no one wishes to claim that Shakespeare's apparent verbal facility reflects no linguistic capacities superior to our own. Surely style, fluency, the ability to pun, to write generative grammars, to read *The New York Times,* are in some way related to linguistic knowledge, and surely these skills vary among individuals. If the concept of competence is valuable (and in our opinion the study of language can scarcely proceed without it), it needs—it deserves—considerable clarification. What is competence competence at?

Not surprisingly, the claim for equal competence is accompanied by a more general nativist approach. Chomsky (1965) and his associates have argued that the faculty of language represents a largely native pattern of predispositions and behaviors in mankind, relatively immune to environmental control and direction, and more or less independent of other aspects of cognition.

> The structure of particular languages may very well be largely determined by factors over which the individual has no conscious control and concerning which society may have little choice or freedom. On the basis of the best information now available, it seems reasonable to suppose that a child cannot help constructing a particular sort of transformational grammar to account for the data presented to him, any more than he can control his perception of solid objects or his attention to line and angle. Thus it may well be that the general features of language structure reflect, not so much the course of one's experience, but rather the general character of one's capacity to acquire knowledge—in the traditional sense, one's innate ideas and innate principles. It seems to me that the problem of clarifying this issue and sharpening our understanding of its many facets provides the most interesting and important reason for the study of descriptively adequate grammars and, beyond this, the formulation and justification of a general linguistic theory that meets the condition of explanatory adequacy. (P. 59)

The question of a native component in language capacity (like the question of equal competence) bears only indirectly on the validity of transformational grammars as psychological models of language. If language capacity is innate and is an expression of the nature of mind and cognition, this does not argue in favor of any particular description of language. Similarly, if language has only a remote relevance to innate cognitive functioning in man, transformational grammars may still be relevant to a psychological theory of language. Nevertheless, the hypothesis of nativism has been advanced by the generative grammarians and it has some clear, if indirect, relevance to the kind of language theory that will ultimately serve psychology.

In recent years, psychologists have begun to study language within the theoretical framework provided by generative grammar. Some of this work has begun to clarify the ways in which the linguistic model may pertain to individual language learning and use and the ways other aspects of behavior may interweave with linguistic organization in linguistic behavior. Other research has been designed to investigate some of the apparent empirical claims of the grammarians. Interpretation of much of the experimental literature is hampered by the considerable difficulty of distinguishing knowledge from various other determinants of linguistic performance.

In the chapter that follows, we review the psycholinguistic literature in so far as it seems to bear on transformational theory. In succeeding chapters, we will present some studies of innovative uses of language and ask how such matters of performance are related to a theory of grammar. We believe our experimental work points to a more direct relation between aspects of speaker and system than might have been expected on theoretical grounds. At the same time, we shall have cause to take issue with some marginal conjectures of the grammarians, particularly the claim for equal competence.

NOTES

1. We use the terms actor-action-object only as a reference to whatever objects and relations may constitute this level of description; no adequate formulation is currently available. More generally, we should

make clear that the descriptive scheme we are outlining here (essentially the 1965 proposal of Chomsky) is in part programmatic and not universally accepted in detail even among transformationalists. The very distinction between this "deep" structural level and a level of semantic organization is quite unclear at this time. For some illuminating recent discussion of these issues, *see* particularly Fillmore, 1968; and McCawley, 1968. In the discussion of the psycholinguistic literature and our own experimental work, these controversies will hardly arise. There is broad agreement that many linguistically and psycholinguistically significant issues can be approached using this formulation.

It should be noted throughout, however, that we restrict our discussion to "constructional" paraphrase and ambiguity. It is a matter of considerable current controversy whether concepts such as synonymity can conveniently be encompassed by the same kind of analysis—whether, for example, the paraphrases *the boy bit the dog* and *the juvenile male human bit the domestic canine* can usefully be said to have the same deep structure.

2. Few today would seriously attempt to defend the radical behaviorism of American linguists of the 1930s and 1940s, who maintained that the forms of spoken language have a unique status among data for a theory of language and that judgments of grammaticalness and the like are mentalistic and, hence, to be rejected. However, in the haste to escape from this restrictive and biasing viewpoint, generative grammarians have often been unduly forgetful of some of Bloomfield's contributions to science and sanity in the study of language. As everyone knows, the empiricist movement was a rather reasonable reaction to the absolutistic and moralistic approaches that had dominated theories of language for two centuries (and still dominate our schools and much lay belief). The episodic character of traditional grammar, its vague, ill-formulated, and untestable pronouncements about correctness and propriety in speech certainly demanded some response; and no doubt the burden of proof lay on those who had postulated an unobservable abstract organization underlying speech. The empiricists believed that the continuing failure to find a linguistic description arose from the traditionalists' tendency to describe language as it ought to be, rather than as it was. This judgment scarcely seems surprising when we consider the grounds on which grammarians at the turn of the century attempted to justify distinctions between what is said and what is somehow "proper" speech. For example, Greenough and Kittredge (1962 ed.) discuss *slang:*

. . . a peculiar kind of vagabond language, always hanging on the outskirts of legitimate speech, but continually straying or forcing its way into the most respectable company. . . . All human speech, even the most intimate, is intended for the ears of others, and must therefore have a certain dignity, a certain courtesy, out of respect to one's hearers if not to one's self. Now slang, from the very fact that it *is* slang, that it is not the accepted medium of communication, has a taint of impropriety about it which makes it offensive. Again the very currency of slang depends on its allusions to things which are not supposed to be universally familiar or generally respectable; and hence it is vulgar, since it brings in associations with what is for the moment regarded as unknown or in bad repute. . . . Finally, the unchecked and habitual use of slang (even polite slang) is deleterious to the mind. (Pp. 72–73)

As a consequence of this concern with nicety, traditional grammars often display a lopsided preoccupation with just those points in the language where class dialects subtly diverge. Similar biases are evident in comparisons among languages; as witness this passage from the great Danish grammarian, Otto Jespersen (1955 ed.), who here compares the "masculine" English language with Hawaiian:

I select at random, by way of contrast, a passage from the language of Hawaii: "I kona hiki ana aku ilaila ua hookipa ia mai la oia me ke aloha pumehana loa." Thus it goes on, no single word ends in a consonant, and a group of two or more consonants is never found. Can anyone be in doubt that even if such a language sound pleasantly and be full of music and harmony the total impression is childlike and effeminate? You do not expect much vigour or energy in a people speaking such a language; it seems adapted only to inhabitants of sunny regions where the soil requires scarcely any labour on the part of man to yield him everything he wants, and where life therefore does not bear the stamp of a struggle against nature and against fellow-creatures. (Pp. 3–4)

Given the tenacity of such views, and the lack of concern for any empirical authority in establishing the rules of the game, it seems hardly surprising that the empiricists tried to find some observable data source (obtained speech) for their inquiries into language. Bloomfield writes, "The discrimination of elegant or 'correct' speech is a by-product of certain social conditions. The linguist has to observe it as he observes other linguistic phenomena" but "this is only one of the problems of linguistics and, since it is not a fundamental one, it can be attacked only after many other things are known." Many of the empiricists seem to have believed that no nonarbitrary formulation of the notion of well-formedness—outside dialectology—would be found; for example, Nida (1949) comments, "If any judgments are to be passed upon the acceptability or so-called correctness of some usage, these are left to the anthropologist and sociologist for an objective statement of the factors in the society which make certain persons more socially prominent and hence make their speech more acceptable, or to the man on the street, who is thoroughly accustomed to forming judgments upon the basis of his own egocentric attitudes and limited knowledge." Study of perceived well-formedness was thus effectively banished as a linguistic topic.

In the overwhelming counterreaction by transformationalists against this position, and with the insight that a study of speech could not in principle provide sources for an explanation of linguistic judgments, it has often been overlooked that Bloomfield was consistently aware both of the innovative aspects of language use and of the centrality of this issue in syntax. He writes (1933):

> It is obvious that most speech-forms are regular, in the sense that the speaker who knows the constituents and the grammatical pattern can utter them without ever having heard them; moreover, the observer cannot hope to list them, since the possibilities of combination are practically infinite. For instance, the classes of nominative expressions and finite verb expressions in English are so large that many possible actor-action forms—say, *a red-headed plumber bought five oranges*—may never before have been uttered. . . . A grammatical pattern (sentence-type, construction, or substitution) is often called an *analogy*. A regular analogy permits a speaker to utter speech-forms which he has not heard; we say that he utters them *on the analogy* of similar forms which he has heard. (P. 275)

When similar programmatic remarks about the content of a generative grammar are made by seventeenth century rationalists, transformational linguists are happy enough to be counted among their heirs.

Bloomfield and his contemporaries avowedly sought a psychological basis for these constructional skills. They were unfortunately content with associationist theories then accepted by many psychologists that not only could not illuminate linguistic judgments, but could not—or so we now believe—support a theory of acquisition. (However, the nowadays much maligned search for explicit "discovery procedures" by these same linguists can perhaps be more sympathetically understood as an attempt to account for the acquisition of language by a device which the behaviorist psychologists had endowed very scantily.) For all the apparent objectivity of the empiricist position, its proponents seem to have failed to see the seriousness of the psychological and linguistic claims that were cloaked by the term *analogy* (or by Skinner's [1957] latter-day equivalent, *latent repertoire*).

But if Bloomfield is to be censured for a complacent mechanism and a bias toward the study of speech forms, he cannot be faulted for lacking insight into the unlimited aspects of language and the relevance of these to a psychological theory. No more should he be burdened with the philosophical enthusiasms of some of his followers who, as a kind of literary conceit, could joyously embrace the very sterility of their conceptualization. Martin Joos (1958), applauding the replacement of phonological explanations by "a sober taxonomy," quintessentially celebrates the demise of mentalism: "Children want explanations, and there is a child in each of us; descriptivism makes a virtue of not pampering that child."

2
Psycholinguistics: The Study of Linguistic Performance

Generative grammar has readily captured the imagination of many psychologists. This is not surprising. The empiricist approach after more than sixty years of effort can boast few insights into human complex processes; it has not even succeeded in pacifying the unruly data of rat behavior. Given this background, the transformationalists' claims have found a ready ear. Chomsky's work presented psychologists with a lucid analysis of some critical phenomena of language (productivity, paraphrase, ambiguity, classification) and a remarkably elegant scheme for their description. Since the early 1960s much of psycholinguistic research has focused upon these phenomena and on various systematic claims about language knowledge that are implicit in generative grammar.

Much of this effort was initially aimed at "validating" some presumptive empirical claims of the grammar. But in the act of empirical validation, psycholinguists have sometimes lost sight of the claims that were to be validated. They have often proceeded as if generative grammar were an explicit model of linguistic behavior. But this is hardly the case, as we have tried to show in the preceding chapter. The grammar attempts to describe an underlying system of linguistic knowledge, or competence. But the relations between such linguistic knowledge (which the grammar purports to describe) and linguistic behavior (about which it is silent) are altogether unclear. In the present idealized form, the theory of competence is immune to test or, rather, tests are irrelevant to the theory. In our view, the critical goal of psycholinguistics must be to clarify these issues: to formulate the competence-performance distinction, to unravel the various performance factors, and to determine how underlying knowledge is related to overt performance.

Currently it is not possible to draw these distinctions with any sort of precision. Since this is so, it is difficult to interpret current work as "testing" or as "validating" one or another of the substantive assertions of generative grammar. Many psycholinguists do state this as their goal, but we believe that their studies are best interpreted in another (and somewhat less ambitious) context. This literature bears on the question of how the various claims about performance and competence may be formulated and what mechanisms might possibly link these two. We certainly do not claim to have understood and disentangled these issues in the brief review that follows; nevertheless we will try to interpret current research in the light of these questions. The relevant work concerns four major assertions that may relate these grammars to the psychology of language: (1) that people can classify sentences as to their grammaticalness; (2) that they can recognize paraphrase; (3) that grammatical patterning is related to extralinguistic aspects of behavior such as memory and recall; and (4) that language is universal and species-specific.

Classification

A basic aim of grammar is to specify the infinite set of sentences "in the language" and to distinguish these from the set of nonsentences. In this sense, a generative grammar is said to mirror the organization of speakers, who are said to be able to distinguish between well-formed and deviant utterances. As prima facie evidence for this skill, transformationalists point out that speakers can produce and understand more new sentences than they can plausibly be expected to have memorized. There is no doubt that novel utterances can be elicited even from very young children. Some psychologists have tried to account for this phenomenon by vague references to generalization of the kind found in the conditioning laboratory. Indeed Pavlov's dog will salivate to previously unheard bells. But the point about language is that no simple dimension can be found to describe the production or comprehension of new sentences that are in certain ways "similar to" previously encountered sequences. Hence the emptiness of the word *generalization* as an account of this ability. Chomsky (1965) makes this argument:

> [Empiricist] speculations have not provided any way to account for or even to express the fundamental fact about the normal use of language, namely the speaker's ability to produce and understand instantly new sentences that are not similar to those previously heard in any physically defined sense or in terms of any notion of frames or classes of elements, nor associated with those previously heard by conditioning, nor obtainable from them by any sort of "generalization" known to psychology or philosophy. (Pp. 57–58)

In contrast, generative grammars do specify the sentences of the language in a way that might plausibly support a description of these innovative skills in the speaker. In effect, the speaker might "refer" putative sentences to "an internalized generative grammar" and note whether the grammar specified these sentences. Thus if the grammar reflects certain human organizing principles, we might expect that the speaker could *classify* sequences according to their grammaticalness. (This is, of course, not to deny that the speaker might be able to classify sequences in many other ways, by, e.g., truth value, length, elegance, and the like.)

Until fairly recently, it was assumed by most grammarians and philosophers of Chomsky's general persuasion that an empirical test of the ability to classify in this dimension would be so simple to conduct and so certain to succeed that to carry it out would almost be a pedantic exercise. In 1957, Chomsky wrote: "One way to test the adequacy of a grammar proposed for [a language] is to determine whether or not the sequences that it generates are actually grammatical, i.e., acceptable to a native speaker, etc. We can take certain steps toward providing a behavioral criterion for grammaticalness so that this test of adequacy can be carried out." Thus it was initially assumed that *acceptability* (to a suitably instructed native speaker) and *grammaticalness* were related in a fairly simple way. During this period of optimism, linguists assumed that everyone would agree that the vexed sentence *Colorless green ideas sleep furiously* would be regarded by English speakers as grammatical, though meaningless.[1]

In practice, it is very difficult to get people to perform this task as in principle they should. Even in the cloisters of the grammarians there are interminable wrangles about the status of individual examples. In 1961, Archibald Hill, a linguist of the structuralist school, reported on an experiment in which he submitted sentences to speakers for grammatical classification. He used as test sentences various examples from transformational tracts: sequences whose grammatical status "every speaker" was said to be able to judge. Hill's subjects, most of them apparently well-educated people, frequently agreed with the grammarians' classification, but sequences as bizarre as *I saw a fragile of* were alarmingly often accepted as grammatical. Maclay and Sleator (1960) conducted a more formal version of the same experiment and they obtained approximately the same result. They found a discernible tendency to classify sentences as the theory of grammar would predict but, to put things mildly, there was a statistical smear in the result. Three of Maclay and Sleator's twenty-one subjects judged *Label break to be calmed about and* to be grammatical!

Have we evidence here of a clear discrepancy between fact and

---

[1] The implication was that "grammar" and "meaning" are in some way separable, however indistinct the line between the two. Recent work in linguistics suggests that the line may be even dimmer than initially supposed. In the formulation we have adopted (*see* chap. 1) syntactic and semantic structure are assumed to be components of a single grammatical description, semantics being the *interpretive* component of the grammar. But these issues have by no means been resolved, as we have noted elsewhere, and they are central topics in current linguistic thought. Throughout this review we use the term *grammar,* as in chapter 1, to refer to an organization that includes phonology, syntax, and semantics as interrelated components. Psycholinguists have generally assumed that these components are distinct and distinguishable, and they ordinarily use the words *grammar* and *syntax* interchangeably.

theory? Is it possible that the organizing principles describing sentencehood in a grammar are quite different from those available to the speaker? The view taken on this question reveals a striking difference in approach among investigators in this area. Maclay and Sleator saw their result as denying a categorical human ability to classify along this dimension. They suggested a more massive empirical attack—using these same procedures—on the classification question. It is worth quoting their conclusion here.

> Very little can be assumed in advance about responses to language, and even the most obvious predictions need to be checked empirically. Judgments must be obtained under controlled conditions from a representative sample of naive native speakers of the language in question. The resulting data will require statistical description along with appropriate significance tests. Such an analysis provides, we believe, the only firm basis for decisions on the acceptability of linguistic forms by native speakers. We are not suggesting that statistics and controls can of themselves make this decision but only that the data needed for the external evaluation of grammars are likely to be ordered in a way that requires statistical treatment. (P. 282)

The reaction of the generative grammarians to such demonstrations was quite different. They rejected the notion that tests of acceptability provided relevant data by which grammars should be (even externally) evaluated. Instead they revised the assertion that acceptability judgments directly reflect the individual's intuitions about grammaticalness, acknowledging that these judgments were not made on such simple grounds as had initially been assumed.

In retrospect, it seems clear that judgments of acceptability may well be tangential to the question of classification. In the first place, few who have suffered through our public school system can be expected to respond with equanimity to the word *grammatical*. More interestingly, acceptability must be affected by comprehensibility no less than by apparent structure. Consider the perplexing responses to the deviant *Label break to be calmed about and*. We can, if the task seems to be one of playing linguistic games, provide a context in which this sentence might be uttered. Someone has a bottle on which appears the label "Break." He asks another to replace this label with a label marked "To Be Calmed About And." Of course he will give the command: *Label "Break" "To Be Calmed About And"*! If a person goes through such a reasoning process and concludes that this sentence is now "acceptable," should we denigrate or admire his grammatical prowess? We would have to distinguish between "blithely accepts as grammatical" and "after deep thought accepts as grammatical" to know how the individual had classified this sentence. The point is that we do not know how to instruct the subject suitably to get at his autonomous notion of grammaticalness, if indeed he has such a concept, and we have no access to the processes that lead him to make these judgments.[2]

[2] In a number of acceptability experiments (Maclay and Sleater, 1960; Pfafflin, 1961) an attempt was made to evaluate the grounds on which the subject accepts or rejects the stimulus sentence. Pfafflin chose sentences in two ways: (1) a computer program consisting of grammatical "rules" first generated permissible sentence types to the level of part-of-speech sequences (e.g., noun, verb) after which a random selection of words from each part of speech was substituted into these sequences. A representative sentence produced in this manner was *A vapid ruby with a nutty fan lies seldom below this tipsy noise;* (2) English speakers, given the instruction to produce sentences that were "meaningful" as well as "grammatical," took the same part-of-speech sequences and substituted words—apparently constrained by the listings in the computer program. An example is *That good fairy from the wild ball rises softly on the sweet music.* It is hard to understand why these subjects produced such meaningless meaningful sentences. At any rate thirty subjects were now asked to judge the sentences produced in these two ways for "grammaticalness." These subjects more frequently accepted the human-generated sentences than the computer-generated sentences. Granting the validity of the procedure, semantic anomaly evidently has an effect on acceptability independent on syntactic anomaly. Maclay and Sleator got much the same result. Sheer sentence length also affected these judgments. Long sentences were less likely to be judged acceptable than short sentences.

One further curiosity in Pfafflin's data ought to be considered, for it is relevant to the empirical work we will discuss later on. In this experiment, subjects were chosen from professional, technical, and secretarial populations working in the same institution. Much of the disagreement among subjects is between, not within, these population groups. If these disagreements arose in the very long sentences, we could assume that the less talented subjects simply broke down when the nature of the materials became memorially or grammatically difficult. However, Pfafflin shows that disagreement occurs primarily in the very short sentences where processing problems would be least likely to arise (e.g., the sentence *This is pushing* yielded large differences in acceptability for different groups, the least-educated subjects rejecting it most frequently). Pfafflin concludes that the difference among populations is a difference in their grammars, or linguistic organization, not a difference in the ability to process complex entities.

Critics of the transformational approach have often argued that the crucial notion of well-formedness is indefensible on these grounds. An ingenious speaker can often conceive contexts for sentences that at first hearing appear deviant (*I ran it out of ink* in the context *The monster has invaded the lovely valley of Ink* or *Why doesn't your pen work?* or *Bake a letter, Miss Jones,* in the context of Sumerian commerce). Given the appropriate context, the sentences no longer seem anomalous. Chomsky (1965) has pointed out that there is nevertheless a class of well-formed sentences that seem to require no special interpretive activity (*I ran her out of town*), and that the very feeling that a context must be provided, that "interpretation" is necessary, reveals a deep difference in the way these sentences are perceived. We suspect this is so, but then the prospects for an operational test for classification seem dismal. If *acceptability* is too complex an activity to reveal much about classification, then *acceptability plus feeling-that-no-interpretation-is-required* holds out little hope.

Later we will take up this aspect of the speaker's creativity: his ability to impose meaningful interpretation on almost any sequence of words in the language, and we will discuss the implications of this kind of activity for the issue of classification. The point here is that acceptability tests are not tests of generative grammar. Such tests cannot invalidate, they can hardly bear on, a theory which when pushed will withdraw into successively deeper reaches of the mind. All that can be said is that, as a matter of historical fact, acceptability tests did not point a simple relation between grammar and this aspect of behavior.

Paraphrase

Given the substance of transformational grammars, a display of paraphrasing abilities would establish a crucial connection between grammars and human linguistic organization; for it is the interweave among constructions that lies at the heart of the transformational hypothesis. If the individual has a procedure for paraphrasing, that is, for providing regular surface alternatives for a single deep structure in a manner consistent with the grammatical description, we have the first kind of evidence that should be looked for in establishing the way that a grammatical dimension underlies language use. If people can provide paraphrases in a principled way, something very like a transformational organization of language must be postulated to account for this skill.

Considering the obvious centrality of the phenomenon of paraphrasing to the transformational view, it is surprising that the psycholinguists have failed to study this question very extensively. An ability to paraphrase is usually taken for granted in psycholinguistic studies, and the act of paraphrasing is taken to be an act of understanding. Most of the experimental literature has, then, only a marginal relation to the question of whether the speaker has a procedure for paraphrasing that is related to systematic formal notions such as base-structure equivalence. Nevertheless, it may be of some interest to consider the findings of experimenters who have used paraphrasing as a task.

Paraphrasing is ordinarily the experimental task in studies of the ways people cope with multiple self-embedding (the situation in which a phrase occurs totally within a phrase which occurs totally within a phrase of the same type); for example:

> *The vase that the maid that the agency hired dropped broke on the floor.*

Although such sentences are technically grammatical (generated by a grammar that recursively embeds sentences into noun phrases), they are not acceptable to most speakers, and they are almost impossible to understand. This striking incompatibility between grammaticalness and acceptability calls for explanation. The grammar is said in general to mirror intuitions about classification, and those who have conducted acceptability tests do find a "significant," though muddy, relation between acceptability and grammaticalness. The grammar and the speaker do not go off in haphazardly different directions. But multiple self-embedding poses a systematic exception in this regard. Yngve (1960) and Miller and Isard (1963) have proposed explanations for this phenomenon related to limitations on short-term memory and processing procedures in the individual, that is, to extralinguistic capacity deficits. On the contrary, Blumenthal (1966) and Stolz (1967) have argued that such sentences should be regarded as ungrammatical because subjects systematically "misinterpret" or incorrectly "decode" them. The grounds are the paraphrases that subjects provide for these sentences.

Blumenthal's college-student subjects (provided with sentences one to two steps more embedded than the example above) were asked "to rewrite each sentence to render it more acceptable or understandable." They could "add punctuation and change or add words if necessary, but they were not to change the meaning of any sentence." In only 24 of 160 observations did subjects do so "correctly." Most of the time they garbled the functional relations (subject, verb, object) specified by the grammar for these expressions, often inserting various conjunctions (. . . *hired and dropped and broke on the floor*). Thus, apparently, some subjects failed to get through to the grammatical structure of these sentences.

Blumenthal's conclusion is that "multiple self-embedded sentences are in fact ungrammatical for *S*s who characteristically perceive them as approximations to sentences containing one compounded clause." Thus he finds the Miller-Isard account of processing difficulties "irrelevant" to account for his result, but it is not clear whether he nevertheless considers the subjects' difficulty to be one of linguistic processing or whether he attributes their failure to problems of grammatical organization (accepting this distinction for the moment). He says both that these sentences "are ungrammatical" and that "perhaps this may be considered a rule of psycholinguistic performance."

Stolz's subjects also were provided with examples like that given above. In some instances, there was internal semantic support for the correct syntactic solution (in the same example, it is unlikely that the maid or the agency broke on the floor). Subjects were asked to "decode" these entities by providing the component sentences (for the same example, the response *The agency hired the maid; the maid dropped the vase; the vase broke on the floor* is correct). Thus a particular kind of paraphrase was asked for. Subjects were given paper and pencil and adequate time to work out their solutions, in an effort to preclude interpretation of the results as effects of memory and processing problems. About half of the college students who served as subjects failed to connect the predicted subjects, verbs, and objects, though they did better when semantic constraints on the choice of relations were available.

Since "the conditions of the experiment effectively relieved the time and memory pressures of real-time processing," Stolz argues, the failure of some subjects must be attributed to a lack of usable linguistic knowledge. He notes that the Miller-Isard experiment involved recall and concedes that limitations on psychological processing mechanisms make self-embedded sentences difficult. But he argues with some justice that this experiment "confounded the effect of these [processing] factors with the *a priori* factor of whether or not the Ss know the sentence structures involved."

But Stolz's own conclusion, like Blumenthal's, confounds the various issues of comprehensibility, paraphrasability, and grammaticalness. Both these experimenters assume that *comprehensibility* is an adequate criterion of perceived *grammaticalness* and that comprehensibility can in turn be judged through *paraphrasability*. They appear to conclude that the formal grammar is here descriptively inadequate, that it has an organization biasedly different from that of the speaker.

Stolz comments that speakers seem to act like "lazy decoders" in this task. They bypass the constructional features that in some abstract sense determine the paraphrastic relations, and they rely instead on pragmatic and semantic probabilities (whatever these may be) for interpretation. While this is undoubtedly so—no grammarian ever doubted that the speaker has a whole bag of tricks, beyond syntax, for comprehension—it does not bear on the question of whether there is a principled approach to paraphrase available to the speaker, should he be suitably instructed to make use of it.

Despite the considerable agility of these experimenters, they do not seem to have evaded the conceptual stumbling blocks that Chomsky has pointed out. "Meaning" or semantic structure may intervene and override gross judgments of syntactic structure, so we cannot tell when a judgment is syntactic (and thus when it may be a wrong syntactic judgment). Memory capacity may be insufficient to allow certain syntactic judgments to take place, and we cannot know whether a particular experimental procedure has circumvented this problem when we know next to nothing of the nature of linguistic processing. That is to say, the irksome performance-competence distinction can be invoked here once again, leaving an intact grammar, a performance-bound speaker, and the relations between the two as mysterious as ever.

It is a curiosity that Stolz finds massive variability among individuals in the ability to cope with this apparently linguistic puzzle. (Blumenthal does not give data on individual differences.) Some subjects did understand the sentences as the grammar might predict. This aspect of the result is reminiscent of Pfafflin's finding of population differences in acceptability judgments (*see* fn. 2, p. 24). But again one may ask whether there is some principled deficit in grammatical knowledge that accounts for the failure of some subjects—as all these experimenters suppose—or whether we see here only linguistically extraneous limitations on calculational skills and memory capacity.

Athough the experiments we have just described use paraphrasing as a measure, they clearly are not adequate tests of the ability to paraphrase nor of the relation of this ability to grammatical knowledge. That such relations will be direct was taken for granted. Further, the very complexity of the stimulus materials makes it difficult to interpret these experiments as bearing on the ability to paraphrase, for surely we are dealing in both instances with a limiting case, not a characteristic one. There is only one study we can cite that appears to avoid this difficulty and to test paraphrasing ability against grammatical knowledge in a revealing way. This is a study by W. H. Livant (1961) on paraphrasing compound nouns; we describe it only briefly here, for we shall take it up in great detail in chapter 4.

Livant submitted a number of compound noun phrases to three subjects and asked them to "interpret," that is, to paraphrase the compounds. He reports that his subjects could in all cases paraphrase the compounds despite the considerable semantic bizarreness and syntactic complexity of some instances. He supposes, on this evidence, that the speaker has a method for paraphrasing which leads to uniform performance; in effect, that the words of the compound can be treated like variables in a known formula. On the basis of the uniform results for all three subjects, he suggests that this is a task any adult can perform. This is evidence for a strikingly direct relationship between grammar and speaker, and it appears to be at variance with the findings of other experimenters (and the provisos of the linguists) that truth value, length, plausibility, and complexity (no less individual capacity) will affect linguistic performance of all sorts. If Livant's results stand up to further inquiry, we have a strong and direct indication that language can be organized along the lines proposed by the grammarians.

It is only fair to add here that some of these results will not bear up in this simple form under close scrutiny, and we shall attempt to show that the subtle ways in which they do not stand up shed some light on the question of how people deal with constructional relations. The task we have set ourselves in our own work is to examine in some detail the nature and extent of paraphrasing skills. Here, if anywhere, introspection tends to confirm the transformational account of language, to support the notion that there are deep and surface levels of syntactic organization. Thus it is here, if anywhere, that we can expect to find direct enough relations between speaker and system to bring linguistic theory back to the level of data.

Labov's (1968) work with black urban children who speak a dialect of English rather different from our own provides a different and revealing glimpse into the workings of paraphrase. Labov asks children (usually about twelve years old) to repeat verbatim (for nickels) various sentences, sometimes cast in "standard" English, sometimes in the children's own dialect. The children find it almost impossible to repeat the standard version when it differs from the regularities of their own speech (such utterances as *I wonder whether he'll come to my house tonight* are "repeated" as *I wonder will he come to my house tonight*). These difficulties persist even when the experimenter points out the repetition error to the subject. Notice that a child who "repeats" in this way has clearly understood the sentence with which he was presented, but he has translated it ("paraphrased" it?). In other terms, the dialects are close enough so that the individual who listens to an utterance (hears the surface-structure output of an alien dialect) can match it to a deep structure in his own internalized grammar; but the transformational systems are sufficiently distinct so that he cannot easily produce the "foreign" surface structure in speech. In listening to Labov's tapes of these sessions, one gathers some inkling of the burdens placed on memory by the (dialectically) deviant instances. "Too long," say the children, "would you say that one again?", while they have no trouble at all repeating long utterances in their own dialect after a single hearing. Further, the mysterious creativity of the speaker—even a twelve-year-old—in imposing meaning and structure on what are to him remote modes of speech does much to convince the skeptic of a "deep" level of organization that transcends the spoken forms.

Extralinguistic Effects of Grammatical Patterning

Recently there have been a number of attempts to show the relation of grammatical organization to well-known psychological variables. In most of these studies some measure such as reaction time or memory loading is used as the dependent variable and linguistic structure is used as the independent variable. Many different measures have been employed in this work, and a number of syntactic relations have been examined. In the review that follows, the work is reported in terms of the linguistic variable under study.

THE REALITY OF SENTENCES

George Miller and his associates (Miller, 1962; Miller and Isard, 1963; Marks and Miller, 1964) set out to study the relevance of syntactic structure to perception and recall. The question is whether grammatical sentences have any special status in these matters. They presented subjects with the following kinds of stimuli (there are some differences between the experiments that we need not take up): sentences that were in all regards well-formed (e.g., *Furry wildcats fight furious battles*);

sentences that were syntactically well-formed but semantically deviant (e.g., *Furry jewelers create distressed stains*); sentences that were syntactically deviant but semantically nondeviant, that is, nondeviant sentences with scrambled word order (e.g., *Furry fight furious wildcats battles*); and sentences that were both syntactically and semantically deviant, that is, scrambled semantically deviant sentences (e.g., *Furry create distressed jewelers stains*).

Some question may be raised about whether these stimulus sentences really exemplify two distinct levels of grammatical organization (syntax and semantics). Nevertheless, it seems obvious that the deviance in these examples is of rather different sorts. In one experiment, subjects were asked to detect these strings in the presence of masking noise and to repeat them; and in another study they were asked to memorize them by the method of free recall. In both cases the results were essentially the same. Well-formed sentences were most easily dealt with and scrambled semantically deviant sentences were the most difficult. The other cases fell properly between. Sensibly enough (given that English is a language in which serial order reflects syntactic relations), when the criterion of recall included order (i.e., when a word was scored as correct only if it appeared in its correct position in the string), syntactic anomaly appeared to be more damaging than semantic anomaly. When the criterion was simply the number of words recalled independent of order, syntactically well-formed but semantically deviant sentences were more difficult than disordered but semantically sensible sentences.

These results show that grammatical patterning is a crucial element in the perception and recall of word sequences. At least in this sense, people can distinguish between grammatical and ungrammatical sentences. In fact—and here the findings are similar to Labov's—it seems that people cannot avoid making this distinction under certain circumstances, regardless of the task requirements.

THE REALITY OF PHRASE STRUCTURE

A number of studies concern the speaker's organization of sentences into linguistically defined subparts—*phrases* or *constit-*

uents. The question is often raised whether "abstract" constituent-structure descriptions have any psychological relevance. Do people, in the normal course of events, make use of similar substructuring in creating and understanding sentences?

A fairly direct display of the psychological relevance of phrase-structure units was given by Johnson (1965). For some reason the experiment was cast in a paired-associate paradigm. Subjects were required to learn paired associates with digits as stimuli and sentences as responses. Responses were scored "for the conditional probability that the words in the sentences were wrong, given that the immediately preceding word was right." The question, then, was whether the sentences were organized word-by-word or phrase-by-phrase, and, if the latter, whether those phrases were just those predicted by the grammar. The result that is of relevance here was that the transitional error probabilities were not equal from word to word; rather the probability of error increased significantly at phrase-structure boundaries.

What is the value of having such "objective" displays of grammatical concepts as Johnson and many others have provided? Surely the issue cannot be verification in any simple sense. If memorization in this experiment had not proceeded in constituent-structure units, we have any number of behavioral displays—performances—that would force us in any case to concede "reality" to phrase structure. We need not even have involved mysterious concepts of tacit competence. The best demonstration is that seven- and eight-year-olds can do a pretty good job of parsing sentences into phrase-structure units despite the fact that they are primitive speakers, primitive understanders of instructions (*pace* Piaget), and gullible enough to believe that their teachers' explanations of such tasks have some dim relevance to performing them. Johnson cannot be asking "Is there phrase structure?" Like Miller in a different context, he must be asking whether phrase-structure units are relevant to rote memorization in particular, and to speech-processing strategies in general. The experimental question may well have some relevance in understanding how the speaker's knowledge of language is involved in various concrete tasks. More centrally, such studies may advance our knowledge of where in the process of comprehending utterances these are segmented in surface-structure terms.

THE REALITY OF DEEP STRUCTURE

Critical to transformational grammars is the distinction between deep and surface organization of the sentence. How can we make manifest the fact, if it is a fact, that speakers perceive deep structure as well as surface structure? Blumenthal (1967) tried to approach this question by exposing subjects to sentences with very similar surface structure but very dissimilar deep structure, for example:

> *Gloves were made by tailors.*
> *Gloves were made by hand.*

He suggests that the surface structure of both sentences is essentially *noun-phrase–verb-phrase–adverbial-phrase,* while the deep structures differ: the first sentence can be taken as the passive equivalent of *Tailors made gloves,* but in the second sentence the *by*-phrase is an instrumental adverbial. Then the final word in the first sentence is the logical subject, but in the second sentence the final word plays a syntactically subordinate role.

After exposing speakers to sentences of both these forms, Blumenthal asked them to recall the sentence when provided with the final word as a "prompt." It turned out that the final noun was a highly effective prompt when it had been the logical subject of the sentence to be remembered and a far less effective prompt when it was involved in the instrumental phrase. Yet there is no obvious way in which one of these sentence types is more difficult to "process" than the other, or less grammatical, less frequently encountered, etc. Thus the study demonstrates that the speaker stores deep-structure as well as surface-structure aspects of the sentence.

Mehler and Carey (1967) also attempted to assess the effect on perception of sentences that differed in deep and surface structure. They considered the following kinds of sentences:

(1) *They are forecasting cyclones.*
(2) *They are conflicting desires.*

(3) *They are delightful to embrace.*
(4) *They are hesitant to travel.*

Note that types (1) and (2) differ in surface structure, that is:

(They) (are forecasting (cyclones)) vs.
(They) (are (conflicting desires))

Types (3) and (4) are identical in gross surface structure, but they differ significantly in deep structure, that is, for (3) there is a paraphrase:

It is delightful to embrace them,

but for (4) there is no paraphrase:

It is hesitant to travel them.

Mehler and Carey attempted to establish a set for the surface structure exemplified in (1) or (2) by presenting ten sentences of the one type or the other in the presence of white noise. They also tried to establish a set for the base structure exemplified in (3) or (4) by the same means. They followed these lists with one "test" sentence of the same or the opposing type. For example, ten instances of type (1) were followed by another instance of type (1) or by an instance of type (2). The task was always recognition. Error scores showed that a sentence was perceived more accurately if it had the same rather than a different surface structure compared to the sentences that preceded it. This result was large and consistent. For the difference in deep structure, the difference between types (3) and (4), the results were very unclear. There was a trend in the expected direction but it was very weak indeed (one-tailed test with a p of .15!). Nevertheless, Mehler and Carey do interpret this result as support for the psychological relevance of the deep-structure notion. They write: "These experiments show that sets for specified types of deep and surface structures can be induced in Ss. Such findings are consonant with the view that representations of sentences that are abstractly related to their physical realization play a role in speech perception."

A sequence of studies (Fodor and Bever, 1965; Garrett and Fodor, 1966; Bever, Lackner, and Kirk, 1969; and many others) examine speech perception in the context of detection. In a dichotic listening situation sentences are presented in one ear, and during this presentation a single click is presented in the other ear. The subjects are asked to judge the point in the sentence at which the click occurred. Judgments in these experiments tend to be displaced toward certain major deep-structure boundaries within the sentence. Spectrographic analysis of the stimulus sentences reveals that these displacements cannot be accounted for by assuming that a physical pause occurs at such boundaries and that the click is simply judged to occur at this silent interval. Similar displacement occurs both for renditions which happen to contain such silences and for those which do not.

The earlier studies of click displacement—like the Mehler and Carey work—seem to have been directed toward establishing that the notions of deep and surface structure were somehow real. And again, it seems to us that such demonstrations are superfluous (when they work) and irrelevant (when they don't). Whatever the outcome of such experiments, there is no reasonable doubt that sentences sometimes consist of partially different overt elements in different orders while having identical logical structure. There is no doubt that people know this, at least in some degree, and there is no doubt that transformational grammar is one way of describing these facts. In so far as these experiments were initially considered to bear on the question of validating the transformational account, some failures with the technique led to a certain amount of chagrin and some tactical maneuvers with the theory of grammar. For example, Fodor and Garrett (1966) could not induce click displacement for some further structure boundaries (specifically, they concluded that only constituents dominated by a sentence node yielded the effect). To explain away the failures, Fodor and Garrett argued that operations in the grammar and operations of the "performance mechanism" might well differ; we will take up this problem somewhat later in the discussion. In more recent work on click displacement, the question of validation has usually been set to rest. Interest has shifted to the question of speech perception, and the primacy of deep-structure units in the immediate processing strategies employed by the hearer has been fairly convincingly established (Bever, Lackner, and Kirk, 1969).

TRANSFORMATIONAL COMPLEXITY

Given the formal and explicit character of transformational grammars, it is possible to propose various measures by which syntactic descriptions of sentences can be said to differ in complexity. For example, in some forms of these grammars (Chomsky, 1957), optional transformations operate successively on base representations of simple sentences (*kernels*). The length (in number of steps) of this transformational derivation seems to be a natural measure of sentence complexity. Sentences can then be said to differ from each other in the number of respects in which their derivations differ.

If the grammar mirrors behavior in this further sense, the individual ought to find simpler constructions more immediate and comprehensible than complex ones. If the sequence of steps in a derivation can be interpreted as a sequence of mental steps, short derivations should be less mentally taxing. Miller (1964) has reviewed a series of attempts to study the relative comprehensibility of affirmative (grammatically simpler) and negative (more complex, i.e., requiring one more derivational step) sentences, when semantic content is controlled. Wason (1961) showed that it takes longer to respond to negative sentences than affirmative sentences, and it takes longer to evaluate them (as to truth or falsity). It is conceivable that in the process of understanding a sentence, listeners recode sentences as base form plus transformational "notes." Miller poses this solution as follows:

> The significant point . . . was that the time differences observed in Wason's experiments might have been attributable, at least in part, to the time required to perform the grammatical transformations from negative to affirmative statements. The implicit assumption here is that, before a subject could respond to a negative sentence, he had to transform it into an affirmative statement and change its truth value, and that the additional time required for negative sentences was occupied with performing these grammatical and logical transformations. (Pp. 103–104)

The next step was to see whether similar effects could be found for instances of transformationally complex sentences of other sorts. McMahon (as reported by Miller, *ibid.*) used an evaluation test closely modelled after Wason's and found a similar difference in time to evaluation between active and passive sentences. He also studied combinations of these types (e.g., passive-negative). The effects of adding transformational complexity seemed to be additive; that is, the extra time necessary for evaluation of the passive and the negative over that of a simple active-affirmative summed to about the extra time necessary to evaluate a passive-negative. Similar results were obtained by Gough (1965). A study by Mehler (1963) showed roughly equivalent results for recall: "kernel" (active-affirmative) sentences were recalled more readily than passives, questions, negatives, and combinations of these.

Miller, McKean, and Slobin, as reported by Miller (1962), also attempted to measure the reaction times involved in relating sentences to their transformational counterparts. The subject was first told what manipulation was required (e.g., active-negative →
passive-negative). He was then presented with a test sentence and asked first to "perform the transformation," that is, determine the counterpart called for, and second, to find that counterpart in a list of sentences. In later versions of this experiment (Miller and McKean, 1964), the sentences were presented tachistoscopically, and subjects pressed a button (stopping a timer) when they were ready to find the match (presumably, when they had performed the transformation). The authors assumed that in this manner search time could be separated from the prior processing time. Reaction times were found to be a function of the number of derivational steps that separated the sentences. Again there was the suggestion of an additive effect of complexity.

Another technique for measuring relative complexity among syntactic forms has been developed by Savin and Perchonock (1965) in the context of studies of immediate memory. The rationale is this: it is presumed that a sentence presented for recall will "take up space" in a small immediate memory bank. A certain amount of space may now be "left over," and this can be loaded with arbitrary material (here, unrelated words). The simpler the sentence, the less space it should take in the memory bank and the more space should be available for the filler words. It was hypothesized that transformational information would be stored somehow separately from a deep-structure representation of the sentence (thus the issue is again the nature of processing, not verification). The longer the derivational history of a sentence, the more space the transformational information should consume. Subjects were presented with a sentence, followed by eight unrelated words pronounced with list intonation. They were required to recall the sentence, and then as many of the words as possible. The number of filler words that were remembered varied inversely with the derivational complexity of the sentence to be recalled. As in earlier studies, the relationship was found to be roughly additive. For most structural types examined in this work, length and complexity were unavoidably confounded. However, for two sentence types used (emphatic affirmatives and *wh*-questions) added complexity is not accompanied by added length and the same effects were obtained nevertheless.

Some results reported by Fodor and Garrett (1966) differ from those found by Miller and his associates in sentence-matching experiments and from those found by Savin and Perchonock in memory experiments. In an unpublished experiment by Fodor, Jenkins, and Saporta, recognition latencies for tachistoscopic presentation of sentences failed to reveal the expected differences between sentences like *John picked the girl up* and *John picked up the girl*. In the grammar, the former is derived from the latter, and thus has a longer derivational history. Miller and McKean had also failed to find the predicted result for differences in the expansion of verb auxiliaries. Similarly, Bever, Fodor, Garrett, and Mehler (again reported by Fodor and Garrett) attempted to extend the Savin-Perchonock technique to further transformational relations, and these attempts failed. Positive results with both these kinds of tests appear to be restricted to relations between affirmatives, negatives, passives, questions, and emphatics.

What are we to make of this? It seems that a variety of measures can be used to demonstrate a reasonably linear relationship between the complexity of certain kinds of sentences (defined as the number of transformational operations involved in their derivation) and various kinds of performance. Yet every one of these relationships seems to break down when other sentence types are studied. Fodor and Garrett suggest that it may have been an error to claim psychological validity for the *operations* by which derivations are accomplished in an axiomatic grammar. Rather, it might be sufficient to claim psychological reality only for the result, the structural descriptions that are the end product of such derivations. By analogy they point out that there are various procedures by which theorems can be tested in the propositional calculus, with large differences in the number of steps involved in the proofs.

As Sutherland (1966) points out in his comments on the Fodor-Garrett paper, the number of steps involved in the proof of a theorem also varies considerably depending on the axioms that are chosen. Sutherland writes: "This suggests a possibility not considered by Fodor and Garrett: namely, that although the type of grammar developed by Chomsky may be one way of axiomatizing language, it is not necessarily the only way nor need it correspond to the axiomatization system (if any) represented in the brain." We seem now to have two choices: (1) we can agree with Fodor and Garrett that the operations defined in an axiomatic description of language need bear no relation (or only a very "abstract" relation) to the operations that the speaker-listener will employ, but then we must be prepared to regard the positive findings (for certain constructions) as trivial or accidental; or (2) we can agree with Sutherland that there may be alternative ways of writing the grammar, ways that may conceivably explain the experimental outcome.

In our view these various mixed results are only superficially embarrassing. Recent reformulations of transformational grammars seem to provide at least a partial descriptive basis for the empirical findings. Katz and Postal (1964) and Chomsky (1965) have suggested on formal grounds that the differences between affirmatives, emphatics, negatives, questions, and passives had to be indicated as base-rule distinctions, that is, differences arising from the options available in deriving an initial deep-structure representation from the formation rules of the grammar. In this view, a special morpheme (e.g., the morpheme of negation) appears in the base component of the grammar, in the deep structure. The appearance of this morpheme later will trigger an obligatory (no longer optional) negation transformation which will in turn affect the derived phrase structure (the surface structure) of the sentence. Beyond formal considerations, the linguists have pointed out, this solution allows us to make the generalization that transformations do not affect meaning. Notice that in the earlier formulation, some transformations (negation, etc.) seemed to change meaning, while others (particle movement, etc.) did not. Now the meaning difference is said to reside uniformly in deep-structure differences.[3]

What is of interest here is that this reformulation involves all those transformational relationships which were empirically found to relate to the proposed complexity measure. It does not involve those for which some predictions from early transformational theory seemed to fail. If this analysis is correct, then perhaps length of derivational history is not the key to the interpre-

---

[3] Notice that while this argument is very useful for negatives, emphatics, questions, and so on, which clearly mean something quite different from their affirmative counterparts, it does nothing to explain the active-passive relation. Except for some unconvincing cases with quantifiers that have been discussed for years by the grammarians (*Every man kissed at least one woman; At least one woman was kissed by every man*), the passive transformation leaves meaning intact. Yet there is a difference between active and passive (the passive morpheme) in the deep structure. Katz and Postal (1964) argue that the deep-structure difference is in this case merely a "dummy" morpheme which can be said to have no semantic consequence: there are deep-structure differences between active and passive but they eventuate in semantic equivalence. In the case of negatives, the morpheme in the base component is not a dummy, but has a semantically interpretable surface manifestation. Similarly, it can be argued, the deep-structure element *sentence* has no semantic interpretation and the surface element *of* (in the nominalization *John's shooting of lions*) has no semantic interpretation. Thus the statement that *be* and *by* of the passive have no semantic interpretation is not unique or necessarily *ad hoc* in this kind of account. Nevertheless, the grammar must eventually account for the direct paraphrastic equivalence between active and passive, just as it does for particle movement. It is true that not all paraphrases are derivationally related (e.g., *Time flies; Life is short*), but the active/passive relation seems much more direct than this. In fact it is the paradigmatic case from which the intuitions about transformational structure grew. In spite of these reservations we have assumed for our present purposes that the formal resemblances between the passive transformation and, for example, the negative, will hold, thus supporting the empirical finding that there is something similar in the way they are perceived. But we do not think that the final word has been said on this matter.

tation of these findings. Rather, what may be critical is the number of base-element differences between the sentences the subject is to match (Miller and McKean) or the number of base elements the subject is to recall (Savin and Perchonock; Mehler) or verify (Gough; McMahon). If there are no base-structure differences between the sentences, no perceptual or memorial effects are found in these experimental contexts. *I turned off the light* and *I turned the light off* presumably differ in the length of derivational history, but not in base-structure elements. Similarly, *wh*-questions and passives differ in number of surface elements but not in number of deep elements—and in fact, space taken in memory is about equal. Negative *wh*-questions are no longer in terms of surface elements than passives, but they contain more base elements; hence they take more space in memory. This description establishes a relation between a formal distinction and an empirically obtained one. Still it offers no hint why optional transformations should have no apparent effect under these conditions. Obviously people can under some circumstances remember which of two stylistic variants they have heard.

SUMMARY COMMENTS

Clearly the psycholinguistic enterprise is no longer aimed at "testing" transformational theory; its goals are elsewhere. No one doubts that this theory is one way of describing productive aspects of language use, but grateful as they must be to the Chomskians for their systematic explication of these phenomena, psychologists of language cannot be satisfied with a system that is neutral with respect to the mechanisms that translate underlying competence into overt performance. The grammar (the competence model) looks like a machine that can specify the set of sentences, define ambiguity and paraphrase, and so on. When psycholinguists attempted to "verify" this grammar, they asked in effect whether the human machine behaved similarly. But clearly a grammar cannot "do" anything that people do when they talk. It cannot comprehend or produce grammatical sentences, decide what to say when, make mistakes about classification, evaluate truth or falsity, lie. In part at least, the psychologist's concern is with the discovery of the mechanisms that underlie such performances. Whatever the mechanisms that are proposed, some "knowledge" (i.e., underlying competence) in the speaker must be presupposed as constraining the way they act. Grammars purport to represent this knowledge. It is our belief that grammars as presently conceived are idealized pictures that go far beyond what the speaker can realistically be supposed to know about his language. Nevertheless, significant insights into mechanisms of speech and understanding have been achieved by working within this idealized framework (particularly the work of Bever, Fodor, Garrett, and their associates), while very little has been achieved either by ignoring the competence model or by going to the opposite extreme and assuming that it is a direct model of performance.

Unfortunately, neither linguists nor psychologists have succeeded in unraveling the various issues of performance and competence, and the mechanism that links these two. Much current work is difficult to interpret because of this conceptual tangle. It is hard to say what kinds of deficit in performance should cause us to revise our picture of the individual's knowledge of the language. In addition, many measures have been used in the psycholinguistic research, and the relation of these measures to language and to each other is quite unclear. Notice that the dependent variable—as well as the language material—differed in almost all the studies we have reported. Reaction time, perceptual set, detectability, various indices of immediate and long-term memory—all are hopefully put forward as measures of the influence of syntactic organization. In the light of our ignorance about what the measures can be measuring, positive results can at best be suggestive and negative results cannot be evaluated at all. One can hardly speculate, for example, as to why sets can be induced for surface structures and not for deep structures (cf. Mehler and Carey, who can discern a faint effect of deep structure only by torturing their data somewhat unmercifully). It is difficult to guess why optional transformations have no discernible effect in the various experimental paradigms involving detection, recall, and evaluation; and conversely why the obligatory transformations are seen to have a large and consistent effect in these situations.

Despite these limitations, psychological studies of language have become remarkably more interesting now that they are conducted within a framework that holds forth some hope of describing the language system itself. There is no reason at present to accept the mournful conclusion of Fodor and Garrett that because certain experiments worked out in a less than simple way, we can expect to find no visible relations between linguistic theory and human language operations; one might as tenably have discarded the claim for psychological relevance when the acceptability experiments failed. On the contrary, the theory of competence seems to illuminate some aspects of performance passing well.

Finally, though, we must admit that the fragmentary psycholinguistic findings now available have not sharpened our picture of the important abilities to classify, paraphrase, and recognize ambiguity. Here the linguistic grammar makes substantive empirical claims about facets of behavior and cognitive organization. Anecdotal evidence for these abilities is incontrovertible but at the same time remarkably resistant to demonstration by simple means. We see the resolution of this apparent discrepancy as a central task for psycholinguistics.

The Universality of Language

Linguists are no longer content merely to describe the particular features of the many natural languages. Their object is to discover those features that are common to all natural languages because it is these, if any, that can shed light on the concept "human language" and give insight into properties of language that may be the consequence of underlying psychological organization. It is in this sense that transformationally oriented students of language are often said to believe that language is "innate" rather than "learned." This is a misleading simplification. While transformationalists are disposed to believe in some fundamental capacities for language behavior that transcend those required for simple forms of conditioning, their suppositions about the extent to which such built-in organizations are specific to language (and thus their beliefs about what is learned about language) differ widely.

Still, a general nativist position is shared by most. For example, consider Postal (1968):

> A substantial portion of the structure of any particular language is not learned, but determined by the innate linguistic organization of the human organism. This innate organization specifies the overall structure of a grammar, the kinds of rules it can contain, the kinds of elements, and the possible interrelations among these. It also determines to an unknown extent part of the actual content of particular grammars, that is, the particular rules and elements these contain. (P. 282)

Nativist positions have been justified primarily on the following grounds: that the structures of all languages are, within close and specifiable limits, identical despite enormous differences in culture; that language is specific to man and always present in man, barring the most extreme pathologies or environmental deprivation; that the emergence of language is for each individual approximately the same in schedule and strategy, despite great differences of environment and intelligence; and that language ability is about the same in all normal adults, again despite pervasive differences of culture and intelligence.

ARE LANGUAGES ALIKE?

A broad study of languages from all over the world has been conducted by linguists during the past thirty years. Although it is often hard to compare the resulting language descriptions (differences in emphasis, format, features studied, etc., are bewildering), there is much evidence that languages are in some ways alike. No one has succeeded in finding a primitive language, although there are certainly primitive cultures. Children do not seem to find some languages easier to learn than others: the age of onset is about the same whatever the language (Lenneberg, 1967). No one has convincingly demonstrated that there is some thought or idea, expressible in some language, that cannot be expressed in another.[4]

Numerous linguists, representing every shade of theoretical opinion, agree that some substantive and formal features of natural languages are universal (*see*, e.g., Hockett, 1966; Greenberg, 1966; Chomsky, 1965) although only the most global (and not necessarily the most important) areas of similarity have been isolated. Every language seems to have pro-forms, singular and plural, something equivalent to the modifier-head relation, something equivalent to the subject-predicate relation, a phonological system of a strikingly similar sort, some large open classes (e.g., noun, adjective) to which new members are freely added, some closed classes with few members (e.g., preposition, conjunction), which seem to resist change in membership. Every language is organized around relationships and relationships among relationships, rather than simply the naming of objects.

No significant revisions of grammatical theory have become necessary as a consequence of turning from the description of one language to another. Given that one subscribes to a transformational account in the first place, one does not encounter any special formal difficulties for any of the (admittedly few) languages that have so far been studied within this framework. The main noteworthy differences among languages, viewed in this way, seem to reside in the particular details of the transformational rules (i.e., in that part of language structure most divorced from meaning) but even here the formal devices employed seem to be much the same.

Since there are such large cultural differences among language communities and since many cultures have been isolated from each other for great periods of time, the fact that languages are so much alike is perhaps surprising. Chomsky (1965) assumes

---

4 Some of Whorf's (1956) suggestions, to be sure, were to the effect that languages differed and that this had cultural and perceptual consequences. But this claim (the so-called Whorfian hypothesis) has never been proved, and in fact appears to be definitionally immune to proof (*see*, e.g., Osgood, 1966, and Lenneberg, 1967). The concept of linguistic diversity as studied by Whorf (and also by Boaz and Sapir) is really orthogonal to the issues of universality as raised here. Except for some extreme statements, this claim concerns differences in habitual modes of semantic organization among cultures, rather than immutable abstract differences among the languages (*see* Hymes, 1964, for a most interesting discussion).

that these similarities imply limitations on what humans have the capacity to acquire, and on the processes and principles involved in acquisition.

A theory of linguistic structure that aims for explanatory adequacy incorporates an account of linguistic universals, and it attributes tacit knowledge of these universals to the child. It proposes, then, that the child approaches the data with the presumption that they are drawn from a language of a certain antecedently well-defined type, his problem being to determine which of the (humanly) possible languages is that of the community in which he is placed. Language learning would be impossible unless this were the case. (P. 27)

Whatever the implications for language learning, it seems clear that natural languages are in some ways similar, that even in the most primitive human setting, language appears full blown in structure and rich in vocabulary. There is, of course, no way of knowing how much of this similarity is ultimately attributable to a single origin of language, to cultural diffusion at an early date, and to physical and cultural identities that may impose limits on the forms of communication. Nevertheless, it seems improbable that the formal resemblances among languages can be altogether explained by historical contact, physical identities, and cultural need. We must therefore accept some native component either for language or for the more general cognitive capacities that underlie language.

The transformationalists have set the discovery of linguistic universals as their central task, and so it must be if linguistic theory is to make a fundamental contribution to cognitive psychology. At the same time, it should be emphasized that the universality of language features does not argue for any particular brand of language description. There is no way to determine whether transformational grammars in particular have captured (or in principle are most suitable to capturing) these essential universal qualities. What is more, we cannot determine at present whether the universal qualities are at bottom linguistic, or cognitive, or the co-incidence of an innate perceptual apparatus and an unchanging physical world.

IS LANGUAGE RESTRICTED TO MAN?

Man is innately endowed with the ability and the propensity to speak. No other animal is believed to be so endowed. That language ability is a function qualitatively different from anything available in the repertories of other animals is a common supposition. Occasionally, the opposing position has been taken. B. F. Skinner (1957) tried to construct a psychologically tenable theory of language by extrapolation from the laws of animal behavior. Such attempts have not been crowned with success (*see* Chomsky's review of *Verbal Behavior,* 1959, for a revealing discussion). In fact, disillusionment with the attempt to extrapolate complex thinking processes from models of animal behavior accounts for much of the interest among psychologists in Chomsky's approach. (*See,* e.g., Bem and Bem, 1968).

Direct attempts to teach animals to speak have failed. The Kelloggs (1933) and the Hayes (1951) adopted infant chimpanzees and brought them up as children, but these animals learned to make only two or three distinguishable grunts. This is in no way surprising (cognitive abilities aside), for the vocal apparatus of chimpanzees is very different from that of man and these animals make more use of gesture than vocalization for communication. Work recently begun by Gardner and Gardner (1968) promises to approach the question of language in primates in a more plausible fashion. The Gardners adopted a young chimpanzee named Washoe, and they are also treating it as a child. They are trying to teach the animal a variety of sign language. Both the experiment and the chimpanzee are still very young, so it is not possible to judge the degree of success this enterprise will have. Washoe is not learning at the rate of a normal child; still, the size of her vocabulary (over forty items) is surprising, and there is some indication that her signing has some nonrepresentational symbols and some rudimentary combinatorial features.

Whether linguists should have a vested interest in Washoe's progress is another matter. Most psycholinguists maintain that the very essence of language is species-specific to man. Lenneberg (1967) presents a massive accumulation of evidence in an attempt to find relevant differences (e.g., in growth rates, in lateralization, in histology) between the brains of men and apes. Should Washoe progress significantly, these data may have to be reinterpreted, at least as they bear upon the species-specificity of language. But while such a result would be of central importance to comparative psychologists concerned with the evolution of intelligence, while it may even point to a genuine prelude to linguistic capacity in infrahumans, the fact remains that the full and natural use of human language is limited to man and is the clearest distinction between man and beast. Even if Washoe should display some stumbling grasp of the rudiments of syntax, this distinction will be in little danger of being muddied.

DOES LANGUAGE UNFOLD MATURATIONALLY?

Were language present at birth, the hypothesis that it is learned would never have arisen. The fact that it is not, coupled with the fact that different children end up speaking different tongues, is the obvious first step of the environmentalist's argument. As we have seen, the nativist counters one of these points by denying its essence: he claims that at bottom different languages are really alike. He deals with the other argument by interpreting language development in the child as an instance of maturation.

This position has been espoused most vigorously by Lenneberg (1964a, 1964b, 1967), who proposes that language abilities unfold maturationally as products of sensory, motor, and especially cerebral development, rather than being learned skills, the products of exposure and training (as Skinner, among others, has suggested). Thus at least some aspects of language development are viewed as analogous to the emergence of such achievements as walking, which appears in all normal children at a relatively fixed chronological moment (although, to be sure, with some minor variations in schedule), often in spite of accidents and pathologies that interfere with the normal course of events. For example, Hopi children who are confined to a cradle-board during the first nine months of life begin to walk at the same time as children whose early activity was not restricted in this fashion (Dennis, 1940). A classic experiment by Carmichael (1926) makes the same point for the development of swimming in salamanders. Lenneberg attempts to show that the emergence of language follows a maturational schedule of the same sort. Thus, he argues, if language development is similar in this sense to walking, it should be resistant to any but the most violent sorts of environmental or pathological interference; it should display a reasonably regular onset (perhaps involving a critical period); and it should show a very similar pattern of development in all individuals.

Developmental Chronology: Maturationally determined behavior patterns typically emerge in a particular, scheduled order: sitting always precedes standing, standing always precedes walking, and all of these appear at roughly the same age in each individual. A similar pattern seems to hold for speech development. One instance concerns certain regularities in the onset of speech. Lenneberg shows that "certain important speech milestones are reached in a fixed sequence and at a relatively constant chronological age." Among the milestones Lenneberg mentions are (1) the development of vocabulary, (2) the beginning of two-word sentences, and (3) the beginning of sentences of five or more words. Rather more striking than the relation between development and age (since correlations here can be expected simply on the basis of similarity of exposure) is the synchrony between speech and motor milestones: babbling and sitting begin at about the same time, as do walking and one-word utterances. As the child learns to run and jump (at about two years of age), vocabulary begins to increase rapidly, and two- and three-word sentences appear. At about the end of the third year, when physical coordination is well-developed, grammatical complexity of the child's utterances roughly resembles that of adults. These synchronies between speech and motor development cannot easily be explained on grounds of equal exposure or change in motivation at given ages. As Lenneberg points out, this chronology seems immune to change by special training procedures: anyone who has tried to "improve" the sentence structure of young children will agree that it is difficult even to get them to repeat what is beyond their spontaneous productive level (*see* Menyuk, 1969, for some experimental evidence).

Even more convincing in this regard is Lenneberg's evidence concerning the development of speech in feeble-minded individuals. Here various linguistic skills emerge at a later point and some are never achieved. What is important is that the developmental schedule is still maintained: the various features of linguistic development proceed according to the same order found in normals, but on a stretched-out time scale. Most important, the synchrony between speech and motor milestones found for normal individuals is still present in retardates. Another argument for a maturational view is that the emergence of language is unusually rapid compared to that of other cognitive skills (Chomsky, 1965; McNeill, 1966b; Lenneberg, 1967). Since language is so complex, since it is not consciously taught, and since the presumed "data" the child has available (utterances heard) are so haphazard and restricted in range, why should the acquisition of language skills be so rapid unless the individual is preprogrammed in this regard?

Evidence for the speed of language learning is somewhat equivocal, in part because we do not know how much real time the child actually puts into acquiring language (or for that matter, anything else), in part because we have no adequate means of assessing the point at which language emergence is complete. Even so, there is little doubt that the initial, and surely the most significant, stages of the process proceed very quickly. But what level is reached in this preschool phase? McNeill (1966b) writes, "At four [children] are able to produce sentences of almost every conceivable syntactic type. In approximately thirty months [from onset], therefore, language is acquired, at least that part of it having to do with syntax." And "on the basis of a fundamental capacity for language, each generation creates language anew, and does so with astonishing speed." But is it really true that the four-year-old has mastered the language system?

There is a sense in which a four-year-old shares the language system of an adult, but it is restricted. To be sure, much of the child's speech is more or less well-formed; still, as a study by Hirsh (1966) demonstrates, there are syntactic complexities in adult speech that are not yet present in the speech of the child. Hirsh collected data on the average sentence length of utterances spoken and written by children aged eight to thirteen. He found that the average length starts to rise rather dramatically (from about ten words) at about the age of twelve, an increase which represents a sudden growth in the use of subordinate clauses. Thus the productive use of certain potentially recursive devices appears to show up in speech some eight years after the age when language organization is asserted by some to be complete. There are considerable (more likely, insurmountable) difficulties in judging system from spontaneous speech, but this criticism applies to McNeill no less than to Hirsh: both base their estimates on this kind of information.

In sum, an impressive body of data by now exists to support the notion that the onset of speech is quite uniform, and that this onset is suggestively related to various indices of brain maturity and to various features of motor development for which there is independent evidence of maturational scheduling. In addition, the early milestones in speech development are reached very rapidly, when we compare these achievements with the acquisition of other cognitive skills, such as adding, understanding of physical relations, and conservation. But we cannot be sure how these milestones are related to language development, which may in part proceed independently from speech development. Even if speech development is regarded as strictly relevant to this more important problem, we do not as yet know how to estimate the significant "completion" of language acquisition. We have almost no tools for assessing speech achievement beyond the point at which the individual is making infantile errors. If we assume that adult language capacity includes, for example, skills such as classification, recognition of ambiguity and paraphrase, and the like, we suspect that "complete acquisition" may not only be slow, but may be forever beyond the reach of most individuals.

Interferences with Language Development: Lenneberg has shown that severe handicaps such as congenital deafness or damage to the articulatory mechanisms fail to suppress the emergence of language in humans of normal intelligence. Consider language in the deaf. Although deaf individuals rarely attain full competence in speech or writing, in most cases they achieve an adequate level of language organization and use. Of course the deaf child must be given special training if he is to vocalize or even learn a conventional sign language. Still, the written language of the deaf is remarkably like our own, if differences in age of exposure, teaching method, source and form of input, and opportunity for practice are taken into account (Lenneberg, 1967). Language of some sort somehow bubbles up in man whatever the external handicaps. Compare this to the struggle involved in trying to teach a few words to the chimpanzee under the best of circumstances.

Environmental deficiencies similarly have some effects on the development of language, but effects that are perhaps less than we should expect if language were simply learned (as chess or tricycle riding are learned) and not in any direct sense pregiven. Children who are institutionalized or hospitalized learn to speak more slowly than do others (*see*, e.g., Brodbeck and Irwin, 1946; McCarthy, 1954), but many of these deficits are easily reversed when the environment is enriched (Lenneberg, 1967).

There is one environmental condition that has been said to suppress language completely and perhaps irrevocably: rearing the child in an animal environment. There have been occasional reports of children brought up as wolves by wolves or as bears by bears (*see* Brown, 1958, for an account of this literature). These children could not be rehabilitated; none of them became normal speakers or, indeed, anything like normal human individuals. Brown points out, however, that there is no way to evaluate the causes of this failure because the evidence is very limited: we have no knowledge of whether the rehabilitation procedures used were adequate, whether the children were originally normal, whether they developed irreversible psychiatric problems through their experiences, whether the effects of malnutrition and the like might not have damaged them beyond repair. On the other hand, Davis (1947) reports on a case of recovery from environmental deprivation that is truly astonishing. The female child of a deaf-mute mother was hidden away in an attic room apparently from early infancy and was given only the minimal attention required to sustain life. For over six years the child's only contact seems to have been with her mute and abnormal mother. Of course the child had no language when discovered, and she showed the cognitive development of a child under two. But within a year this child learned to speak and was almost indistinguishable from children her own age (who had six more years of practice). Amazingly enough, this child's intelligence test performance became normal, and she took her place in a normal school.

In sum, language development seems to proceed despite severe sensory and environmental obstacles, although it is not unaffected by them. Recovery from such deprivations is in many cases remarkable. Language is apparently difficult to suppress in man.

Critical Period: The ability to acquire language even in the face of extreme obstacles is not unlimited—generally speaking, it declines with age. Lenneberg (1967) states that the capacities for learning and recovery become atrophied approximately at puberty. He views the development of language as that kind of maturational process characterized by a "critical period." In biological usage, this term refers to certain innately determined complexes of behavior that appear at a chronologically fixed stage in the animal's development. These behavior patterns may require some environmental catalyst for their appearance (e.g., "imprinting" behavior in the duck). If the environment is sufficiently abnormal to preclude the emergence of the behavior at the maturationally appropriate time, it will never appear at all. Lenneberg suggests that language emergence may be an example of this kind of process (though of course not all maturationally determined features of behavior have critical periods). In its strongest form, this argument would lead to the prediction that a healthy individual who had not been exposed to language until the age of fourteen could never learn it.

One line of evidence comes from data on recovery from aphasia. According to Lenneberg, the prognosis for recovery is very good in childhood but very poor after puberty. Lenneberg relates this finding to the phenomenon of lateralization. For most normal adults, speech function is localized in the left (dominant) cerebral hemisphere.[5] In adults, serious damage to

---

[5] There is some evidence which shows that not all language functions are restricted to the major hemisphere. Sperry's work (1968) suggests that, while speech is highly localized, some linguistic capacities coexist in the minor hemisphere. Sperry's split-brain patients can follow rather complicated linguistic instructions presented exclusively to the minor hemisphere, but they cannot speak of them.

the dominant hemisphere often produces aphasia with little hope for significant recovery. The case for children is dramatically different. A unilateral lesion in either hemisphere rarely produces a lasting aphasic effect. When aphasic symptoms do occur in early childhood, recovery is usually rapid and complete. The older the child, the more his prognosis becomes like that of an adult. Furthermore, aphasic symptoms subside rather differently for adults and children. In the adult, the process seems to be recovery of some functions, while in young children there is a recapitulation of the original acquisition process. The very young aphasic may go through the normal course of learning, including a babbling stage, though at an accelerated rate.

Lenneberg suggests that a critical biological concomitant of language emergence is lateralization of cerebral function. When this process is completed (at about puberty), the critical period is over. Thus the minor hemisphere can take over language functions in the child but not in the adult. Clearly there is a critical period for lateralization. Whether this implies a critical period for language acquisition is a more difficult question.

A more direct consequence of the hypothesis that language acquisition has a critical period is the assertion that language learning stops after puberty.[6] This is difficult to test with normals since we are not clear on how to assess progress beyond the achievement level usually present at that age. Lenneberg, Nichols, and Rosenberger (1964; as reported by Lenneberg, 1967) found an ingenious solution. They studied a group of mongoloids whose achievement levels were sufficiently low so that progress (or its absence) could certainly be evaluated. They found that in this group language development continued until puberty and then ceased *regardless of the level achieved at that time*. It appears that, at least in retardates, the acquisition period comes to a halt at a point determined by age and not by level of achievement.

[6] It is not always clear what points in the chronology are meant when a critical period for language emergence is proposed. Two different points are usually singled out: first, the period from three to four; second, puberty. The first is usually referred to in discussions of regularity of onset, and it is often implied that language learning is "essentially complete" at the end of this period. The second is referred to in discussions of recovery from aphasic symptoms and development in retardates. Presumably the earlier dates are thought of as a kind of "most critical" period, with some residual potential for language growth available to the early teens.

Is there any way of studying this question with normal adults? Perhaps not when we consider first-language acquisition, but second-language learning may provide a better clue: if an individual is still a Language Learning Device, he should perhaps acquire a second language more readily than one who has already passed out of this stage. Thus Lenneberg suggests that "automatic acquisition from mere exposure to a [second] language seems to disappear" after puberty, and "foreign languages have to be taught and learned through a conscious and labored effort" after that time. The evidence for this is anecdotal, but unfortunately it does not even cover all of the anecdotes. It is only the acquisition of a native accent—almost surely a peripheral feature of linguistic competence—that seems to trouble most adults. There are innumerable reports of adults who learn foreign languages without apparent pain (some talented individuals accomplish the task within a few months) and, indeed, write novels in the new tongue.[7]

Some of Lenneberg's evidence is very persuasive; certainly he has made an interesting case for the maturational approach by arguing the ties between developmental history and various aspects of learning and recovery. But the case for a critical period has as yet not been established. That language acquisition in adulthood is harder than before puberty may well be true; that it is impossible (except perhaps in retardates where limits are set to so many other cognitive functions) has not been shown.

Speaking more generally, one can argue that the maturational factors Lenneberg has pointed to may not be specific to language but may underlie a whole host of cognitive factors upon which language development may be dependent. Indeed, there is a

---

[7] It is sometimes claimed that children easily learn new languages merely by running about in the streets with other children, while their parents are still struggling with rudiments of the new tongue. But perhaps it is the opportunity to speak with children, rather than the developmental level, that facilitates this learning. We suspect that one of the best cures for an adult who has difficulty with a foreign language is to sit in a kindergarten classroom for a few weeks. During the past few years we have had four successive baby sitters living with us (German, Swedish, and Dutch speakers). Their job was to run about with our children. These women learned English with little apparent effort (and with conscious teaching only by one kindly six-year-old). After all, children speak more simply, and to that extent may be better teachers of English than learned professors of linguistics.

developmental schedule for language emergence, but tricycle riding, chess playing, knitting, and even grammar writing also develop in harmony with the maturational process. No doubt a native component must be postulated for any of these, and surely there must be fairly specific kinds of environmental interaction for these skills to emerge. Maturational processes are involved for all these achievements, but the extent to which these processes are specifically relevant to language is not so easily estimated at this point. Still, even in the absence of conclusive evidence, there is something very attractive about a theory of language behavior that emphasizes its biological roots, stresses its intricately organized structure, and tries to discover an orderly pattern in its development. In part, this appeal may be attributable to disillusionment with present-day approaches to the psychology of learning. Attempts to account for linguistic organization (and other cognitive skills) through mechanisms of association by contiguity or reinforcement without regard to species-specific capacities and dispositions cannot explain even the simplest phenomena of human speech. But the failure of modern learning theory offers no guarantee for the success of a maturational approach.

Language Patterns in the Child: Attempts have been made to buttress specific hypotheses about innate features of syntactic organization by an analysis of the spontaneous speech productions of young children. Psycholinguists with a nativist orientation want to search the child's language for evidence of linguistic universals. Given the notion of an innate capacity for language, the features acquired first must be precisely those shared by all men.

> It is necessary to suppose that the features of language that correspond to the linguistic universals are among the first acquired. This hypothesis leads us to expect that children's first grammatical efforts will include the abstract features contained in linguistic theory. (McNeill, 1966b, p. 101)

If McNeill is correct, it would seem that studying the speech of children may get us closer to the real essence of language than studying that of adults: the older the speaker, the harder it is to detect the original universals which eventually get overlaid with the diverse specifics of the different natural languages. The actual evidence on this point is rather sparse. Reasonably systematic sampling of spontaneous speech has been undertaken with only about a dozen two-year-olds, leading to some preliminary hunches about the mechanisms of acquisition (*see* Braine, 1963, 1967; Brown and Bellugi, 1964; Miller and Ervin, 1964). However, with such limited data, the choice of theory is largely a matter of taste.

Braine, for example, takes the position that language development is essentially based upon learning and discovery. He argues that regularities in adult speech provide an adequate basis for the discovery of critical syntactic features, for example, that the child can determine word categories by observing positional restrictions on the occurrence of words in the utterances of adults. However, whether such distributional restrictions can readily be observed in a real sample of speech is open to serious question, and Braine's work has led to considerable controversy (*see,* e.g., Bever, Fodor, and Weksel, 1965; McNeill, 1966a). In fact, it is on the supposition that no such inherent pattern *can* be discovered in spontaneous speech that linguists assert that the grammar cannot be learned by organisms "initially uninformed" about its structure.[8]

McNeill (1966a) has attempted a more detailed description of the course of acquisition, drawing heavily on the samples of spontaneous speech collected by Braine and others but approaching the data with a strongly nativist orientation. All those who

[8] Evidence against a reinforcement theory of language acquisition has been presented by Brown and Hanlon (1968). Skinner (1957) had previously suggested that syntactically correct sentences come to predominate in speech because the adult speaker selectively reinforces grammaticalness and disapproves of ungrammaticalness. But Brown and Hanlon have shown that in samples of mother-child dialogue, approval is contingent on the truth-value of the child's remarks and is unrelated to the syntactic niceties of his utterances. Of course there may be reinforcing factors of an entirely different sort in the language learning situation. And to say that learning does not proceed by reinforcement hardly implies that learning does not proceed. More important, as Harris Savin has pointed out to us, even if it could be shown that one was reinforced only and always for talking grammatically, Skinner would still be unable to explain (without begging the question) how it happened that generalization was always from grammatical sentences to new grammatical sentences.

have worked with such materials agree that even in the rudimentary two-word "sentences" constructed by these children there is evidence for word classes: there are restrictions on the relative distribution of vocabulary items within these utterances. McNeill comments further on the nature of primitive constructions. He argues that children's speech directly reflects deep structure (which surely they have never heard); that is, children are said to behave from the beginning as though they know and respect certain universal grammatical relations.

McNeill's claim is very important; if true, it would have a crucial bearing on a wide variety of linguistic questions. However, the evidence does not seem to warrant this kind of assertion. Consider the grounds on which McNeill's interpretation is based. He first discusses the universality of such relations as modifier-head (e.g., adjective-noun) and subject-predicate in all known natural languages. He claims that the two-year-olds, whose utterances consist mainly of two or three words, combine words in accordance with these relations and avoid combinations (e.g., subject-object) which violate these relations. But consider one of the obtained utterances: *Adam two boot.* On the face of it, this seems to be an instance of subject (*Adam*) object (*two-boot*), which violates the postulated universal grammatical relations. There are many such instances in the data. McNeill has an explanation: "it has been assumed that verbs can be omitted from [predicate phrases] as in *Adam two boot,* which to most adults means *Adam has two boots.* This assumption accounts for noun-noun, noun-preposition-noun, and noun-noun-noun as patterns all corresponding to the subject-predicate relation."

This argument can prove no more than that adults interpret children's speech as though it is in accord with known grammatical relations. It thus suggests no more than that adults understand these relations and impute them to the child. Whether such imputations have any objective justification is totally unclear. This is precisely the question here at issue, and this question is begged. It is true that children often accept our expansions of their primitive utterances with some complacence but perhaps they are simply preserving the peace. (After all, if they don't know our grammatical relations, they may not know that we have violated theirs.) McNeill's view does not seem implausible and it may prove to be correct, but he has provided no empirical evidence.

Another approach to the study of linguistic development concerns the order of appearance of various constructional types. If the maturational position is valid, the pattern of development should be similar for all individuals. For example, Bellugi (1965) has shown that approximations of interrogative structures appeared in a similar chronological order in the spontaneous speech of three children. Despite the limited sample size this result offers suggestive evidence of similarities in strategy of acquisition.

All of the studies we have considered here have concerned the spontaneous speech of children. It is worth noting that reliance on overt speech samples represents a novel posture for transformationally oriented psycholinguists. We have already discussed the altogether sufficient reasons why modern grammarians have turned from such data to a consideration of judgmental features of language organization. If the character of spontaneous speech were sufficiently transparent to provide data for a theory of language, the empiricists would themselves have discovered transformational grammars, thus avoiding a lot of useless controversy. These arguments were valid when considering the language of adults; are they any less valid when we turn to children? The methodological problems in getting to the "competence" of the child are self-evident (can a two-year-old classify for grammaticalness?), but this does not change the theoretical issues. Studies of children that emphasize language organization as opposed to overt speech are still rare but even their limited results allow one conclusion: spontaneous speech provides a shaky basis for a description of how linguistic skills emerge.

In an attempt to get at this issue, Shipley, Smith, and Gleitman (1969) have tried to ask children for "judgments of grammaticalness." They asked mothers to present commands to their children. These commands varied in structure but not (presumably) in meaning. Among the structural types were rudimentary sentences of the sort the children themselves spoke (e.g., *Talk telephone!*) and well-formed sentences (e.g., *Talk on the telephone!*). Shipley et al. found that children respond most readily to well-formed commands (at a period during which they cannot or will not speak them) and less readily to the rudimentary forms they themselves speak. Thus grammars based on children's overt speech seriously underestimate the kinds of linguistic discriminations the children can make.

To sum up this discussion of language emergence, it seems probable enough that the development of language depends on unique neurophysiologically determined features of human cognitive function. Lenneberg's penetrating studies of the relations between maturation and the emergence of language skills leave us in little doubt on this point. It appears that as yet there is no evidence to support conclusions about whether these innate endowments are specifics about language structure or about more general capacities for organizing and processing information. We have no way of knowing, then, in what sense language reflects the nature of the mind.

For these reasons, we can take no position on the far stronger claims made by some linguists about the innateness of syntactic organization. Nativist assertions at this level seem to us to add little to our knowledge of how language emerges. After all, something is learned in the learning of language. The question of what that is and how it happens ought not to be submerged even by the very credible claim that much about language need not be learned at all.

DO ALL MEN SPEAK EQUALLY WELL?

Many transformational linguists assert that, except where pathologies are present, language competence is equal in all men. Recall Katz's claim (see chap. 1) that variation in performance with intelligence in nonlinguistic tasks "contrasts with the performance of speakers with respect to some purely linguistic skill, where no significant individual differences are found." In a similar vein, Putnam (1961) asserts the independence of language ability from intelligence as an argument for "the model of [the speaker] as a Turing machine who is processing each new sentence with which he is provided according to some mechanical program."

Even a person of very low-grade intelligence normally learns both to speak his particular dialect grammatically and to recognize deviations from grammaticalness . . . a moron whose parents happen to speak the prestige dialect may have serious vocabulary deficiencies but he rarely has grammar deficiencies. He too learns to speak the prestige dialect, and to feel that there is something wrong with sentences that deviate from the grammatical regularities of the prestige dialect, even if he does not have the extremely complicated skill (parsing) which is required to say what is wrong. But an ability of this kind, which can be acquired by practically anyone . . . independently of intelligence level, is almost certainly quasi-mechanical in character. (P. 40)

Given the known variability of intelligence, culture, and environment, a finding of adult equivalence might give credence to a strict nativist hypothesis. However, evidence for uniform linguistic competence is virtually nonexistent. Lenneberg (1967) has tried to support this position by pointing to language achievements in feeble-minded children: "Children whose IQ is 50 at age 12 and about 30 at age 20 are completely in possession of language though their articulation may be poor and an occasional grammatical mistake may occur." Here Lenneberg is on slippery ground. There is at present no known basis on which to judge "complete possession of language" in anyone.

In the main, evidence for equal competence is anecdotal (anyone can and does read *The Daily News, ergo* everyone is linguistically competent). Anecdotal evidence for inequality in linguistic competence is far easier to provide, and it is equally unconvincing (only the very best people can read Dylan Thomas, or make a good pun, or write a grammar, *ergo* some are more linguistically competent than others). Further we have the peculiar individual differences reported by Pfafflin (1961) and Stolz (1967) in presumptively linguistic tasks. At the moment one can wriggle around all of these findings by invoking the performance-competence distinction; but there is no substance in arguing one way or the other from such evidence.

In the development of transformational grammars in all their variety and richness, linguists must necessarily make use of the most exquisite judgments of the sentences and semisentences of the language. They claim with considerable justification that such judgmental precision is necessary in describing any language, and that the ability to render such fine judgments is in itself evidence of the remarkable competence of the speaker. Were such delicate decisions excluded in the process of writing or justifying a grammar, grammars could not sensibly be devised or tested, nor would there be as much reason to exalt the complexity of syntax, for this complexity would never have been discovered. But oddly enough the mere production of a few, or a few hundred thousand, dull but "previously unheard" sentences by the average speaker is taken as sufficient reason to endow him with all the wealth of the English language. Presumably the fact that a linguist's butcher can say "Good morning, professor; the liver is fine today," serves as sufficient proof that in every butcher there have emerged the subtlest features of English syntactic structure. It seems to us that the matter cannot rest on such flimsy evidence. As mentioned in chapter 1, this problem has serious methodological ramifications: if the grammarian's introspections do not refer to a system shared by all speakers, the grammars derived through such introspections will not reflect a common knowledge about the language.

An Experimental Approach

The following chapters describe some systematic attempts to reveal speakers' tacit knowledge of certain linguistic abstractions. We have not, in these experiments, circumvented the conceptual problems that Chomsky has raised. In principle, the grammarians' complaints about the pitfalls of operational procedures seem legitimate enough. And, as we have argued throughout, we have in hand more than sufficient evidence for innovative, rule-determined, linguistic activities in normal adult speakers (even if, as we suspect, there may be some individual differences in the range of these activities). No one can seriously deny that generative grammar is an elegant and persuasive account of some of these abilities nor that this theory may ultimately be of relevance to cognitive psychology. If all this is so, some explanation is required for why further "objective" evidence is to be collected.

Granting that certain activities of the speaker force us to suppose that he can classify, paraphrase, and perceive ambiguity, it is still surprisingly hard to demonstrate these skills by direct means, except with specially trained subjects (grammarians). Some difficulties of demonstration surely arise from the fact that there can be no "pure" linguistic performance, that the behavioral context is always complex. But we cannot sidestep all questions of linguistic behavior simply by reference to the problem of distinguishing knowledge from performance in some task. No more can we accept without further question the description of competence, as received from the grammarians, without some further review or clarification. It hardly seems reasonable to accept every convincing display of incompetence as one of the many masks of uniform competence. The most interesting advances in psycholinguistics to date have come from studies that attempt to understand actual performance by developing some specific hypotheses about speech processing mechanisms that might link competence to performance. We see this as a central step in developing a psychology of language: while recognizing that competence and performance are in some ways independent, the job is to sort out the two in some less obscure way, to relate them through some explicit mechanisms.

Our studies were undertaken within the theoretical framework of generative grammar which we treat here as an idealized system of constraints that shows us what to look for in the linguistic behavior of people. Our aim was to provide some clarification of what empirical claims are being made about the ability to paraphrase. We will try to account for some deficits in paraphrasing performance in terms of the ways people process linguistic inputs, but we propose as well some limitations on the way the generative model should be interpreted as a description of actual knowledge in the speaker. We have tried to dodge some of the more obvious difficulties of relating grammars to performance by several means. We have used tests that are direct enough to have some face validity for the theoretical position. We have tried to obtain data rich enough in internal detail to bear on the question of what task the subject thought he was performing. Finally, we have aimed at a mild democratization of linguistic inquiry:

since we cannot evaluate the contribution to psychological theory of the linguists' study of elite populations (specifically, the population of grammar writers), we look at more representative samples.

The experiments are addressed to two general questions:

(1) In what ways does a linguistic grammar describe the capacities of individuals? Although the informal evidence for some projective device in individuals is overwhelming, a private grammar may be more limited than that which describes the Ideal Grammarian.

(2) If people "have" such grammars, what linguistic activities does this make possible for them? Can they make decisions about grammaticalness? Can they paraphrase? We know that a grammar is a description of something now called competence, but competence at what?

More specifically, we examined the ability of individuals to paraphrase compound nouns and certain related structures in English. Compounds offer a very convenient aspect of English for a study of this sort. They are a relevant constructional type, for apparently they can be described only by reference to the kinds of recursive processes that provide the basis for novel syntactic behavior. At the same time, their complexity and internal structure can be varied considerably without adding to the phrase either in length or in vocabulary, a fact which will prove useful in designing suitable experiments. Further, they are a central combinatorial device in English. The creation of complex compounds is a frequent and familiar productive activity, one that shows up at a relatively early stage in linguistic development, and one that is used without restraint even in the most rudimentary discourse.

In earlier discussion, we suggested that paraphrasing might legitimately be considered a feature of performance relevant to linguistic competence. Some proponents of the theory of competence may disagree with this estimate, although they have themselves rested much of the claim for grammatical intuition on the presumptive ability to paraphrase. In our opinion, the ability to recognize regular sentential relationships follows from the assumption that there is an internalized generative grammar, granting only that this hypothetical competence makes the individual linguistically competent to do anything at all.

We present in chapter 3 a brief sketch of compound nouns from a transformational point of view. No claim is made there for any population, nor for any mechanism that may relate the description to linguistic performance. In chapter 4, we provide some studies of the actual availability of these abstractions to the speaker.

3

A Grammatical Sketch
of Compound Nouns

In The Pub, a restaurant in Philadelphia, there is a plaque that reads:

VOLUME FEEDING MANAGEMENT
SUCCESS FORMULA
AWARD
1963,

a tribute, not only to the managers of The Pub, but also to the productivity of the noun-compounding process in English. Our admiration is only slightly dampened when we discover that the search for a success formula was made by a trade journal named *Volume Feeding Management*. This finding makes it appear less likely that the six-word complex above arose whole cloth as a paraphrase of

> the award given for discovering a formula for succeeding at man-
> aging the feeding of people in large volumes.

Since neither phrase nor paraphrase comes trippingly off the tongue even after decipherment, the question arises in what sense the use of such recursive devices is open to the individual. In general, we are pursuing the attempt to sharpen our understanding of the relations between Language and linguistic behavior, to inquire how a theory of competence (a grammar) bears on the individual's abilities to form and understand utterances and make linguistic judgments. Specifically, we provide in this chapter an overview of some compounding processes current in American English. In chapter 4 we will present evidence concerning the tacit knowledge of these processes in speakers.

The aim of the grammatical account that follows is to provide a general definition of an (unlimited) set of expressions in English, typically called *compounds*. We can give no advance definition of the set of expressions being considered—the definition will ultimately be the grammatical rules that purport to generate all such expressions. Some examples may serve to hint at the general features of English we will be trying to describe. Intuitively, the following are compound expressions: *milkman, spoilsport, five-day-after-Christmas money-back guarantee, lighthouse keeper, light housekeeper, housekeeper, blackberry, pushcart.* Compounds will be treated in part as a special product of the more general transformational process of *nominalization,* in part as a generative process of word-formation that differs in several respects from transformational processes. We proceed by first showing some obvious relations between compounding and various nominalizing processes, second by introducing some generative rules for compounding, third by discussing the relation of these rules to transformations.

Nominalizations

In English, there are many sentences containing noun phrases whose internal structure reflects that of independent sentences, for example:

> *That he was drunk was clear to us.*
> *The resumption of nuclear testing was*
>   *greeted with hostility.*
> *Rolling stones is dangerous.*
> *Rolling stones are dangerous.*

We call the sequences in boldface *nominal* or *substantive* phrases because, for one thing, they occupy the same positions in sentences as do simple noun phrases:

> *The problem was clear to us.*
> *Helen was greeted with hostility.*
> *The shark is dangerous.*
> *The sharks are dangerous.*

Furthermore, the complex nominal phrases, just like simple noun phrases, determine other features of the constructions in which they appear, that is, if in subject position, they determine the number of the verb; they have selectional effects on the choice of following verb, and so on.

In short, it is convenient to suppose that these complex entities play a constructional role similar to that of noun phrases in the constituent structure of sentences. However, the sentential character of these phrases is also apparent to the speaker: *that he was drunk* seems to be related to *He was drunk; the resumption of nuclear testing* seems related to *Nuclear testing was resumed;* and *rolling stones* seems related to *Stones roll,* or, alternatively, to *(Someone) rolls stones.*

As we noted in chapter 1, sequences like these, having sentential character but phrasal function in the sentences in which they appear, are said to be related to or "derived from" underlying sentential constructions, through formal operations that "transform" them into noun phrases when they are embedded in larger matrices (e.g., *see* fig. 2). When the complex forms are treated on the one hand as instances of the category *sentence,* and on the other hand as instances of the category *noun phrase,* the description of sentence structure is materially simplified, and selectional restrictions that are identical for a large number of sentential and nominal forms need not be restated for each constructional type, for example:

> *Helen was greeted with hostility.*
> *Wasn't Helen greeted with hostility?*
> *Greeting Helen with hostility amuses them.*
> *It is treason to greet Helen with hostility.*

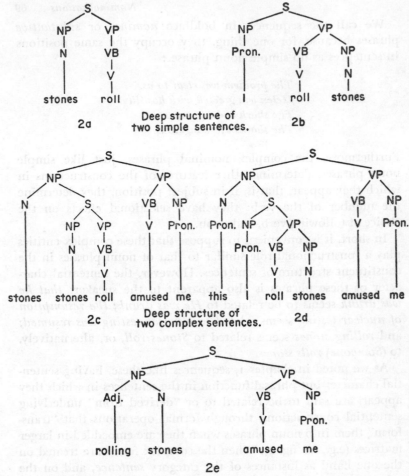

FIGURE 2. PHRASE MARKERS ILLUSTRATING THE AMBIGUITY OF THE SEN-
TENCE *Rolling stones amused me.* These highly simplified diagrams
show: presumed deep structures for the simple sentences *Stones roll*
(*Fig. 2a*) and *I roll stones* (*Fig. 2b*); the deep structures for these
sentences when they are embedded in the matrix sentences *Stones
amused me* (*Fig. 2c*) and *This amused me* (*Fig. 2d*); and the surface
structure—identical for both deep sources—for the two sentences
(*Fig. 2e*). For a description of the transformational operations that
relate the various deep structures (*Figs. 2a, b, c,* and *d*) to the surface
structure (*Fig. 2e*), the reader can consult any of a number of source
texts (e.g., Jacobs and Rosenbaum, 1968).

Compounding [1]

Compounding is a device in some ways analogous to nominalizing transformations:

> *Helen-greeting* is a worthwhile hobby.
> *Test-resumption would be folly.*
> *Shark-bait can be useful.*

Base sentential functions (subject-of, object-of, and the like) are preserved at least in part in compound forms; that is, intuitively *a freight train* is *a train* (subject) *that carries* (verb) *freight* (object). An immediate semantic kinship is noticed with relative clause and prepositional phrase constructions. Traditional accounts of compounds make constant reference to these regular paraphrastic relations (Marchand, 1966; Jespersen, 1961) but provide no systematic account in terms of paraphrase. In part, this is a simple consequence of the discredited view that paraphrase plays no role in syntactic description. On the contrary, transformational grammars specifically explicate such sentential relations. The grammar described here is essentially a hypothesis about quasi-paraphrastic relations between compound nouns and relative clauses.

---

[1] Classical grammarians often speak of compounding whenever two or more words are joined together in such a way that their independent status is not altogether obliterated. Thus Webster II distinguishes *copulative* compounding, for example, *lions and tigers,* in which the elements are coordinate; *dependent* or *attributive* compounding, in which one element stands in an oblique (e.g., genitive or instrumental) relation to the other, for example, *the lion's foot;* and *descriptive* compounding, in which one element qualifies or describes the other, for example, *houseboat, pea pod.* We use the terms *compound* and *compounding* to refer only to this last process, descriptive compounding.

There is a further reason why compounds have traditionally been treated quite differently from nominalizations. Compounding seems to result in a morphological unit, a word, as opposed to a construction. Both syntactically and semantically the compounding process reflects a more intimate and irreversible relation among its elements than do nominalizing transformations. The constructional relations between compounds and sentential structures are in some ways systematically obscure, that is, *the doghouse* is equivalently *the house for dogs,* or *the house where a dog lives;* worse, it is sometimes not a house at all, but *ill favor.* Semantically, there seems to be a "permanent" association between the elements of a compound, rather than the momentary, one-time-only, relation that may be implied for the elements of a phrase. One can speak both of *a man who brings garbage* and *a man who takes away garbage,* but since the economy does not recognize a continued occupation of bringing garbage, we presumably reserve the compound *garbage man* for the second sense. And although every garbage man is a man who takes away garbage, not every man who takes away garbage is a garbage man (the soldier who removes the garbage when the garbage men strike is a soldier, not a garbage man). We will consider these matters in more detail later on.

The paraphrastic relations between compounds and phrases are bewilderingly varied, as witness *doghouse* (a house for a dog); *blackberry* (a berry that is black); *money-back guarantee* (a guarantee that you will get your money back). The tendency of many linguists to treat compounds as nonconstructional features of the language is in part a consequence of this apparent proliferation of forms and semantic patterns. We hope to show that a generative account can provide some major simplifications here (the best extant example is the heroic pacification of these data undertaken by Lees, 1960).

Our purposes will be limited: some grammatical features will be described informally, hopefully in a way that is accessible to readers not acquainted with the intricacies of formal linguistics. Special descriptive problems with compounds also make it inconvenient to describe them in orthodox transformational terms. The "rules" we will provide roughly characterize certain relations between compounds and relative clauses, but they are not "rules of grammar" in a strict sense. For a discussion of the form of rules for linguistic description the reader is referred to Chomsky, *Aspects of the Theory of Syntax*, 1965.

Similarly, we have not attempted to characterize anywhere near all of the compounding processes current in American speech, but only to sketch some broad outlines so as to provide context for the studies of paraphrase that we will describe in chapter 4. For a more exhaustive description, the reader is referred to R. B. Lees, *The Grammar of English Nominalizations*, 1960; to Otto Jespersen, *A Modern English Grammar*, 1961; and to Hans Marchand, *The Categories and Types of Present-Day English Word-Formation*, 1966. Many insights attributable to these writers are incorporated in this description. Particularly, we borrow freely from Lees' transformational grammar, simplifying wherever details go beyond our present scope. Some general questions about the structure and meaning of compounds will be raised, and here the description will differ more seriously from previous generative accounts.

STRESS

Descriptive compounds can be characterized in part by a special pronunciation. The actual physical properties of the defining intonations are not easy to describe. The relations between the acoustic and perceptual facts are very complicated, in part because higher-level grammatical considerations interact with acoustic cues to determine the perception of what was said. We speak here in terms of certain perceptions about syllable prominence that are more or less reliably associated with such constructions, but the reader should bear in mind that these are acoustically ill-defined. The naive English-speaking listener generally reports that prominence ("stress") is a function of relative loudness and pitch, but Bolinger (1958) has shown that *pitch prominence* (generally, but not always, high or rising pitch) is in English the major cue for stress—loudness seems to have little real effect. Further, *tempo* (temporal distance between syllable centers) seems to be a major cue to the constituent structure of compounds (Bolinger and Gerstman, 1957).

For the purposes here, it is sufficient to speak in terms of three levels of relative "stress" that the speaker can judge fairly reliably in clear renditions of compounds: *primary* (strong), *secondary* (intermediate), and *tertiary* (weak). Simply note that these are apparently realized physically in terms of relative pitch and tempo. Compounds characteristically have a strong stress on the first element (primary or secondary, depending on the sentence context, on the syllable length of the compound, etc.), and a relatively weaker stress (secondary or tertiary) on the last element.[2] Thus, for the simplest case of a two-word compound composed of monosyllabic nouns (e.g., *milkman*), we can write these features:

$$N^1 \; N^2 \; (milk^1 man^2).$$

Not every phrase consisting of two nouns is a compound. For example, the sequence:

lady killer

may be a compound (with the meaning—metaphorical or not—*slayer of ladies*), or it may be a phrase (with the meaning *slayer who is a lady*). But if this latter sense is intended, the pronunciation will be characteristically different from the intonation almost invariably associated with *milkman:*

$$N^2 \; N^1 \; (lady^2 killer^1).$$

The stress here is intermediate (2) on the first word and primary (1) on the second. Such change in meaning as a function of

2 For a systematic account of the phonological system of English, and of the phonology of compounds in particular, *see* Chomsky and Halle (1968). In the notation used here, primary stress is indicated by the superscript *1*, secondary stress by *2*, and tertiary stress by *3*. Thus, for example, in a colorless rendition of the phrase *an old man*, the stress would be indicated as *an* 3 *old* 2 *man* 1, and the pattern of the phrase would be called a *321* pattern.

change in stress [3] is a pervasive feature of English, occurring within single words (e.g., con^1sort^2 vs. con^2sort^1) and in constructions, for example:

$lady^2bug^1$ (= *a bug lady*)
$lady^1bug^2$ (= *a species of bug, both*
            male and female)
$lady^2bird^1$ (= *a bird lady*)
$lady^1bird^2$ (= *a first lady*)

When the stress pattern of such constructions is essentially that of the adjective-noun sequence in English (the pattern *21*), we will call the collocation *phrasal;* then the term *phrase* applies to $lady^2bug^1$ just as it does to old^2bug^1. When the primary stress appears instead on the initial word of the sequence, for example, $lady^1bug^2$, we call the sequence a *compound*.[4]

[3] Bolinger (1968) notes the specific determinants of perceived "stress" here:

Ideally, with a three-syllable sequence like this the supposed "stress" feature is realized mainly by pitch, the difference being how the -*dy* syllable is treated. As

$$lady\ kil_{ler}$$

with -*dy* at the same pitch as *la-*, the primary is on *kil-*. With

$$^{la}dy\ killer$$

and -*dy* on the same level as *kil-*, the primary is on *la-*. . . . A shape such as

$$lady\ _{killer}$$

can be heard either way, and this is one of those ambiguities that are tolerated because we so often don't need the phonetic information anyway.

[4] Objections can be raised to the decision to characterize compounds by intonation pattern. Lees (1960), in a very revealing discussion of these matters, points out that there are sequences that take phrasal rather than compound intonation without any obvious difference of semantic or syntactic function (e.g., *Third* 2 *A1venue* vs. *Fourth* 1 *Street* 2; *ap* 2 *ple pie* 1 vs. *cheese* 1 *cake* 2). A similar objection is raised by Jespersen (*op. cit.*), who notes that the distinction becomes extremely sticky because of co-existent pairs like *ice* 1 *cream* 2 and *ice* 2 *cream* 1, which both mean the same thing. There is no doubt, however, that in current English there is a functional relationship between stress pattern on such collocations and meaning. Exceptional cases— even systematic ones, as we note for *Street* vs. *Avenue*—complicate but do not alter this fact.

The reader will by now have objected that the notion of fixed stress in words and especially in constructions is something of a fiction. There are certainly occasions on which the patterns specified here are superseded:

$$I \ said \ eye^2brow^1, \ not \ eye^2lash^1!$$

There are, then, overriding considerations of sentential stress (ordinarily called *emphatic* or *contrastive* stress patterns) that cause the usual, or colorless, stress patterns of words and constructions to be submerged. (For a discussion of contrastive stress, *see* Bolinger, 1961.) As we will show later on, the colorless stress pattern is ordinarily assumed by the speaker in the absence of contrastive context.

Another difficulty in specifying the pronunciation of compounds arises because there is only a very small number of stress distinctions that can be maintained reliably by listener and speaker. As soon as the compound becomes longer (has polysyllabic elements or has more than two elements), these features become confusing and distinctions wash out. As the compound grows longer there are insufficient distinctions available for keeping some sequences apart. For example, in a simple three-word compound, three levels of stress have to be distinguished, but it is not always easy, at least in quick speech, to pick them out. Consider the compound $lady^1bug^2$. When this compound is embedded in a larger compound, the stress on *bug* will usually be reduced (from *2* to *3*), so that the new terminal element can receive the intermediate stress. But, in normal speech, it is no easy matter to tell whether the outcome, say $lady^1bug^3house^2$ is a house for the (species) *Ladybug* or a house for female bugs. Occasionally, even in this simple case, the hearer may report the paraphrase *asylum for females,* suggesting that he heard $lady^2$ bug^1house^3. These difficulties for the hearer rapidly become insurmountable; it is impossible, without further context, to know what *an old lady bug house keeper* does for a living.

THE STRUCTURE OF COMPOUNDS

The fragment of a generative grammar describing compound nominals attempts to explain the sense in which *a wood-box* (a compound noun) [5] is palpably akin to constructions with radically different constituent structure such as *a box for wood* (a prepositional phrase) and *a box that holds wood* (a relative clause). As stated in chapter 1, the perceived semantic relationship is partially explicated if we can show a deep-structure relation among these forms. Further, a complete grammar would seek to explain relations to even more distant forms such as *A box holds wood* and *Does a box hold wood?* The network binding all these sentences does service, of course, for an unbounded number of sequences, such as *bird-house* and *teak-wood box*, which differ morphologically but not structurally from this example. The grammar describes both the wealth of possible instances in the language and the organizational principles accounting for their rather uniform comprehensibility.

Among base rules centrally involved in the derivation of deep-structure representations for sentences containing nominalizations are these:

---

[5] We now shift to hyphenation as a device for marking intonation when we cite these forms. In certain cases, hyphenation is used in ordinary English orthography to mark intonation, or to mark internal constituent structure. Thus in *132* and *213* compounds, a hyphen generally is used to "unite" the *13* pair, for example, *dog-house guest = dog* 1 *house* 3 *guest* 2 = *the visitor to the dog-house;* and *dog house-guest = dog* 2 *house* 1 *guest* 3 = *the canine visitor.* We follow this convention. However, the English orthographical conventions for hyphenation of two-word compounds are peculiarly unmotivated either by grammatical or intonational features, as far as we can discern. We defy the reader to make sense of the "rules" for hyphenation provided in traditional texts (*see*, e.g., the fantastical recipes under the items *compound* and *hyphenation* in Webster II). Our conventions for cited forms will be:

(1) a compound with the usual stronger-weaker (*12*) stress will be marked by hyphenation, for example, *model-farm* (a farm where models are grown); and

(2) space will be used to indicate phrasal intonation, for example, *model farm* (a farm that is a paragon); except

(3) solid print is used for a well established proper noun when that is the convention, for example, *Blackberry*, and space when that is the convention, for example, *White House*.

Thus when we cite known compounds, our usage may differ from the typical except for proper names. This may sometimes be jarring to the eye, but it is more important to our purposes that the reader be aware of the intonation pattern to which we are referring. Of course conventional spelling is intended except when citing forms.

[i]   S   → NP VP
[ii] NP → (T) N (S)
[iii] VP → VB (NP)

Rule [ii] specifies that sentences (*S*) can be embedded into noun phrases (*NP*). Transformational rules will then specify surface structures of various sorts (*see* fig. 3) for the embedded sentences.[6]

As a first approximation to the definition of compounds, we provide some generative rules that express relations between compounds and relative clauses. As we go along, we will take up some issues that will force us to distinguish between these rules and the meaning-preserving transformational rules that describe nominalizing processes.

The deep-structure representation of the relative clause is derived by taking the following option from phrase-structure rule [ii]:

A partial deep-structure phrase marker for one kind of relative is given in figure 3a. This phrase marker is (obligatorily) subject to a *relativizing* transformation, which produces the derived

---

[6] These "rewrite" rules take a symbol on the left and expand it as two or more symbols on the right (*see* chap. 1). For a description of rewrite rules, *see,* for example, Chomsky, 1957. For our purposes, it is sufficient to notice that these rules are an explicit way of stating the kinds of generalizations about phrase structure made by traditional grammars. At the end of this chapter we list all symbols used in the various rules.

Parentheses in rules indicate an optional element. Thus, for example, rule [iii] states that a verb phrase (*VP*) consists of a verbal (*VB*) which may or may not be followed by a noun phrase (*NP*)—either *John disappeared* or *John read the book.* Braces indicate a choice between two expansions of the symbol on the left. In all of these rules, details of many sorts are omitted. For example, [iii] does not reveal that *VB* may be expanded in a variety of ways, for example, *eat* (simply a verb) vs. *rely on* (verb plus some particle). Further, the rule is incomplete in various ways. For example, some verbs accept more complex objects than we have shown: *I elected him president; The preacher married John to Mary;* and so on.

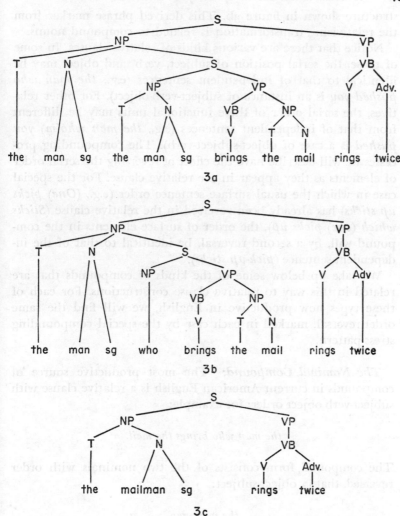

FIGURE 3. SOME REPRESENTATIONS OF *The man who brings the mail rings twice* AND *The mailman rings twice*. (a) Is a partial deep-structure representation of *The man who brings the mail rings twice;* (b) is a partial surface-structure representation of the same sentence; (c) is a partial surface-structure representation of *The mailman rings twice*. It is possible that (c) arises from the base structure (a) by a rule [iv] operating on (b).

structure shown in figure 3b. This derived phrase marker from the relativizing transformation is related to compound nouns. Notice that there are various kinds of relative clauses. In some of these, the serial position of subject, verb, and object may be identical to that of independent sentences (e.g., *the man who pushed you* is an instance of subject-verb-object). For other relatives, the serial order of these functional units may be different from that of independent sentences (e.g., *the man who(m) you pushed* is a case of object-subject-verb). The compounding processes we will describe have the effect of reversing the serial order of elements as they appear in the relative clause. For the special case in which the usual surface sentence order (e.g., *(One) picks up sticks*) has already been reversed in the relative clause (*Sticks which (one) picks up*), the order of surface elements in the compound will, by a second reversal, be identical to that of the independent sentence (*pick-up sticks*).

We take up below some of the kinds of compounds that are related in this way to relative clause constructions. For each of these types now productive in English, we will find the same order-reversal, marked in each case by the special compounding stress pattern.

The Nominal Compound: The most productive source of compounds in current American English is a relative clause with subject-verb-object order; for example:

> *the man who brings the mail.*

The compound form consists of the two nominals with order reversed, that is, object-subject:

> *the mail-man.*

The relation can be stated roughly as follows: [7]

---

[7] Here particularly we have collapsed into one rule a number of relations that in a formal grammar (Lees, 1960) might have to be distinguished on the grounds that sometimes N_2 of the relative clause is object of the verb (e.g., *man who brings the mail*), sometimes object of a prepositional phrase (e.g., *bird that lives in the house*), and so on. In part we are simply avoiding issues that have no obvious relevance to the discussion of chapters 4 and 5. In part,

$$(T_1)\ N_1\ \text{-}\#_1\ \textit{wh-}\ \text{proVB}\ (T_2)\ N_2\ \text{-}\#_2\ \rightarrow\ (T_1)\ N_2^1 N_1^2\ \text{-}\#_1,$$

where T = article, N = noun, $\text{-}\#$ = number (singular or plural), $\textit{wh-}$ = any relative (*which, that,* etc.), $\textit{proVB}$ = a "pro-" or unspecified verbal expression. Parentheses indicate optional elements, superscripts indicate stress features, subscripts index elements, and hyphens indicate prefixes (*wh-*) and suffixes (*-#*). Thus, for example:

a box wh- (some indefinite verbal relation) *wood* → *a wood-box.*

Speaking more informally, the compound is generated by a manipulation of its immediate paraphrastic kin, the relative clause:

> *a box that holds wood* → *a wood-box*
> *the dog who brings the mail* → *the mail-dog.*

Notice that this rule, as we have stated it, gives no account of why *hold* is a good guess at the underlying verb in *wood-box* but a bad guess for *mail-dog*—why we doubt that a wood-box is a box that brings the wood, or a mail-dog a dog who holds the mail. Thus at best the rule is only a partial characterization of the relations between compound and relative clause. Reserving this problem for the moment, we can provide similar partial characterizations for further classes of compounds. Certain compounds are related to prepositional phrases that are sentence transforms. For completeness, let us rewrite the rule to reflect this fact:

$$[\text{iv}]\ (T_1)\ N_1\ \text{-}\#_1\ \left\{ \textit{wh-} \ \substack{P \\ \text{proVB}} \right\}\ (T_2)\ N_2\ \text{-}\#_2\ \rightarrow\ (T_1)\ N_2^1 N_1^2\ \text{-}\#_1,$$

where P = any preposition; for example:

---

however, the decision made here is motivated by our supposition that the verbal relation underlying the compound is only minimally specified.

To specify the appropriate article (definite, indefinite, or none) of the compound as well as its number (singular or plural), we have had to break up the noun phrase in these rules as article-noun-number ($T\ N\ \#$). Use of the symbol N to describe the whole noun phrase saving the article and the plural morpheme of course is simply schematic. As we shall see presently, far more complex sequences may appear in this position.

> *a block of wood* → *a wood-block*
> *a house for bugs* → *a bug-house.*

The source or prior structure for compound nouns is thus said to be a noun phrase containing a relative or a preposition. The output structure (*see* fig. 3c) is again a nominal construction, a constituent of the larger (*matrix*) sentence. The recursive property of the base rules implies that such nominals can be embedded into sentences without limit. In effect, the compounding rule comes to be applied again on its own outputs. For example, if *bug-house* is an output of [iv], that output is a noun, so it may appear in the left hand of a rule meeting the condition for [iv], for example:

> *a bug-house for ladies* → *a lady bug-house*
> *the lady who runs the bug-house* → *the bug-house lady.*

Note again that under these circumstances stress on one element is reduced (here, apparently, by reducing the temporal interval between *bug* and *house* relative to the interval between *house* and *lady, see* Bolinger and Gerstman) so as to mark the internal constituent structure. The sub-unit *bug-house* receives *13* stress, and the external element *lady* receives the intermediate, *2* stress: *bug^{1}house^{3}lady^2*. The mechanism of compounding, then, is essentially inversion of the two nouns, marked by the addition of a characteristic (stronger-weaker) intonation pattern.

It should be noticed in reading rule [iv] that if N_2 is plural, the plural affix is lost in the compound form (*birds who live in houses* are *house-birds,* not *houses-birds*). *House* plays the role of a modifier in the compound, and this is reflected in the absence of inflectional affixes. There are isolated exceptions, such as *purple people eaters.* Such exceptions seem to occur only in case the noun involved does not take the usual *-s/es* plural suffix, but has instead an irregular infixed plural. Thus *purple person eaters* is (in either reading) permissible, if stodgy, while *purple persons eaters* is distinctly deviant.

Compounds with Verbal Components:　Many compounds contain one or more verblike components. A large class of instances (e.g., *inn-keeper, dog-catcher*) can be subsumed under rule [iv] if we assume a prior rule that takes verbs into agentive nouns— a rule that is independently necessary in treating prepositional phrases of the form *keeper of inns, catcher of dogs:*

$$[v]\ \text{Indef}\ \text{-}\#\ wh\text{-}\ \begin{Bmatrix} V & \text{-Tns} \\ V_t & \text{-Tns NP} \end{Bmatrix} \rightarrow V\text{-Indef-}\#\ (of\ NP),$$

where $Indef$ = the indefinite pronoun, V_t = transitive verb, $-Tns$ = the tense affix.[8]

In further detail, we assume here that the indefinite subject noun phrase (*one*) becomes under [v] the agentive suffix (*-er*), for example:

one who keeps inns → keeper of inns,

whence, by [iv]:

keeper of inns → inn-keeper.

Of course a lower level rule will specify that $Indef$ is realized phonologically as the word *one*, while the suffix $-Indef$ is realized as *-er*. [9]

[8] Recall that in our notation a symbol followed by a hyphen (*wh-*) is a prefix, and a symbol preceded by a hyphen (*-Indef*) is a suffix. Rule [v] moves the symbol $Indef$ to the right of the verb to which it is suffixed. Note that we have restricted the statement to intransitives, where it seems to work uniformly (*eater, sleeper*), and to transitive verbs without particles (to exclude such cases as the complex *rely-on, relier on of luck*). Note also that intransitives with noun phrase "objects" are excluded (*one who becomes an actor* is not *a becomer of an actor*).

[9] A further problem is the absence of the agentive suffix in such compounds as *chimney-sweep* and *boot-black*. Given the large number of instances of this sort, it would seem at first glance that we should allow "zero" phonological realization of the suffix *-Indef* for specified verbs. But notice that this zero case occurs only in compounds (e.g., *bar-keep*) and is not an alternative when the same verb is used in other contexts (*one who keeps something* is *a keeper,* not *a keep*). Further, the use of this zero suffix in compounds of this type is not productive. Despite the large number of extant expressions of this form, they are probably no longer freely introduced into the language: we create *poll-watcher, pill-pusher,* but not *poll-watch, pill-push.* Expressions with this apparent shape, for example, *car-wash,* often are instances of another (productive) process (*a car-wash is a place where they wash your car, not a washer of cars*), discussed below. We assume, then, that instances like

Further compounds with verbal components are formed on relativized phrase-markers with object-subject-verb serial order; for example:

> *a cart that one pushes* → *a push-cart*
> *sticks that one picks up* → *pick-up sticks*
> *a house where one bakes* → *a bake-house.*

This relation can be expressed as:

$$[\text{vi}] \ (\text{T}) \ \text{N -\#} \ \textit{wh-} \ \text{Indef VB Tns} \rightarrow (\text{T}) \ \text{VB}^1 \ \text{N}^2 \ \text{-\#}.$$

The subject-predicate relation can also be expressed by a compound when the verb can be used intransitively:

$$[\text{vii}] \ (\text{T}) \ \text{N -\#} \ \textit{wh-} \ \text{VB Tns} \rightarrow (\text{T}) \ \text{VB}^1 \ \text{N}^2 \ \text{-\#},$$

for example:

> *a baby who cries* → *a cry-baby*
> *lines that drag* → *drag-lines.*

Note that for a verb that can be used both transitively and intransitively, there is a general ambiguity between rules [vi] and [vii], that is, a *drag-line* may be *a line that one drags* or *a line that drags*.

We have so far ignored one kind of compound with verbal elements that does not show the usual order-inversion. We refer here to verb-object constructions of the type *kill-joy, pick-pocket, cut-throat, catch-penny*. Although this model was extremely productive in English over an extended historical period (*see* Jespersen, *op. cit.*), it is apparently no longer used to create new forms. Presumably, today we would not form *snatch-child* on this anal-

---

chimney-sweep have equivocal status in a grammar of American English and often must be dealt with as idioms. However, notice that it is quite simple to recover their constructional properties; thus in some sense they are not "mere" words psychologically—as, for example, former compounds like *breakfast* are. Distinctions between "dead" forms as exemplified by *breakfast* and "half-dead" forms as exemplified by *chimney-sweep* will be discussed more fully when we ask (chaps. 4 and 5) how people paraphrase compounds.

ogy (but rather *kidnapper* through [v] + [iv]) nor *push-pill* (rather *pill-pusher*).[10]

Compounds with Adjectives: Noun phrases with adjective and noun modifiers are derived from relative clauses much in the same way that compounds are derived from such clauses when the clause contains the copula *be* (*see* fig. 4). But note that the intonation pattern prescribed for the output noun phrase is phrasal, not compound:

$$[\text{viii}] \ (T_1) \ N_1 \text{ -\#} \ wh\text{-} \ be \ \left\{ {A \atop (T_2) N_2} \right\} \rightarrow (T_1) \ \left\{ {A \atop N_2} \right\}^2 \ N_1^1 \text{ -\#},$$

for example:

> *a bird that is black* → *a black bird*
> *actors who are children* → *child actors.*

However, there are numerous cases of adjective-noun collocations and noun-noun collocations with an underlying copulative

---

[10] Notice that compounds of this type differ in yet another way from those previously cited. While a *Blackbird* is *a bird* and *a rainbow* is *a bow*, a *pinch-penny* is not *a penny*, but *one who pinches pennies, a miser*. Compounds with this feature are called *exocentric*. Although the type *pinch-penny* is apparently extinct, there are productive exocentric compounds in American English, but these seem to share the general feature of order inversion (*see* fn. 11, p. 88).

Marchand (1966) provides an interesting description of semantic constraints on compounds of the type *pick-pocket*: "Personal substantives have at all times had a pejorative tinge, so the type has never been a rival of suffixal agent substantives. A very few combinations only are neutral terms designating the holder of an office, but even then the occupation is always an inferior one: *turnspit . . . scarecrow. . . .* All other personal substantives are contemptuous or ridiculing terms (in slang there are many more of them), designating disreputable persons, as criminals (*cut-throat* 1535, *pick-lock* 1553), drinkers, gluttons, parasites (*fill-belly* 1553, *fill-pot* 1616, *tosspot* 1658, . . . *lickspittle* 1629), slanderers (*pickthank* 1412, *telltale* 1548, *find-fault* 1577), idlers (*donothing* 1579, *donought* 1594), mischiefmakers (*killjoy* 1776, *spoilsport* 1821), sluggards, stupid or ignorant persons (*lackbrain* 1596, *lackwit* 1667, *lacksense* 1881, *lackmind* 1887, *knowlittle* 1651, *knownothing* 1739), scoundrels, ruffians (*rakehell* 1550, *rakeshame* 1599, *lack-grace* "reprobate" 1817), unreliable persons (*turncoat* 1557, *turnskin* 1831), prodigals and misers (*pinchback* 1600, *spendthrift* 1601, *pinch-belly* 1648, *pinch-gut* 1659, *turn-penny* 1824), the least objectionable quality being perhaps that denoting one who is a *dare-devil* 1794." (P. 37)

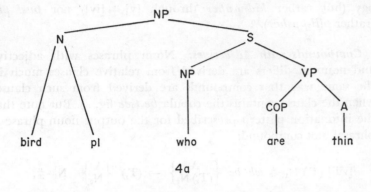

4a

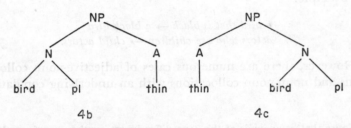

4b   4c

FIGURE 4. PARTIAL DERIVATION OF A NOUN PHRASE WITH AN ADJECTIVE
MODIFIER.
The phrase *thin birds* is derived from an underlying relative clause
(a); first the relative (*who*) and the copulative (*are*) are deleted (b);
then, in case the adjective has no complement, the word order is necessarily reversed (c).

verb, as in [viii], which have the compound, not the phrasal, intonation pattern, for example, *Blackbird, White House, girl-
friend*. This pattern is used most often (though not exclusively)
to indicate that a proper name—some particular species or type
—is intended. Thus, for example, while:

a pure² blue²bird¹

must certainly be blue from tip to tail,

a pure² blue¹bird³

is a pure Bluebird and thus can (and does) have a distinctly reddish breast. Certainly the Bluebird was so named because it is a bird that is blue, but the expression *Bluebird* does not refer to all birds who are blue, but only to a particular species. Notice in addition that the name *Bluebird* is a noun, and hence cannot be directly preceded by *very* (an adverb): *very Bluebird* is deviant, but *very blue bird* is not. Here again is something of the "permanent" nature of the relations among the elements of compounds, as opposed to relations among the elements of a phrase: the compound, by being a compound, implies a name, some unitary character to the relationship among the elements. In some sense, the outputs of this constructionally regular process tend to lose their constructional character. In effect, this is what is said by lexicographers when they list and define the compound *Bluebird* but do not list the phrase *blue bird*. The latter can be understood by reference to its element words and rule [viii]. The special meaning of the former must be given. In some cases, paraphrastic relations of the compound to its presumed source may be obliterated. If the White House were to be painted blue, it might conceivably be renamed *Blue House* but this is by no means certain; it might well be the blue White House.

This problem exists similarly for various kinds of compounds. Most adults when asked, "What would you call *a dog who brings the mail?*" will respond "*a mail-dog,*" but young children will often respond "*a dog mailman.*" The compound becomes a name, and a name need not make sense. Compound names are invented in a linguistically systematic way. No language description can safely ignore this fact. It does no good to claim that *Bluebird* is a species name, unrelated to the relative clause *bird that is blue*. But *Bluebird* is not related paraphrastically to just any relative clause of the form *bird that is blue* but only to generic readings of this clause. The system for word-formation is generative:

$$A^2\ N^1 \rightarrow A^1\ N^2,$$

but the result is not quite meaning-preserving, that is, the relationship is not transformational. Perhaps a more revealing description of these inconvenient facts might be:

[ix] (T) N_1 -# *wh- be named* $\left\{\begin{matrix} A \\ N_2 \end{matrix}\right\}^2$ $N_1^1 \rightarrow$ (T) $\left\{\begin{matrix} A \\ N_2 \end{matrix}\right\}^1$ N_1^2 -#.

However these regular semantic relations are to be accommodated in a language description, the rule as given above is a reasonable approximation to the observational facts. Anticipating the more systematic inquiry to be reported in chapter 4, we can cite a typical response of subjects asked to provide a meaningful equivalent of a phrase like *black-house:*

> *a house that is called* black-house *and it is called*
> black-house *because it is a black house.*

For this semantic function, we again find an earlier stage of the language in which the opposite serial order for head and modifier was acceptable, for example, *Little Boy Blue, The Billy-Goats Gruff* (note the internal plural here). Thus turn-of-the-century hotels are often so named (*Hotel Astor, Hotel Ritz, Hotel Plaza*) but more recently we find *Hilton Hotel, Sheraton Hotel, Holiday Inn,* according to the models of [viii] and [ix]. Only summer camps (and these are Camp) still seem to prefer the older pattern (*Camp Sunshine, Camp Turtle Mountain, Camp Kee-Wah-Kee*).[11]

Compound Adjectives: This additional construction must be described here although it is syntactically distant from those we have discussed. The outputs of this process are often word sequences identical to compound nouns simply because of the extensive lexical ambiguity in English among common nouns, adjectives, and verbs.[12] This construction will show up fre-

---

[11] Exocentric compounds on a similar model are also productive, for example, *egg-head, flat-foot, green-horn, pot-head, pale-face, long-hair, loud-mouth, wet-back* (again the pejorative tinge with exocentric constructions, *see* fn. 10, p. 85).

[12] As a practical matter, there are difficulties in deciding what construction a speaker is using (what he means) because of the extensive lexical ambiguity we have just mentioned: the same overt word may be a noun on one occasion and a verb or an adjective on another, for example:

> *I saw a yellow parchment.*
> *Yellow is my favorite color.*
> *The parchments yellow.*

We would obviously be missing a significant generalization about meaning

quently enough in the experiments of chapter 4 that we ought to have a descriptive model:

$$[x] \begin{Bmatrix} as \text{ A } as \text{ N} \\ \text{A } like \text{ N} \end{Bmatrix} \rightarrow N^2 \; A^1,$$

for example:

> *as cold as ice* → *ice cold*
> *as thin as paper* → *paper thin*

Notice that this adjective phrase is often subject to nominal interpretation (*a cold conceived while sitting on ice*). The intonation pattern is different in careful speech from that of compound nouns, but the difference is so slight that there is some difficulty in distinguishing between the two constructions when they are presented in isolation.

SYNTAX OR SEMANTICS?

We now take up in more general terms the question of where compounds stand in the continuum from construction to word. We have so far expressed some generative principles relating compounds to relative clauses and prepositional phrases. For ease of explication, we have spoken as though the relationship was derivational. But we have not asked whether these principles

---

if we claimed that we had here three different words, alike only in phonemic shape.

Words can regularly be reclassified syntactically by addition of a fixed form. For example, verbs can act as nouns in sentences when they have the suffix *-tion*. A common assumption among grammarians is that *yellow* as verb or noun is simply a special case of the same process: a "zero" suffix is added to make *yellow* a noun or a verb. This explanation reflects the intuition that *yellow* is really, basically, an adjective. Accordingly, we assume here that words have a *basic* part-of-speech classification, but that they are assigned further *derived classifications* through various affixing transformations. For some words, there seems no easy intuition about basic classification. For example, *dry* seems to be equivalently a verb and an adjective. Neither use seems prior; this is a case of *multiple classification*. The distinction between derived classification and multiple classification will come up critically in the experimental work.

are transformational, in what sense they are meaning-preserving, and where and how these generative principles might be reflected in a grammar of English. Some of these questions must rest on more general considerations of the form of a grammar, which we cannot pretend to solve here. Without taking a stand on how various issues in grammar construction may be resolved, we will try to describe the problems that will have to be faced in accommodating compounds within a revealing overall description of English. Most generally, the problems are these: (1) some apparent compounds are not constructional items at all, but are "frozen" lexical forms; (2) while surely a generative process, compounding may very well not be a transformational process.

Frozen Forms: Very different expressions are related to the same compound. In principle *horse-cart* may mean *cart that is shaped like a horse* (as *box-car* means *car that is shaped like a box*), and similarly it might mean:

> *cart that is drawn by a horse* (as in *dog-sled*)
> *cart that a horse rides in* (as in *passenger-car*)
> *cart for a horse* (as in *hay-wagon*)
> *cart that is as big as a horse* (as in *horse-radish*).

In devising rules for compounding, we recognized this fact by claiming that the verbal or prepositional relation is unspecified; that it is to be understood as a pro-form. However, this claim ignores the fact that the speaker-listener often knows more than the rule grants: a horse-cart is just a cart that is drawn by a horse. In this instance, the compound has become a lexical item with a *set* or *frozen* meaning.

A compound is properly considered a construction only to the extent that the paraphrastic relations for the item are appropriate, and in case the usual alternative interpretations are available. Set compounds, on the contrary, must be entered into a grammar as lexical items and they may be expected to be handled psychologically in ways quite different from compound constructions. Experimental work with children (Livant, 1961; Berko, 1961) shows that frozen compounds are, in general, perceived initially as simple nouns, and their constructional features are only "discovered" later in development (our children say that a blackboard is called a *black-board* because you write on it).

A problem arises because the distinction between set forms and constructions is not really clear-cut, but is a matter of degree. Consider, for example, the problem of deciding which of the following compounds with *dog* have constructional status (all these are listed by Webster II as lexical items): *dog-ape (a baboon)*; *dog-bane (genus* Apocynum); *dog-cart (a cart drawn by a dog)*; *dog-days (the sultry part of the summer)*; *dog-fight (a melee of airplanes)*; *dog-fish (any of several small sharks)*; *dog-paddle (a swimming stroke similar to that used by dogs)*; *dog-rose* (Rosa Canina); *Dog-Star* (Sirius); *dog-tooth (the tooth of a dog)*; *dog-trot (a gentle trot, a dance)*; *Dog-wood* (Cornus); *dog-watch (a watch of two hours on ship-board)*.

An ingenious speaker who had never heard some of these words could conceivably puzzle out the sense intended for some of them, to some extent because the constructional principles that gave rise to them are retrospectively clear, and to some extent because certain semantic relations between the elements may be transparent. There may be some point in making the following distinctions among frozen forms: (a) those that exemplify a process still productive in the language, for example, *cart-wheel* (through [iv], *the wheel of a cart,* though the meaning *(an acrobatic trick)* cannot be reconstructed through the rule); (b) those that exemplify a process that is no longer productive, but is retrospectively obvious, for example, *pinch-penny;* and (c) those whose constructional properties are entirely lost, for example, *Charley-horse (stiffness from muscular strain).*

Is Compounding a Transformational Process? We return now to the various problems involved in treating compounds as *derivationally* related to relative clauses: the material said to be "deleted" in rules like [iv] is apparently not recoverable, but at the same time we seem to make suspiciously good guesses about what is "missing" in the compound form; further, the relation between compounds and relative clauses is not strictly meaning-preserving.

The person who says *owl-house* does not expect his hearer to interpret this as *a house that owls fall on* or *the house my owl flew by*. Houses are not generally characterized by a regular tendency to be fallen upon by owls. As we have previously mentioned, the elements of a compound are felt to form a unit that is somehow integral, generic, or necessary, not one that is short-lived or capricious. Your mailman is the man who brings your mail. The man who burns your mail is not your mailman unless, perhaps, you are with the CIA. The man who burns your leaves in the fall might conceivably be called your *leaf-man,* but the vandal who burns your leaves in the spring is not a leaf-man, at least he is not *your* leaf-man. It appears that while we cannot determine the exact identity of the "deleted" verb we at least can tell some verbs that it is not. In Zellig Harris' terms (1963) there is an "appropriate verb," or at any rate there are some verbs that are more appropriate than others.

What determines the choice of the appropriate verb? Grammarians have surprisingly different opinions about the sources of such intuitions. Marchand (1966) believes that they are semantic, not syntactic, and sees no hope for any systematic account.

> It is no use trying to exhaust the possibilities of relationship; many combinations defy an indisputable analysis. It may be that we have instrumental relation in *footstep, handwriting* . . . but it cannot be proved. We will always try to classify, but it should be borne in mind that the category of compounding is not one that fills the need for classification. Whether a *nightshirt* is "a shirt for the night" or "a shirt worn at night" is quite unimportant. In forming compounds we are not guided by logic but by associations. We see or want to establish a connection between two ideas, choosing the shortest possible way. What the relation exactly is, very often appears from the context only. (P. 22)

By referring to "association" Marchand restates the problem, but suggests no solution. Note that the proposal we have adopted so far shares this difficulty: the verb or preposition is unspecified in rule [iv].

Alternatively, Zellig Harris (1963) has suggested that there are distributional constraints in the language (i.e., limitations on co-occurrence) that serve to disambiguate compounds formed on the basis of rule [iv]. He points out that certain verbs are very generally associated with compounds (e.g., *bring, yield, shaped like, look like*). Attempts to choose some such verbs or phrases as specifics to the compounding process are not, however, altogether convincing intuitively. Lees (1960) has discussed this problem and rejected the possibility of literally stating a fixed set of verbs underlying the subject-object compounds.

> In many compounds the omitted verb itself is one only of a very small set, all similar in meaning, and it might be possible therefore to formulate the rules for generating these compounds in terms of one or a few individual verbs. . . . Unfortunately, however, it seems quite unlikely that all the members of one large, productive class of subject-object compounds can be so treated in terms of just a few specified verbs.
>
> For example, while *disease germ, oil well, credit union,* and many others in this group might be taken from sentences with one [of the] "cause"-verbs, it is at least difficult to so construe *hour glass, gas stove, sunflower,* . . . *car thief.* The most natural source to choose for the latter would, of course, be the sentence: The thief steals the car., and the second member would be the subject of a transitive verb of which the first member is the object. . . .
>
> In a few cases one could construe the compound with a different, antonymous verb and thus as belonging to [another] class; e.g., *police dog* might be either *dog which the police use* or else *dog which serves the police.* In other cases it is quite difficult to think of any appropriate verb for the source-sentence, yet the relation subject-object still seems to be grammatically correct. For example, most speakers, unless they happen to be professionally familiar with ordnance, will not have available any convenient verb for the sentence: Proximity _____s the fuse., but yet they will recognize that such a sentence exists and provides the proper relations in its subject and object for the compound *proximity fuse.* (Pp. 143–44)

Lees' rule for subject-object compounds (mechanics and details aside) converts a symbol *V* to a gerund, after which "the nominal compound is generated simply by ellipsis of the intervening gerund." The difference between this formulation and our own (again, mechanics aside) seems to be small: Lees would delete a symbol *V* (which he does not specify) and we have deleted a symbol *proVB* (which we *define* as unspecified). But this apparently small difference in statement is consequential in the question of how and where compounding is to be described in a grammar of English.

Lees treats compounding as a transformational process, differing only in detail from other nominalizing transformations. There is little doubt that a *transformational* account of compounding requires a solution along the lines he proposed. It is by now generally accepted (*see,* for discussion, Chomsky, 1964*a;* Katz and Postal, 1964) that recoverability of deleted material must be a requirement on transformations—this is part of the generalization that transformations do not alter meaning. For those transformations that have been studied extensively, what is missing from foreshortened forms is perfectly clear. Thus *Peace and prosperity vanished* means the same thing as *Peace vanished and prosperity vanished;* no verb other than *vanished* is recoverable from the short form. In *Believe in the Lord!* an instance of *you* is again uniquely recoverable. For ambiguous sentences, there is, of course, more than one way of recovering the omitted items, but recovery is unique on a reading—if the sentence is *n*-ways ambiguous with respect to *x,* there are just *n* ways of recovering *x.* For transformations that are well understood, this *n* has been found to be mercifully small, in fact it is usually two or three. If Lees' proposal is taken quite literally, and the requirement of recoverability is accepted, compounds will turn out to be quite novel in this sense: each compound on rule [iv] is *v*-ways ambiguous, where *v* is approximately the number of simple transitive verbs in the language. If, on the contrary, we do attempt the staggering job of specifying the underlying verb, we may reduce this number somewhat—but the prospects in that direction are uninviting at best. This argument does not in principle preclude a transformational analysis of compounds, but it does lend some impetus to a search for another treatment.

A more serious problem is posed by the supposition that the many possible readings of a compound represent constructional ambiguity. Undoubtedly ambiguity in this sense is sometimes present. For example, recall *drag-line* which can be read as a *line that drags* or as a *line that one drags.* These two alternative readings refer to two different base structures, and the difference between them is reflected in the distinction between rules [vi] and [vii]. But compounds raise some further problems that may not be adequately described in this manner.

Consider the compound *lion-house*. This may be *a house for a lion, a house belonging to lions, a house that lions live in, a house suitable for lions,* and so on. The paraphrases of the compound are many, but perhaps in the cases above these do not reflect constructional ambiguity: it is quite possible that this is not a case of different base structures transformed to yield the same (compound) surface structure. On the contrary, the compound may perhaps be said to be related to a *partially* specified base structure.

To make this point concrete, consider the ambiguous sequence *Pushing policemen can be provocative.* This has alternative readings which are incompatible. Only under the most special circumstances would the speaker be indifferent to the listener's interpretation. This is a genuine constructional ambiguity—different bases fall together into the same surface structure due to a particular derivational history. The case may well be different for compounds, for here we find different readings that are not incompatible. We suspect that the person who says *lion-house* would consider it rather odd if someone asked him: "Did you mean *a house for a lion, a house suitable for lions,* or *a house lions can live in?*" Obviously the speaker meant any of these indifferently, though all seem to differ in syntactic structure. In this instance, the compound seems vague rather than ambiguous. A syntactic analysis of compounds that distinguishes among forms derived from different kinds of objects, instrumentals, and so forth, may miss the fact that these distinctions only make sense for specific verbs, and thus it seems reasonable for the compounding rule to specify only a maximally indefinite ("pro-") verbal.

Nevertheless, in some way (unknown to us) a partial semantic specification does seem to be associated with *lion-house*. All of the relative clauses we gave as examples above had the sense of *dwell, occupy.* If one conceives a grammar in which only such general semantic features, and not specific verbs such as *dwell, live,* are the elements of base structure, then the objection we have raised is effectively countered, and our decision to treat the verb in [iv] as unspecified again seems questionable. Hopefully, even Lees' recalcitrant police dog might submit to a semantic theory of this scope. More important, there are innumerable cases where compounds are amenable to many incompatible, semantically distinct, interpretations. For example, *Eskimo Dog* might be read *dog used by Eskimos* (the usual interpretation), or *dog that looks like an Eskimo* (the sense of *Bulldog*), or *dog that lives in igloos* (*dog that has the living habits of Eskimos*), and so forth. Here *ambiguity,* surely not *vagueness,* seems the better descriptive term. A rule like [iv], which specifically calls for a pro-Verb, does not explicate this ambiguity. On these grounds, it might pay to return to Lees' solution, which has the virtue of reflecting a real (though mammoth) ambiguity, recoverable by the list of verbs itself. But there is yet another objection.

Transformations, nominalizations among them, do not alter meaning. This generalization is too important to be discarded because of difficulties with the (already murky) compounding processes. But there is definitely a problem in saying that relative clauses and compound nouns mean the same thing: not every man who removes the garbage is a garbage-man. Only a man who occupationally, customarily, eternally, removes the garbage is a garbage-man. On the other hand, every garbage-man (on this reading) is a man who removes the garbage. More to the point, *man who removes the garbage* is a definition of *garbage-man,* but the converse is not sensible. If we wished to hold that the two are derivationally related, that they arise from the same base structure, we would at minimum have to rewrite the rules so as to specify that the compound always arises from bases marked *generic,* while the relative clause may arise from bases so marked and from other bases. Some sticky descriptive problems would then be involved in accounting for, say, *seven garbage-men,* as there is no generic of the form *Seven garbage-men (do so-and-so), Seven men who remove the garbage (do so-and-so).* The problem is how to derive a compound with the determiner *seven* from a generic, which can only have an indefinite determiner.

In brief, then, there are two problems that make it difficult to treat compounds as transformational processes: there are systematic difficulties in recovering deleted material, and the association between relatives and compounds is not symmetrical, not quite meaning-preserving. At the same time, what is deleted is not utterly unknown (good guesses can be made at the appropriate verb), and there is a quasi-paraphrastic, close to meaning-preserving, relation. We have reflected the systematic, generative, nature of the relation in rule [iv], and we have claimed as well (by specifying *proVB*) that the underlying verb is not recoverable by any generative process that we know of. We have thus implicitly relegated the problem of the appropriate verb to the semantic component of the grammar, where we have much company in our ignorance.

A further word can be said about the special relation of compounds to generics. Notice that compounds are exactly equivalent to all other nouns in the sense that they are in a definitional relation with generic relative clauses. That is, the simple noun *Husky,* identically to *Eskimo Dog,* must be related in the semantic component of the grammar (or in some alternative theory of semantic structure) to the phrase *dog of no particular breed that is used by Eskimos. Eskimo Dog* and *Husky* are synonyms (neither is a definition of the other), that is, both are defined by the same generic relative. Whatever the special relation of compounds to generics, it is no different from the relation of all nouns to generics.

The only difference remaining between nouns and compound nouns, then, is that the latter are formed by a recursive generative process that is partially recoverable. We cannot know at this stage exactly where the rules for compounding will fit into a grammar, but we regard it as unlikely that compounds and relative clauses will be found to be in a derivational relation. We suspect that this process of word formation will appear as a systematic part of the lexicon, along with the various affixing rules (e.g., [v]) which it closely resembles.

To sum up, only a generative description will account for the fact that there are regular quasi-paraphrastic relations between compounds and relative clauses, and that these are partially recoverable. Only through this kind of description can we account for the fact that new instances are invented systematically, and that they can be combined so lawfully that monstrosities like *Volume Feeding Management Success Formula Award* can be at least partially understood. These organic relations can be expressed by rules that show a rather uniform pattern: compounds are meaningfully related to certain relative clauses and prepositional phrases in which the surface elements of the compound appear in reverse order. Yet this description by no means exhausts the descriptive problem, for there are semantic issues that no proposed grammar has accounted for adequately. Some of these issues are the same as those involved in describing the semantic structure of the simple noun, but the issue of knowledge of the appropriate verb must partially involve the semantic specification of the noun pair that appears in the surface structure: a "plausible" generic relating a particular pair can often be reconstructed without external context.

In the experiments we report in the next chapter, the subjects' knowledge of syntactic and semantic features of compounds will be displayed, and we will offer some hypotheses about the way these factors interact when a person interprets a novel compound. To a surprising degree, we will find that people can retrieve the generative relation, the relative clause construction that mirrors the compound; and we will find (yet without being able to offer a psychologically or linguistically revealing explanation) an astonishing uniformity in the verb "reconstructed" in interpreting these compounds.

Explanation of Symbols Used in the Rules and Figures

S	sentence
N	noun
A	adjective
V	verb
V_t	transitive verb
P	preposition
T	article (*the, a*)
VP	verb phrase
VB	verbal
proVB	pro-verbal
NP	noun phrase
Indef	the indefinite pronoun (*one, -er*)
wh-	any relative (*which, who, whom, when*, etc.)
-#	number affix (singular or plural)
-sg	singular affix
-pl	plural affix
-Tns	tense affix
→	is rewritten as
(x)	x appears optionally
$\begin{Bmatrix} x \\ y \end{Bmatrix}$	choice between x and y

4

The People vs. The Grammar

The grammar that we have been describing makes claims about structural relations among phrases in the language. More specifically, it claims a special relation between compound nouns and relative clauses. But what is the psychological status of such "rules of grammar"? We have shown that transformationalists assume these rules to have more than a mere formal relevance to the study of language: it is supposed that the speaker is in some sense aware of these relationships, that rules of this kind reflect something of the way language is organized in the mind. Since surely the speaker does not know the rules in any conscious way, we ask in what ways his alleged tacit understanding of the underlying relationships becomes manifest in his use of language.

Because the grammatical description is built so intimately on paraphrastic and similar meaningful relations, it would seem that a study of paraphrase itself might be particularly revealing and direct in the context of these questions. It is plausible that an individual "in possession of" a transformational grammar might recognize meaningful and formal relations among phrases with closely related morphology and deep structure. But we need not consider the act of paraphrasing to be a test of the reality of syntax to find this ability interesting, for it cannot be irrelevant to questions of linguistic organization, whatever the axiomatic description. Our purpose was to find out something about how people perform this feat. We use the linguistic grammar as a starting point for this attempt because it describes regular constructional variations that seem to qualify in this intuitive way as paraphrastic.

It was pointed out in chapter 2 that psycholinguists have given little attention to the question of paraphrasing abilities in the speaker. In studies by Blumenthal (1966) and Stolz (1967) speakers were asked to interpret or rephrase some multiply embedded sentences of a complexity rarely found in speech. In these studies the ability to paraphrase was taken for granted; when the subjects failed to provide appropriate paraphrases for the test sentences, it was assumed that they could not understand those sentences and not that they understood but could not paraphrase. But the ability to paraphrase cannot be granted to the speaker so offhandedly. The dimensions and limits of this ability are central to a psychological theory of language.

If paraphrase is to be studied, constructional monstrosities must be avoided, but at the same time the stimuli used must be sufficiently complex to nudge the speaker's effective capacity. Compound nouns of the sort we have been considering offer a convenient tool for this purpose. They can become extremely complex even when only three or four words long, they are ambiguous in overt structure, and they are used productively in speech. New instances are created and understood every day.

Can people paraphrase compound nouns? We know from episodic questioning that even children can manage simple instances like *dog-house*. In fact, our six-year-old brought home a "work paper" from school that obliged her to match two-word compounds of this sort with corresponding relative clauses; the first grade seems to find this task congenial. But notice that in these simple instances the issue of recursiveness of the rule system is not raised. These forms can be iterated on their outputs to create yet more complex constructions, that is, *the egg-plant is the plant shaped like an egg;* and *the egg-plant plant is the plant on which the egg-plant grows;* and *the egg-plant-plant plant is the place where they make egg-plant plants;* and *the egg-plant-plant-plant plant is the spy in the egg-plant-plant plant,* and so forth. We want to know whether people can in practice unpeel such constructions.

It seems that such a test has been made, with astonishingly positive results. W. H. Livant (1961) reports that he provided three individuals with three-word compounds, some of them quite bizarre in interpretation, and these subjects were all, and all uniformly, capable of providing the appropriate paraphrase in every case. This experiment was mentioned briefly in chapter 2, and it is described here more fully, along with a replication we have performed because this work suggested the starting point for the empirical study of paraphrase described later in this chapter.

Livant constructed three-word compounds in the following way. He chose three simple words (*black, bird,* and *house*), arranged them in all six possible serial orders of three, and imposed on them either of two stress patterns common to such compounds (*213* and *132*). Thus he derived, for example, *black bird-house* and *house-bird black.* (All twelve compounds are listed in the first column of table 1, which describes our replication of Livant's study.) He now asked three individuals to "interpret" these items and he reports that in each case they devised paraphrases of exactly the sort the grammatical description (chap. 3) might predict, for example, *a bird-house that is black, a blackener of house-birds.* This is all the more surprising because some of the compounds lack a certain semantic transparency. (A list of possible correct paraphrases for each of these compounds appears in the second column of table 1.)

The implication of Livant's study is that speakers are able to retrieve sentential structures related in very special ways to compound nouns, despite the presumed unfamiliarity of particular instances, and often despite their semantic and even syntactic novelty. The results suggest, in short, that speakers may have an effective procedure for paraphrasing.

Livant's test was, of course, very restricted in range, and the results hang on special features of the word *black* (which can be adjectival, as in *I saw a black bird;* nominal, as in *Black is not a color;* and possibly verbal, as in *He blacked the shoes*). Nevertheless, we attempted to replicate this experiment, for it represents a crucial step in establishing a connection between the grammar and its users. Our findings were quite different from Livant's even though we used the same stimuli and a haphazardly selected group of twelve subjects.[1]

Livant's three subjects performed perfectly. In contrast, none

---

[1] Livant does not report the conditions under which he presented these compounds to subjects. We assumed that the only realistic test would be oral presentation, since the intonational cues for these constructions are not uniformly reflected in English orthography.

TABLE 1. Replication of Livant's study of paraphrasing

Stimulus	Sample Correct Responses	Rule Describing: Subcompound *	Total Compound *	Frequency of Correct Response (N = 12)
bird[2] black[1] house[3]	a black house for birds	[ix]	[iv]	10
black[2] house[1] bird[3]	a pet bird that is black	[iv]	[viii]	10
house[1] black[3] bird[2]	a bird for blackening houses;	[v]	[iv]	2
	a bird as black as a house	[x]	[viii]	
bird[2] house[1] black[3]	a blackener of houses who is a bird	[v]	[viii]	0
house[2] black[1] bird[3]	the black bird that lives in the house	[ix]	[iv]	12
bird[1] house[3] black[2]	as black as a bird-house;	[iv]	[x]	8
	paint for bird-houses	[iv]	[iv]	
bird[1] black[3] house[2]	a house which is black as a bird;	[x]	[viii]	2
	a house where those who blacken birds live	[v]	[iv]	
black[1] house[3] bird[2]	a bird who lives in a black house	[ix]	[iv]	10
house[2] bird[1] black[3]	one who blackens birds who lives in the house	[v]	[iv]	2
house[1] bird[3] black[2]	as black as a house-bird;	[iv]	[x]	7
	blackening stuff for the bird that lives in the house	[iv]	[iv]	
black[2] bird[1] house[3]	a bird-house painted black	[iv]	[viii]	11
black[1] bird[3] house[2]	a house for birds who are black	[ix]	[iv]	10

* "Subcompound" refers to the pair joined under *13* stress. "Total compound" refers to the combination of the subcompound with the word under *2* stress. Rules refer to those listed in chapter 3.

of our twelve subjects performed perfectly, and some of them did very badly. Some subjects thought that a *house bird-black* was a *black bird-house*. Such a response cannot be predicted or explained by the rules of grammar; at least the explanation therefrom is going to be very circuitous indeed. In the last three columns of table 1 are shown the rules of grammar related to the correct sample paraphrases and the sometime tendencies of our twelve subjects to submit to these rules.

Since Livant's results are not generally repeatable, some further inquiry is necessary to establish what individuals know about paraphrasing. The first experiment that we will report was designed along lines rather similar to Livant's study, and again our results were very different from his. To be sure, some of our findings provide persuasive evidence for community-wide linguistic patterning, and suggest that grammars of the sort sketched in chapter 3 are fruitfully regarded as predictive statements about the ways people form paraphrases. At the same time, the findings point to various other major factors—by no means linguistically external—that determine people's perception of the meaning of a phrase. Further, the results cast considerable doubt on some of the equalitarian assertions of the transformational linguists.

Paraphrasing Compound Nouns

DESIGN OF THE EXPERIMENT

Our question is whether people can devise phrases that are related to compound nouns. As a working hypothesis, we suppose that responses will be related systematically to the rules of grammar described in chapter 3. Although we know that this hypothesis will fail in part, it provides some convenient principles for organizing the actual results. In general terms, we wanted to put the question of paraphrasing to subjects in the simplest and most natural fashion we could think of so as to reveal their capabilities as fully as possible.

A. Stimuli: We constructed three-word compounds in the following way. We first chose two "constant" words, *bird* and *house* (henceforth called the *C-terms*), which appeared in each of 144 compounds. Both of these are unambiguous nouns.[2] In addition we chose twelve other simple monosyllabic words (the *X-terms*) to be combined with the two *C*-terms. Three of the *X*-terms were basically verbs, three were basically adjectives, two were basically nouns, and four had more than one basic classification (see table 2 for a listing of the *X*-terms and their presumed

[2] We are speaking here, and at all times, of spoken forms. Thus the verb *house* is not homophonous with the noun *house*.

classifications).[3] Clearly, the choice of lexical class (noun, verb, adjective) should affect the subject's choice of paraphrastic construction if the rules of grammar reflect his behavior at all. Thus, for example, if the stimulus contains a verb (*bird-wash house*), the subject might "refer to" rule [v], [vi], or [vii] of the grammar in devising his paraphrase (*a house where you wash birds*).

A total of 144 different compounds was generated by using all possible permutations of position for the *X*-terms, the order of the two *C*-terms, and stress. The *X*-term could be in one of three positions; for the two remaining positions *bird* could occur either before or after *house;* and the stress could be either *132* or *213*. (All 144 stimuli are listed in the appendix.)

We now had compounds for study that met the following four requirements: (1) most were novel, unfamiliar at least in part, so that the issue of productivity could be raised; (2) all involved two applications of the compounding rules, so that recursiveness could be examined; (3) all were of equal length, both in words and in syllable count, and all consisted of simple vocabulary

---

[3] The distinction between basic (or primary) part-of-speech membership vs. derived (or secondary) classification made in table 2 follows a suggestion in the grammatical discussion: although words serve various functions in sentences, one or two functions may seem to be fundamental for a word. The reader may disagree in certain respects with the lexical classification as proposed in table 2. This would not be surprising since the classification is entirely intuitive and has no further justification, either experimental or formal. For example, the reader may regard the use of *glass* as an adjective more "basic" than its use as a noun. Furthermore, many of the words which are classified identically here differ somewhat in their syntactic functions. For example, we treat both *glass* and *black* as in one use adjectival. Yet one can say *a very black house* but cannot as naturally say *a very glass house;* one can say *a blacker house* but not so easily *a glasser house* or *a more glass house.* Thus even if our classificatory distinctions are sound, they are not subtle enough for the purpose of composing a grammar.

However, the gross distinctions made here are fruitful in describing the experimental results. Subjects do behave similarly for words that we have categorized similarly, much more so than for words we have categorized differently: thus in all instances the within-category differences in response type (e.g., the differences for *black* and *thin*) are very small when compared to cross-category differences (e.g., the differences between *black* and *kill*). This is so when we compare the sheer number of errors made and when we compare the kinds of error with which each presumed class is associated. Thus these lexical classifications achieved some empirical support in the test situation. Presumably other procedures would bring out the more subtle syntactic distinctions, but this is of no relevance to the issues we are discussing here.

items so that certain trivial explanations of differences among them could be excluded; and (4) all were so short as to make it unlikely that we were taxing immediate memory.

TABLE 2. LEXICAL CLASSIFICATION OF THE X-TERMS

Test Word	Basic Classifications	Derived Classifications
boot	noun	verb
foot	noun	verb
black	adjective	noun, verb
bright	adjective	
thin	adjective	verb
eat	verb	
kill	verb	noun
wash	verb	noun
glass	adjective, noun	verb
stone	adjective, noun	verb
dry	adjective, verb	
shut	verb, past participle	adjective

The stimuli were randomized by blocks of twelve according to X-term and according to structural type (the stress and order of words). They were then recorded on tape to assure that all subjects received the same acoustic information.[4] Three orders for the presentation of stimuli were chosen, and subjects within each group (see below) were assigned at random to these orders of presentation.

[4] The stimulus tape was pretested and modified several times before it was ready for experimental use. The first problem was to insure that only two stress patterns, *132* and *213*, were utilized. As it happens, the stress pattern for *pea-soup green* (the vegetable you put in *pea-soup*, the pattern *132*) is sometimes difficult to distinguish from yet another stress pattern, the one found in *pea-soup green* (as green as *pea-soup*, the pattern *231*). We first trained three judges to distinguish the consistently between these two patterns, using the two versions of *pea-soup green* as the training stimuli. We subsequently used these judges to pretest all relevant items for this distinction, modifying the pronunciation if necessary until there was agreement that the appropriate *132* stress had been produced.

A final pretest was conducted on all items. Two members of our staff were trained to indicate stress and then they judged each item for *132* vs. *213* pattern. There was 95 percent agreement. The remaining stimuli were re-recorded and retested until complete reliability of interpretation was achieved.

B. Subjects: In the replication of the Livant study, we had noticed that subjects who were highly educated were more successful at this task. Our first supposition was that the less educated subjects might have had trouble understanding or accepting the instructions. After all, some of the responses called for are rather bizarre (e.g., *a bird who blackens houses* for *houseblack bird*). On the other hand, less educated subjects seemed to answer "correctly" for some semantically anomalous compounds that we could on formal grounds characterize as constructionally simple. It therefore seemed possible that there were intrinsically linguistic distinctions among populations in the ability to paraphrase compounds without contextual recourse. To test this possibility, we chose subjects from three educational groups:

Group A: Seven graduate students and Ph.D.'s in various fields.
Group B: Seven undergraduates and college graduates who
          had no intention of doing graduate work.
Group C: Eleven secretaries with high school degrees who had
          no intention of going to college.

All subjects were essentially monolingual white female English speakers. Most were midAtlantic and midWestern in linguistic background, but one was Canadian. All were between the ages of nineteen and thirty-six. All subjects were recruited to "participate in an experiment about the way people use English," and all were paid at the same rate for participation. Four secretaries were later discarded because of possible failure to understand the instructions. (*See* note 1, p. 141) We thus ended up with twenty-one subjects, seven in each of three groups. As noted earlier, subjects within groups were further subdivided into order groups that received the stimuli in different serial orders.

C. Procedure: Subjects were instructed to provide for each of the 144 compound nouns a phrase that "meant about the same thing" as the compound. (The formal instructions read to each subject appear in the appendix.) We provided known and novel compounds, along with their paraphrases, as examples. Subjects were told that some of their responses had to be semantically odd since some of the stimulus compounds were odd. We made every effort to assure that the task was understood, and the experimenter often repeated and amplified parts of the formal instructions. Other sorts of information were not provided. In practice, the subjects seemed to understand what they were being asked to do.

After reading the instructions, the experimenter played the stimuli one by one, and the subject gave her paraphrase for each. The subject could (and often did) ask for a replay of the stimulus. There was no time limit for responding. The subject was never told whether or not her answer was correct. The experimenter tried to respond neutrally in each instance, and the subject was informed in advance that this was a condition of the experiment (but even with the best of intentions the experimenter occasionally broke up on an ingenious solution). The entire experimental session was taped. After every fifty stimuli, or whenever the subject requested, a fifteen-minute break was taken. The sessions lasted from $2\frac{1}{2}$ to $3\frac{1}{2}$ hours.

Subjects sometimes repeated the stimulus aloud before or after giving a response. Occasionally the repetition was inaccurate (the subject misreported the stress or order of words, or even misheard a word). In these cases, the experimenter said, "Let me play that one for you again," and the subject was encouraged to give a new response.

After the session was over, the experimenter asked the subject about her educational background and age. These questions were delayed until after testing so that subjects would not construe the situation as an intelligence test (perhaps it was).

D. Scoring: The methods used to score subjects' responses are in a very intimate way the basis for all our interpretations of the findings. Since this is so, it is necessary here to describe the methods of scoring in more than ordinary detail.

1. Did Subjects Err?   A linguist and a graduate student scored the responses on the basis of the grammatical descriptions provided in chapter 3 and on the basis of their intuition about the correctness of the paraphrases. Both judges scored the responses for three subjects and reliability was found to be high.[5] Thus a correct paraphrase was taken to be one that the grammar predicted, the left-hand "source" of the compound-noun constructions described by the rules of the grammar.

Often, a response can be taken in two ways, only one of which is in our sense correct. Thus a response to *bird black-house* might be *a house for a bird that is black.* Does the subject mean that the house is black (the correct interpretation) or that the bird is black (the incorrect interpretation)? Little attempt was made during the experimental sessions to clarify such responses, because pilot work showed that any such probing tended to confuse and mislead the subject. We always gave subjects the benefit of the doubt in scoring these ambiguous responses, even though we sometimes did suspect that the subject meant what she shouldn't have. Interestingly enough, A-group subjects often spontaneously explained such responses while other subjects did not.

The particular verb or preposition chosen by the subject when giving responses related to rule [iv] (in which verb or preposition is "deleted" in the compound) was not considered of relevance in scoring. For example, in response to *black-house bird,* a subject might say:

> *a bird who lives in a black house*
> *a bird from a black house*
> *a bird for black houses*
> *birds who hang around black houses*
> *birds who build their nests in black houses*
> *a bird of black houses.*

All of these responses are equivalently described by rule [iv], and all were scored identically. Responses were often expanded. The

[5] There was greater than 92 percent reliability between the independent scorings for three subjects made by these judges. Most inconsistencies arose from a failure by one judge to notice ambiguity in either stimulus item or response. Thus the inconsistencies in scoring were usually easy to resolve. Scoring was also checked to see whether a response scored as correct for one subject was scored the same way for other subjects. There was a slight (not statistically significant) "halo" effect, a tendency to score "good" subjects leniently, possibly because their responses were more fluent and literate. Inconsistencies of this kind were also corrected.

"internal" compound (the two words joined under *13* stress, the hyphenated pair) was also paraphrased, for example:

> *birds that live in a house that is black.*

Expansion of the internal compound was not required, simply because requiring subjects to take this further step would have involved more complicated instructions. However, if the subject did expand and made an error in expanding, her response was called incorrect. Then only if a subject responds to *black-house bird:*

> *a bird who lives in a house and he, the bird, is black*

or:

> *a black bird who lives in a house*

do we claim that she has erred.

  2. How Did Subjects Err? Subjects made various kinds of error, and we now asked whether we could distinguish among them. Sometimes the response seemed utterly far-fetched, given the structure of the compound, while other responses seemed to be only a bit off the mark. We found that we could make this distinction very fruitfully by asking what compound the phrase given as response was a paraphrase of. In other words, *while the correct response is a paraphrase of the compound we provided, the incorrect response is a paraphrase of something else.* We could now compare the two source structures: the one we actually gave to the subject and the one she acted as though we had given her. And we could ask what distinguished between these two sources: perhaps they were both compound nouns but differed in the order of the words or in the stress feature; perhaps the paraphrastic source of the response given by the subject was not a compound noun at all. Since we are assuming that perceived paraphrastic relations tell us something about the subjects' linguistic organization, we made use of this device in distinguishing among response types. On this basis, we could isolate four kinds of error:

   a. Errors of Order (E_o):   If the response the subject gave would have been correct had the order of the *13* to the *2* stressed word in the stimulus been reversed, we say that the subject made an (O_1) error of order, for example:

ERROR OF ORDER (O_1)

STIMULUS	*bird-house boot*
CORRECT RESPONSE	*a boot you wear in a bird-house*
ERROR OF ORDER (O_1)	*a bird-house that has a boot in it*
ALTERNATIVE STIMULUS (stimulus for which this response would have been correct)	*boot bird-house*

Similarly, when a single change of order within the *13* (internal) compound would make the response correct, this inversion was considered an (O_2) error of order, for example:

ERROR OF ORDER (O_2)

STIMULUS	*bird-house boot*
CORRECT RESPONSE	*a boot you wear in the bird-house*
ERROR OF ORDER (O_2)	*a boot for house-birds, pet birds*
ALTERNATIVE STIMULUS (stimulus for which this response would have been correct)	*house-bird boot*

Analysis showed no interesting differences between O_1 and O_2 errors of order (although intuitively the O_1 error usually seems to do less violence to the semantic structure of the compound). These two categories of error-type were therefore collapsed in the analyses of results.

   b. Errors of Stress (E_s):   If a change in the stress feature of the compound would make the wrong answer the right answer, we say there was an error of stress, for example:

ERROR OF STRESS (E_s)

STIMULUS	*dry-house bird*
CORRECT RESPONSE	*a bird who lives in a dry-house*
ERROR OF STRESS (E_s)	*a house-bird who is dry*
ALTERNATIVE STIMULUS	*dry house-bird*
(stimulus for which this response	
would have been correct)	

Just as with errors of order, a single change in the compound is here sufficient to repair the responses.

    c. Errors of Chaos (E_{ch}): Where more than one change of stress or order or both would have to be made in the compound to make the wrong answer the right one, the error is called an error of chaos, for example:

ERROR OF CHAOS (E_{ch})

STIMULUS	*bird-house black*
CORRECT RESPONSE	*paint for blackening bird-houses; as black as a bird-house*
ERROR OF CHAOS (E_{ch})	*a house for a black-bird*
ALTERNATIVE STIMULUS	*black-bird house*
(stimulus for which this response	
would have been correct)	

Note that in order to transmute *bird-house black* into *black-bird house* we have to (1) put *black* in first serial position; and (2) join *black* to *bird* intonationally. We termed such responses "chaos" because they seemed to play so fast and loose with the syntactic determinants in the stimuli, and because they completely garbled the presumed meaning. There is another reason: notice that any relative clause or prepositional phrase response containing the three words of the stimulus can be repaired by two changes, of order and stress. Thus E_{ch} can be regarded as the ceiling on error.

    d. Errors of Format (E_f): If the subject fails to provide a nominal response at all, we call the error an error of format, for example:

ERROR OF FORMAT (E_t)

STIMULUS	*bird wash-house*
CORRECT RESPONSE	*a house where birds are washed;*
	a laundry for birds
ERROR OF FORMAT (E_t)	*Somebody is telling the bird to*
	wash the house;
	Wash the house-bird!;
	An Indian is saying:
	"Bird: wash house!"
ALTERNATIVE STIMULUS	*Wash the house, bird!*
(stimulus for which this response	*Wash the house-bird!*
would have been correct)	*Bird: wash house!*

How are we to regard responses of this sort? We expected a relative clause or a prepositional phrase, but we were given an imperative sentence.[6] To repair responses of this kind, that is, to find the phrase for which these responses are paraphrases, is a more complicated matter. For one thing, we have to insert the word *the* (thus the hypothetical stimulus phrase would be *Bird—wash the house!*). It is hard to think why the subject thought she was listening to an imperative sentence in light of this fact: the conditions under which *the* fails to appear in such sentences are rather well fixed (in headlines; when Tonto speaks; when babies babble), and indeed, one subject here seems to have captured one of these conditions. But, in addition to the absence of this "function" word, the stress of the compound is all wrong for such an interpretation. We would have to impose a totally new intonation contour on the stimulus to account for the response by our substitution method. Also it is of some minor relevance that the subjects were told that the stimuli were compound nouns, and were given examples of them. We will not anticipate discussion of the findings by explaining here our interpretation of why subjects made this strange response. For scoring purposes we stand on simply intuitive grounds: though we may not know

---

[6] Almost all errors of format of this kind were imperatives. However, there were a very few sentential, as opposed to relative, responses when the compound contained a prenominal adjective, for example, the subject occasionally responded *The bird-house is black* when presented with *black bird-house*. Although this is semantically just right, we had to stick to our requirement that in form as well as content the response be a paraphrase. At any rate, errors of this latter type were so rare as to be statistically invisible.

precisely what a compound noun is, surely it is not an imperative sentence. (*See* note 2, p. 142.)

E. *Overall Design of the Experiment:* A total of 144 compound noun stimulus items were presented to twenty-one subjects to paraphrase. The basic independent variables were: (a) phrase category (see below), and (b) population differences (three groups of subjects: graduate students, undergraduates, and secretaries). The basic dependent variables were: (a) correctness or incorrectness of response, and (b) the type of error (E_o, E_s, E_{ch}, E_f).

The phrase categories are listed in Table 3. We will use the following notation. The two constant terms (*house, bird*) will be denoted by *C*, and the X-term will be denoted by the symbol of its lexical class (*N, A, V, AV* or *NA*).[7] Hyphenation will be used to indicate stress pattern as described in chapter 3. For example, *C N-C* indicates a compound in which the X-term is a noun in second position, and the stress pattern is *213* (e.g., *bird foothouse, house boot-bird*). *A-C C* describes a compound with an X-term that is an adjective in first position, and with a *132* stress pattern (e.g., *black-bird house, thin-house bird*).

RESULTS

The effects of most variables described here are so large as to make statistical analysis unnecessary. Most results are displayed in graphic or tabular form in the text. Nevertheless, for the sake of completeness we did submit the data to statistical analysis, primarily through the analysis of variance technique. The tables on which these analyses are based appear in the appendix wherever they are not included in the text.

A. *The Effects of Group Membership:* The result that stands out immediately is an overwhelming difference among the three groups of subjects. The mean error rate per item was .13 for group A, .45 for group B, and .62 for group C. Figure 5 presents the individual error scores for each subject. There is no overlap at all between groups A and C and almost no overlap between

[7] These symbols refer to the basic lexical classification of the words, as given in table 2. Thus N = noun, A = adjective, V = verb, NA = noun/adjective, AV = adjective (or past participle)/verb.

TABLE 3. PHRASE CATEGORIES AND SAMPLE PARAPHRASES *

X-Term	Phrase Category	Stimulus Item	Sample Correct Paraphrase
NOUN:	N C-C	foot bird-house	the nethermost bird-house
(foot, boot)	N-C C	foot-bird house	a house for birds with big feet
	C N-C	bird foot-house	a foot-house for birds
	C-N C	house-foot bird	a bird of the species house-foot
	C-C N	house-bird foot	the foot of your pet bird
	C C-N	bird house-foot	a foot disease common to birds
ADJECTIVE:	A C-C	bright house-bird	an intelligent parakeet
(bright, thin,	A-C C	bright-bird house	a house for gaily colored birds
black)	C A-C	bird bright-house	a university for birds
	C-A C	bird-bright house	a house for polishing up birds
	C-C A	bird-house bright	as bright as a bird-house
	C C-A	bird house-bright	brightening material for houses, used by birds
VERB:	V C-C	kill bird-house	the bird-house used for slaughter
(kill, eat,	V-C C	kill-house bird	the bird who lives in a slaughter-house
wash)	C V-C	bird kill-house	a slaughter-house for birds
	C-V C	house-kill bird	a bird who murders houses
	C-C V	house-bird kill	the prey of the house-bird
	C C-V	bird house-kill	murder in houses, conducted by birds
ADJ/VERB:	AV C-C	dry bird-house	a bird-house that is not wet
(dry, shut)	AV-C C	dry-house bird	the bird who lives in a dry house
	C AV-C	house dry-bird	the thirsty bird who lives at home
	C-AV C	house-dry bird	the bird who is dry when indoors
	C-C AV	house-bird dry	as dry as a house-bird
	C C-AV	bird house-dry	a drying of houses done by birds

X-*Term*	*Phrase Category*	*Stimulus Item*	*Sample Correct Paraphrase*
NOUN/ADJ:	NA C-C	glass bird-house	a bird-house made of glass
(glass, stone)	NA-C C	glass-house bird	a bird who shouldn't throw stones
	C NA-C	bird glass-house	a glass house for birds to live in
	C-NA C	house-glass bird	a bird made from house-glass
	C-C NA	house-bird glass	the drinking-cup of the pet bird
	C C-NA	bird house-glass	the monocle used at home by the bird

* The same X-term from each lexical class is used in all the examples to clarify the overall design.

groups A and B. The appendix provides the actual responses for the median subject in each population group, and also gives responses of all subjects to one stimulus in each phrase category. Examination of these sample responses is perhaps the most convincing way to see the very large and consistent differences among these subjects of differing educational background. Mean error scores are at best a pale reflection of these pervasive differences.[8]

The subjects differed, not only in the absolute number of errors made, but in the kinds of errors they committed. To analyze this effect, we computed for each subject the ratio of each of the four error types to the total number of errors made by that subject. Table 4 presents the means of these ratios by group and by error type. Several analyses of variance showed reliable group differences for errors of order and of chaos: A-group subjects made proportionally more errors of order and fewer errors of chaos than did the B- and C-group subjects.[9] This result is of

[8] Analysis of variance shows that the group effect reaches a massive level of statistical significance ($F = 38.1$, $df = 2$ and 18, $p < .001$). According to Duncan's Multiple Range Test, the difference between group A and the other two groups is significant at the .001 level, that between groups B and C at the .01 level.

[9] For errors of order, $F = 5.01$, with $df = 2$ and 18, $p < .025$. For errors of chaos, $F = 5.72$, with $df = 2$ and 18, $p < .025$. Statistically significant differ-

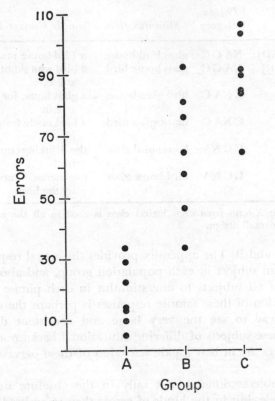

FIGURE 5. ERRORS OF PARAPHRASING AS A FUNCTION OF GROUP

particular importance because, as we shall later discuss, it implies qualitative differences among the populations in the way they approached the paraphrasing task.[10]

ences among groups were not obtained for errors of stress and format. (Of course this holds only for the *ratios* of one kind of error relative to the others, not for their *absolute* number.)

[10] It will be recalled that in addition to the population groups, subjects (within groups) were further subdivided into "order groups" that received the stimuli in different serial order. This difference did not affect the final error scores. An analysis of variance showed no trace of an order effect ($F < 1$).

A related question concerns item difficulty as a function of serial position: does the subject get better at the task as she proceeds? To deal with this

B. *The Effects of Syntactic Pattern:* We have now demonstrated that an experiment of the sort Livant has described will generally have results quite different from those he obtained. None of our subjects performed perfectly. However, before we turn to a description of the circumstances that led our subjects to err, one backward note is in order. We cannot be blind to the fact that in about half the instances, our subjects did provide syntactically determined responses, responses that conformed in form and content to the description we have proposed. Out of all the indefinitely many expressions in the language, subjects surprisingly often found one that is a constructional paraphrase in this strong sense. If the reader does not find this surprising, let him consider whether any other theoretical description would

TABLE 4. GROUP MEMBERSHIP AND ERROR TYPE

	Mean Percent of Total Error		
Error Type	Group A	Group B	Group C
Order	60	42	35
Stress	26	29	33
Chaos	8	24	21
Format	6	5	11
All Errors	100	100	100

allow us to predict in any precise way what form paraphrases would take.

On the other hand, subjects did err very often. Although the less-educated subjects erred more often than members of group A, the results display a remarkable correspondence among all groups in the syntactic and semantic determinants of error: the same phrase categories made trouble for all subjects, regardless

---

point, we considered mean error scores for test items 1–36; seven subjects received these as the first 36 items, seven others received them in position 96–132, seven others in position 109–144. The mean error scores do decline very slightly for groups that received the items later in the test, but the effect does not begin to reach statistical significance. An analysis of variance for the 36 stimuli shows the usual high effect of groups ($F = 42.2$, $df = 2$ and 12, $p < .001$), but neither the main effect of serial position nor its interaction with the group effect met anything like the usual criteria of statistical acceptability (both p-values were larger than .25).

of their educational background, although, as we showed earlier, the response to difficulty (the particular error type) differed with population group. We now consider the syntactic and semantic features of compounds that led to error.

1. The Relation of Phrase Category to the Number of Errors: Tables A and B of the appendix list the various phrase categories and the errors and error types associated with them, for compounds containing N, A, and V X-terms.[11] It is clear from an examination of these tables that errors are distributed unequally among the phrase categories. In order to isolate some of the factors involved here, we can lump the phrase categories together in various ways. For example, if we consider the phrase categories by lexical class of the X-term (either N, A, or V), we find that this basic classification is a strong determinant of error: the mean error for compounds with noun X-terms was .27 (per item); for compounds with adjective X-terms it was .44; and for compounds with verb X-terms it was .42.[12]

Since English is a language in which sequential patterning is a central syntactic feature, analysis by lexical class is obviously too crude a description of what is happening here. In table 5 we

[11] In this and some of the following analyses we are considering only the compounds containing unambiguously classified X-terms. Thus we exclude for the moment stimuli containing the X-terms *glass, stone, dry,* and *shut.* We are now dealing with ninety-six stimulus items. An analysis of variance was performed for these ninety-six items to assure that the population effects were still there, and the result was again enormous ($F = 30.3$, $df = 2$ and 18, $p < .001$).

[12] This result is highly significant ($F = 11.5$, $df = 2$ and 331, $p < .001$). It is worth noting that there is no interaction between population group and lexical class ($F < 1$). In this and all of the subsequent analyses of these data, we have statistically corrected for the huge absolute differences in total error scores among the three groups. The mean error score of C-group subjects was 4.9 times greater than that of the A-group subjects, and 1.4 times greater than that of the B-group subjects. Accordingly, all scores of A-group subjects were multiplied by 4.9, and all scores of B-group subjects were multiplied by 1.4; those of the C-group subjects were left unchanged. Without such an equalizing procedure, the C-group data would have had a disproportionate effect on the overall analyses. It should be noted that while data transformed in this fashion form the basis for the statistical analyses, all tabular and graphic presentations are based on untransformed scores. A final point: the results here presented are very robust and are largely unaffected by data transformations. Most of the analyses reported have been performed on both transformed and raw scores, with virtually identical results.

TABLE 5. PERFORMANCE AS A FUNCTION OF SOME SYNTACTIC GROUPINGS

Lexical Class	Phrase Categories *	Relevant Rules	Mean Error per Item (× 1000)
Nouns	N C-C, N-C C, C N-C C-N C, C-C N, C C-N	[iv], [viii]	266
Adjectives			
prenominal	A C-C, A-C C, C A-C	[viii], [ix]	278
postnominal	C-A C, C-C A, C C-A	[x]	595
Verbs			
prenominal	V C-C, V-C C, C V-C	[vi], [vii]	471
postnominal	C-V C, C-C V, C C-V	[v]	373

* When adjectives or verbs were in second position, they were classified as prenominal or postnominal according to their function in the subcompound. This is determined by the stress pattern. The X-term is prenominal in *C A-C* and *C V-C* (*bird black-house, bird kill-house*), postnominal in *C-A C, C-V C* (*bird-black house, bird-kill house*).

display the error associated with compounds containing adjectives and verbs in prenominal and postnominal positions. (Of course, no such distinction is made when the X-term is a noun, since here all three serial positions in the compound are filled by nouns.) For adjectives, the distinction between prenominal and postnominal positions is precisely the distinction between rules [viii] and [ix] of the grammar on the one hand and rule [x] on the other. For verbs it is the distinction between rules [vi] and [vii], and rule [v]. We see in table 5 that, apart from compounds consisting of three nouns (rule [iv]), subjects found compounds with prenominal adjectives (rules [viii] and [ix]) and nominalized postnominal verbs (rule [v]) distinctly easier to deal with. Thus *black bird-house* was very much easier than *bird-house black* and *house-bird kill* was easier than *kill house-bird*.[13]

[13] The difference in error scores for prenominal and postnominal adjectives is enormous: nineteen subjects erred more often with postnominal than with prenominal adjectives, while only two showed the reverse trend. (A t-test yielded the preposterous t-score of 7.50, with $df = 20$, $p < .001$.) The difference between prenominal and postnominal verbs is less impressive, but still statistically significant: of the twenty-one subjects, fifteen made more errors for prenominal than for postnominal verb X-terms; four subjects showed the reverse trend, and two did not differ ($t = 2.32$, $df = 20$, $p < .025$).

In sum, some kinds of compounds are easier to paraphrase than others. Notice that this does not necessarily imply that some of the compounds are "more grammatical" than others. Rules [vi], [vii], and [x], associated so strongly with error in paraphrasing, appear to be rules of grammar nevertheless. We will return to this question in chapter 5 after all the experimental findings are in.

2. *The Relation of Phrase Category to Error Type:* We can ask further whether certain phrase categories lead to differences in the *kind* of error that is made. Table A of the appendix shows that error types as well as total errors were distributed unequally among the phrase categories. Figure 6 shows this effect as a function of the lexical class of the X-term. We found hardly any differences for errors of stress, which were distributed rather equally among nouns, adjectives, and verbs. On the other hand, errors of order were more predominant with adjective and verb X-terms (particularly adjective) than with nouns. Errors of chaos were more predominant with verbs and adjectives (especially verbs) than with nouns. Finally, errors of format were primarily associated with verb X-terms.[14]

In sum, the error type, as well as the sheer number of errors, is partially determined by lexical, stress, and positional features of the compounds, which are in turn embodiments of the various grammatical rules we have described.

Notice that these obtained relations between error type and phrase category are in a sense already implied by the finding that the phrase categories differ in difficulty: error types can generally be understood if we assume that the subject "acts as

---

[14] All comparisons are based on Duncan's Multiple Range Test, performed subsequent to separate analyses of variance which were carried out on each of the four error-type scores. For errors of order, the difference between nouns and adjectives was highly significant ($p < .005$), that between nouns and verbs rather marginal ($p < .05$), while the difference between adjectives and verbs was not significant. For errors of chaos, the difference between nouns and verbs yielded a p-value of less than .001, that between nouns and adjectives a value less than .05, and that between adjectives and verbs barely reached the .05 level. For errors of format, verbs were more difficult than either adjectives or nouns, with a p-value of less than .001, and no difference between nouns and adjectives.

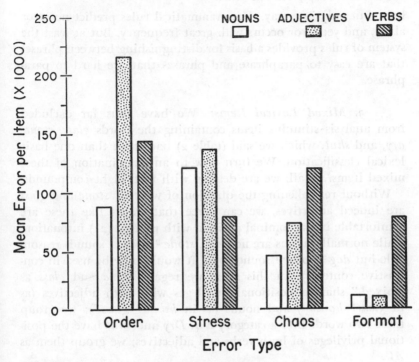

FIGURE 6. ERRORS AS A FUNCTION OF LEXICAL CLASS

though" a difficult stimulus was in fact an instance of some easier type. For example, since prenominal adjectives are easier to deal with than postnominal adjectives, the subject behaves as though postnominals that she hears are really prenominals, thus effectively changing the order of the words in the stimulus compound and committing an error of order (the mean error of order per item was .38 for postnominal adjectives, and only .08 for prenominal adjectives and .09 for nouns). Similarly, the prenominal verb (associated with the "difficult" rules [vi] and [vii]) tends to be construed instead as an imperative sentence in which, obviously, the verb precedes its object. In so misconstruing the item, the subject commits an error of format (mean error of format per item was .11 for prenominal verbs, .05 for postnominal verbs, and only .01 for both nouns and adjectives).

In a way, the grammatical description is working rather well here, but only in a way. The grammatical rules predict no error at all, and yet error occurs with great frequency. But at least the system of rules provides a basis for distinguishing between phrases that are easy to paraphrase and phrases that are hard to paraphrase.

3. Mixed Lexical Items: We have thus far excluded from analysis stimulus items containing the words *glass, stone, dry,* and *shut,* which we said (table 2) had more than one basic lexical classification. We turn now to an examination of these mixed items. In all, we are dealing with forty-eight compounds.

Without reawakening the question of whether *stone* and *glass* are indeed adjectives, we can agree that words like these are comfortable in prenominal position with phrasal (*21*) intonation, while normally nouns are not (e.g., *stone* ^{2} *house* ^{1} sounds reasonable but *dog* ^{2} *house* ^{1} sounds odd. It would only be used in contrastive contexts). In this sense we regard *stone* and *glass* as "mixed," sharing positional privileges with both adjectives (as in *glass* ^{2} *house* ^{1}) and nouns (as in *house* ^{1} *glass* ^{2}); we group these two words into a category *NA*. *Dry* and *shut* have the positional privileges of both verbs and adjectives; we group them as *AV*.

Our initial supposition was that stimuli with these mixed *X*-terms ought to lead to less error than stimuli with simple *X*-terms. After all, we know that for whatever reason it is difficult to deal with an adjective in third serial position (rule [x]), while a noun in third serial position leads to no special problem (rule [iv]). This being so, an adjective that may alternatively be viewed as a noun ought to be easier to deal with in this position than a simple adjective.

To test this notion, we compared the mean number of errors when the *X*-terms were simple (*N, A,* or *V*) and when they were mixed (*NA* or *AV*). Our initial notion turned out to be false: mixed *X*-terms did *not* lead to fewer errors than simple ones. Compounds with *AV X*-terms led to slightly more errors than those with either *A* or *V X*-terms (mean error of .48 compared to .44 and .42). Compounds with *NA X*-terms led to more errors than those with *N X*-terms though to fewer than those with *A*

X-terms (.34 compared to .27 and .44 respectively). Considering error scores separately for prenominal and postnominal position, we find that both *AV* and *NA* X-terms tend to act like adjectives: the prenominal position is easier. With *AV* X-terms the mean error was .40 and .56 for prenominal and postnominal positions respectively. The corresponding figures for *NA* X-terms are .22 and .45. The subjects evidently tended to construe such items as adjectives, even when the less troublesome noun interpretation was available.[15]

C. The Effects of Semantic Pattern:　The differences among the phrase categories are not abolished even if we (statistically) remove the effects of lexical class, the position of the X-term, and the interaction between them. Two major sources of variation still remain. The *semantic plausibility* and *prior familiarity* of subparts of the stimuli influenced the tendency to err.

1. The Effect of Semantic Plausibility:　Certain consistent patterns of meaning appear in the compounds we have used. Consider stimulus items with serial order *XCC* (the X-term followed by the two *C*-terms) and *CCX* (the two *C*-terms followed by the X-term). Two stress patterns (*132, 213*) occur with both these serial orders in our stimuli. The stress patterns have the effect either of "unifying" the two *C-terms* (i.e., $C^1C^3X^2$ as in *bird-house boot*, $X^2C^1C^3$ as in *boot bird-house*), or "disunifying" them (i.e., $C^2C^1X^3$ as in *bird house-boot*, $X^1C^3C^2$ as in *boot-house bird*). In other words, the *13* stress subpattern (whether it precedes or follows the secondary [2] stress) conjoins two of the words into a subcompound (e.g., *bird-house*).

Suppose there is a tendency for subjects to expect that the two *C*-terms will be a sub-unit (i.e., will have the *13* subpattern). Given the *C*-terms we used, this would not be surprising. *Bird-*

---

[15] Neither the difference between *A* and *AV*, nor that between *V* and *AV* X-terms achieved statistical significance; for the first, $t = .94$, for the second, $t = 1.41$. On the other hand, *NA* X-terms led to a level of difficulty that was reliably midway between that for *N* X-terms and that of *A* X-terms (for both comparisons, $t = 2.52$, $df = 20$, $p < .01$). A sign-test showed that the superiority of prenominal to postnominal position was reliable both for *NA* ($p < .001$) and *AV* X-terms ($p < .02$).

house is a familiar unit, known to speakers as a lexical item; *house-bird* is not familiar in this way, but it requires no great flight of the imagination to connect it, by analogy, with known items (e.g., *jail-bird, house-cat, field-mouse, barn-owl*). At any rate, both of these pairs, when intonationally unified, are semantically plausible. When, on the other hand, a *C*-term is unified with an *X*-term, a selectional restriction in the language may or may not be violated (e.g., *black-bird* and *wash-house* are familiar and plausible; *bird-boot* and *dry-house* are unfamiliar but plausible; *house-foot* and *bird-thin* are unfamiliar, implausible, and just possibly violations of real selectional constraints in English).

We would expect fewer errors where there is no semantic anomaly. Since for "unified" *CC* there is *never* a violation, and for "disunified" *CC* there is *often* such a violation, unified *CC*, on average, ought to be easier. Notice that if *CC* is disunified, and in fact *CX* or *XC* does violate a selectional restriction, this phenomenon might be further enhanced: not only must the subject deal with an eccentric semantic event, but she must take care not to be beguiled by a normal semantic event that she can bring into existence by just a slight flim-flam with the stress pattern. Presented with *foot-bird house* (clearly *a home for livery birds*), one might be tempted to respond *a basement apartment for birds,* although that is *a foot bird-house,* as we know, and an altogether different story.

To determine whether such a phenomenon actually exists, we compared error scores and error types for stimuli with unified and disunified *C*-terms. For these purposes we of course did not consider items in which the *X*-term is in second position (where the *C*-terms cannot possibly be unified). Again, we excluded the lexically ambiguous stimuli, leaving sixty-four stimulus items for the following analyses. The bar graph of Figure 7 shows that the stress difference indeed produced enormous differences in the tendency to err: the number of errors for items with disunifying stress was almost double that for items with unifying stress.

If this effect can in fact be interpreted in this way—as a reflection of semantic patterns in the stimuli—then the errors produced by this factor should be primarily errors of stress and chaos. As figure 7 suggests, this turns out to be so. The factor of

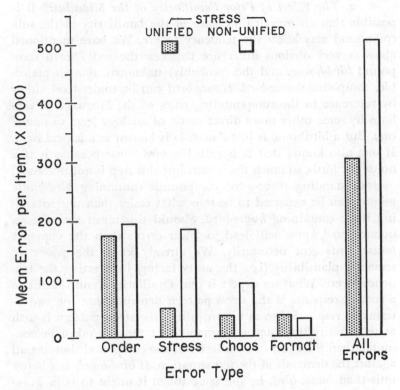

FIGURE 7. ERRORS AS A FUNCTION OF UNIFIED AND NONUNIFIED STRESS

semantic plausibility (i.e., the unity factor) interacted significantly with error type, an interaction which is attributable to a sharp increase in E_s and E_{ch}.[16]

[16] A highly significant effect of unity was found for errors as a whole ($F = 14.9$, $df = 1$ and 228, $p < .001$). When considering separate error types, significant effects of this factor were found for errors of stress ($F = 17.0$, $df = 1$ and 228, $p < .001$) and of chaos ($F = 15.4$, $df = 1$ and 228, $p < .001$). (It will be recalled that an error of chaos is said to occur when a response reflects both an error of stress and an error of order. Since we therefore expect some co-variance of E_s and E_{ch}, we here expect a rise in both.)

It is worth noting that there was no trace of an interaction between the unity effect and group membership ($F < 1$). Apparently, graduate students are as prone to such semantic interference as are secretaries.

2. *The Effect of Prior Familiarity of the Stimulus:* It is possible that an overall difference in the familiarity of the subcompound may affect the tendency to err. We have mentioned above a very obvious difference between the well-known compound *bird-house,* and the (probably) unknown, though plausible, compound *house-bird. House-bird* can be understood either by reference to the compounding rules of the language or perhaps by some other more direct mode of analogy (e.g., to *house-cat*). But a birdhouse is just a nest. It is known as a lexical item. If one also knows that it is called a *bird-house* because it is a house for birds, so much the better, but this step is not necessary.

Understanding three-word compounds containing *bird-house* might then be expected to be somewhat easier than understanding those containing *house-bird.* Should this mean that the sequence *bird/house* will lead to fewer errors than the sequence *house/bird?* Not necessarily. We already know the power of semantic plausibility (i.e., the unity factor) in affecting the tendency to err. What we expect is that familiarity should facilitate a correct response if the stress pattern demands that the two *C*-terms be responded to as a unit; but if the stress pattern is such as to disunify the *C*-terms (demand that they be taken as nonunits), then the effect of familiarity of the compound should pull against the demands of the test situation. If *bird-house* is a better unit than *house-bird,* by the same token it ought to be a worse nonunit (e.g., *bright-bird house* should lead to more stress errors than *bright-house bird*). In short, we expect that the two factors of familiarity and semantic plausibility will interact. Given unifying stress, familiarity should help; given disunifying stress, it should hinder. This effect is shown in figure 8 which presents error scores for the same sixty-four items, now grouped by both familiarity of compound and by stress pattern.[17]

D. Summary of the Results: We have found massive differences in the ability of the three population groups to provide syntactically determined paraphrases of the compound noun stimuli. The less-educated groups make more errors, and to a significant extent make different errors than the most-educated group.

[17] This interaction led to an *F*-ratio of 11.7 ($df = 1$ and 54, $p < .001$).

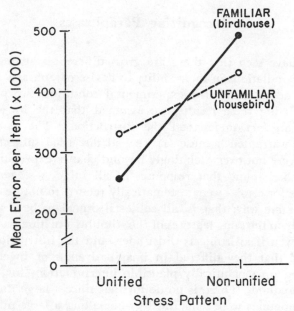

FIGURE 8. THE EFFECT OF FAMILIARITY UNDER CONDITIONS OF UNIFIED AND NONUNIFIED STRESS

At the same time, all population groups are affected similarly by certain syntactic features of the compounds. Some syntactic types are easier to paraphrase than others, and certain compounds are associated with certain kinds of error.

The added flexibility of meaningful interpretation available for stimulus items containing mixed lexical items did not, as was predicted a priori, aid the subjects in finding paraphrases. For all groups, stimuli with mixed lexical items were at least as difficult to paraphrase.

Finally, the semantic plausibility and, to a lesser extent, the prior familiarity of features of the compound affected the nature of responses. Plausible and familiar sub-units within the compounds were "created" by the subjects, even when the stress feature of the compound in some abstract sense should have militated against such interpretations.

Recognizing Paraphrases

We have seen that there are gross differences among educational populations in their ability to devise paraphrases for compound nouns under the experimental conditions we provided. In reporting these results, we assumed that the less-educated groups in fact understood the instructions. The assumption seemed warranted because (1) we had discarded subjects whose scores were not overwhelmingly beyond chance expectations and (2) we had found that responses of all subjects—regardless of baseline for error—were systematically related to phrase category in the same way; that is, all subjects seemed to be responding similarly to the same features of the stimulus situation.

Yet even if all subjects did understand the instructions, it is possible that they differed in imaginativeness or ingenuity in dredging up semantically plausible interpretations for some of the compounds. There is no doubt that since a large number of the compounds were semantically anomalous, a large number of correct paraphrases had to be anomalous also. Ingenuity aside, perhaps the less-educated subjects were uncomfortable (at being wrong, at seeming foolish) and suppressed odd interpretations that occurred to them. Further, the inability to devise paraphrases need not necessarily bear on the question of whether the subjects understood the phrases. Although our intuition was that the measure of understanding is being able to say it in one's own words, that requirement might be too strong.

In short, a number of *performance* problems that might be unequal for the various groups might have been present in the experimental situation. For this reason, we had to consider whether the paraphrasing task had been well designed to display the subjects' maximal comprehension, and to display it equally for all subjects. To clarify some of these questions, we performed a forced-choice experiment with the same stimulus materials. If the results so far reported have any bearing on underlying *competence*, they ought to be resistant to modification by this further technique.

DESIGN OF THE EXPERIMENT

Given a compound noun, can subjects choose appropriately between two proposed paraphrases? When the subject's task is merely to indicate a preference between two alternative paraphrases, issues of verbal imaginativeness and temerity are removed from the situation: the subject need not actively devise and endorse a context in which the novel compound has some plausible interpretation. Some of the subjects from the previous experiment, and some new subjects, were now run under this forced-choice condition to determine whether group differences were abolished, whether absolute improvement occurred, and whether subjects' behavior was consistent with their performance in the free-paraphrasing experiment. As it happened, these experimental findings gave us some further understanding of the extent and limitations of paraphrasing ability.

A. Stimuli and Response Alternatives: The same taped series of stimuli was used. The subjects were provided with a pair of alternative paraphrases for each of the 144 compounds. So that these alternatives would be plausible, they were derived from subjects' own responses in the previous experiment. As the correct alternative, we provided the modal response of group A to each of the original stimuli. As the incorrect alternative, we provided the modal incorrect response of group C (more often than not, this modal error was actually the modal response of this group—for all responses, correct and incorrect—since errors were so frequent). Thus both correct and incorrect alternatives were paraphrases that had frequently appeared as the spontaneous responses of the subjects themselves.

The alternatives for each stimulus were typed on separate index cards. Stress was indicated (for compounds in the paraphrase) by hyphenation, as in ordinary English orthography. The pair of alternatives for each compound is given in the appendix.

B. Subjects: Subjects were eight secretaries and five graduate students chosen from essentially the same populations that had previously been sampled. Four of the eight secretaries and two of the five graduate students had participated in the original (free-paraphrasing) experiment. The seven additional subjects were run through the free-paraphrasing experiment approximately three weeks prior to being run in the forced-choice study. (Approximately a year intervened between test and retest for members of the original subject populations.)

C. Procedure: Subjects were first pretested to assure that they understood how to pronounce the phrases on the cards; this seemed to create no difficulty. Two nouns joined by a hyphen were uniformly pronounced with compound intonation after minimal instruction. Subjects were now reminded of the previous task and were told that this time they were being asked merely to choose the card that "meant most nearly the same thing" as the compound they heard. The instructions from the free-paraphrasing task were now read to the subject, with minor modifications (*see* the appendix for the formal instructions).

At the beginning of each trial, both correct and incorrect alternatives for the stimulus item of that trial were exposed (of course, positions were randomized). A few seconds later, the stimulus item was played, and the subject made her choice. As in the previous experiment, replay of the stimulus was allowed at the subject's request, there was no time limit for responding, and the subject was given no knowledge of result.

After the choice was made, the two cards bearing the response alternatives were removed, and the next pair was exposed. All 144 stimulus items were presented in this manner to all subjects.

RESULTS

Two questions are of major interest here for the eventual determination of subjects' ability to paraphrase: (1) are the differences among groups abolished by this procedure; and (2) are subjects consistent in their behavior under the two experimental conditions?

A. Group differences: Error scores for each subject are shown in figure 9. Just as in the free-paraphrasing situation, we find

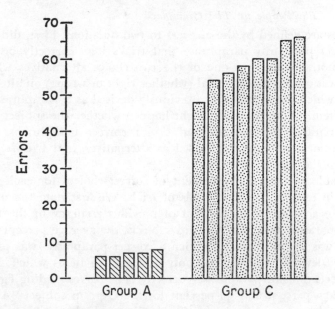

FIGURE 9. FORCED-CHOICE PERFORMANCE IN A-GROUP AND
C-GROUP SUBJECTS

that the two distributions do not overlap. There were 144 trials.
On these, the worst A-group subject made 8 false choices, while
the best C-group subject made 48 false choices. The mean error
per item for group A was .05 as compared to .40 for group C.
Given this result, it is very difficult to explain the results of the
free-paraphrasing study by assuming that the A-group differed
from the C-group only in being more imaginative, that the less-
educated subjects could not "think up" paraphrases. One trivializing explanation of the paraphrasing results is thus excluded.

B. Consistency of Subjects Between the Tasks: We now ask
whether the subjects erred under both conditions for the same
stimuli, and whether they tended towards the same kinds of error
they had made before. A comparison of the response patterns
characteristic of these two tasks may give us some idea of how
systematic subjects are in their approach to paraphrase.

For any one subject, trials in the forced-choice task can be
classified into four distinct categories, related to her performance
on the free-paraphrasing task undertaken earlier. The four cate-

gories are defined by the answers to two questions. First, did the subject previously paraphrase that trial's item correctly or did she not? Second, was one of the two choice alternatives which she was offered on that trial (whether right or wrong) an alternative which she herself had previously devised as a paraphrase to the item? (Note that this might happen whether the subject had paraphrased correctly or had erred: correct paraphrases that were not modal were not used as alternatives, and likewise for nonmodal errors.) [18]

Table 6 presents the percent of correct choices for each subject in each of the four kinds of trials. We first note the mean choice accuracy as a function of previous accuracy in the free-paraphrasing task: for A-group subjects, the average percent correct was 97 for items on which a correct paraphrase was previously devised, while it was only 61 for those items which these subjects did not paraphrase correctly. The corresponding figures were 70 percent and 50 percent for the C-group subjects. Apart from the group differences already discussed, there was a clear-cut consistency in performance on the two tasks. Items that tend to be paraphrased correctly are also items for which the subject chooses correctly.[19]

An explanation of this consistency is not hard to find. One factor that is certain to play a role is the differential difficulty of the items themselves. As we have already seen, some stimulus items (e.g., *black bird-house*) are enormously easier to paraphrase than others (e.g., *house-black bird*). This being so, one would expect that correct choice among the alternatives would also be easier for the one kind of item than the other. The fact that

[18] Judging whether an alternative was a subject's "own" turned out to be a rather difficult matter, for we could not possibly require word-for-word identity. The chief criterion used was syntactic identity. For example, *a bird who lives in a black house* and *a bird who hangs around black houses* were for these purposes considered identical. However, *a bird of the species "black-house"* was considered a different answer. All questionable cases were considered nonidentities. Judgments were made without knowledge of the subject's actual forced-choice response. (By these criteria, the subject's own responses were available as alternatives between 42 percent and 81 percent of the time.)

[19] This effect was highly reliable for both groups. Analysis of variance yielded an F of 36.2 ($df = 1$ and 21, $p < .001$) for the C-group, and an F of 10.8 ($df = 1$ and 12, $p < .001$) for the A-group.

TABLE 6. CHOICE ACCURACY AS A FUNCTION OF PARAPHRASING
SUCCESS AND ALTERNATIVES OFFERED (IN PERCENT)

Trial Category

	Gave Correct Paraphrase		Gave Wrong Paraphrase	
	Presented with "own" alternative	Not presented with "own" alternative	Presented with "own" alternative	Not presented with "own" alternative
Group C				
* S-15	79	57	36	49
* S-18	76	66	53	69
* S-19	75	64	51	65
* S-21	84	80	36	67
S-22	68	54	38	66
S-23	77	75	24	52
S-24	56	50	50	57
S-25	89	72	33	57
Mean	76	65	40	60
Group A				
* S-5	97	95	0	100
* S-2	100	96	82	78
S-26	96	100	88	90
S-27	94	94	20	100
S-28	98	100	0	50
Mean	97	97	38	84

* Original subject in the free-paraphrasing study.

choice accuracy is a function of previous accuracy of paraphrase
can then be attributed simply to the fact that the same stimulus
items appeared in both tasks.

Some other features of the results presented in table 6 are
more interesting. Is there a difference between trials on which
the subject's own free paraphrase (right or wrong) is available as
an alternative, and trials on which the subject's own paraphrase
is not available to her? First consider trials for which the stimulus items had been paraphrased correctly by the subject in the
previous task. We note that accuracy on the forced-choice task

is *greater* when the correct alternative is the subject's own paraphrase than when it is a paraphrase the subject did not herself
devise. For C-group subjects, the mean percent correct was 76
and 65 respectively; the direction of this difference was the same
for all eight subjects. The situation is exactly reversed for trials
containing stimulus items that the subject had paraphrased incorrectly in the free-paraphrase task: here, choice accuracy was
less when the false alternative was the subject's own previous
paraphrase, and *greater* when it was a paraphrase devised by
others. Again for the C-group, the mean percent correct was 40
and 60 respectively under these conditions; every subject showed
a difference in the same direction. The conclusion is perfectly
clear. The subject prefers her own way of saying things regardless of whether it is right or wrong by *our* criteria. When offered
her own correct paraphrase, she tends to choose it, thus increas-
ing her choice accuracy score. When offered her own incorrect
paraphrase, she tends to choose that, thus decreasing her choice
accuracy score. Essentially the same results were obtained for
the A-group subjects, though with less reliability.[20]

Can this effect be explained by assuming that the subject
merely recalled her own previous responses? Undoubtedly not.
Some subjects were retested after an interval of a year; some
others after an interval of only three weeks. The effects were the
same regardless of test interval (*see* table 6). Furthermore, subjects were generally quite unable to recall and distinguish among
the stimuli after even a few seconds following their presentation.
Very frequently they would insist that they had heard some
stimulus item earlier in the list, though in fact no item was ever
repeated. Further, as noted in footnote 18 (p. 134), the subject's
own paraphrase was only very rarely available verbatim; in most
instances to say that the subject's "own" alternative was avail-

---

20 The preference of the subject for her own alternative is manifested as an
interaction between the two determinants which defined the four kinds of
trials: was the subject's prior paraphrase correct; and was it offered as an
alternative? This interaction was highly significant for the C-group ($F = 21.7$,
$df = 1$ and 21, $p < .001$) but failed of significance for the A-group ($F = 4.3$,
$df = 1$ and 12, $p < .10$). It should be noted that the data for the A-group
are very limited, given the relatively few trials on which they made errors
both in paraphrasing and (especially) in choosing.

able meant that the same syntactic structure was available, not a word-for-word repetition. Under the circumstances, the hypothesis that consistency was due simply to the recall of a prior response becomes untenable.[21] The subject's response in the forced-choice task is similar to her response in the free-paraphrasing situation because both reactions reflect the same features of her linguistic organization. (*See* note 3, p. 143.)

The Reality of Group Differences

Massive population differences in the ability to cope with paraphrastic relations were displayed in the forced-choice situation, just as they were in the free-paraphrasing situation. Moreover, subjects—particularly the less-educated group—showed a bias toward choosing their own previously devised paraphrases, whether these were wrong or right by our criteria; thus the choice of an incorrect paraphrase is systematic, not a random response to the unknown. (*See* note 4, p. 146.)

Contrary to some theoretical expectations, subjects—from all populations—err, and err systematically, in the paraphrasing tasks. Before discussing some possible interpretations of these effects, it is appropriate to ask in some detail whether there is reason to suppose that basic linguistic skills were being tapped. Several procedural and methodological questions are most conveniently discussed here in terms of the one countertheoretic experimental outcome: population differences.

Inescapably, these populations differed in their responses to the experimental questions. We have seen that many generative grammarians suppose individuals to be equally competent in linguistic matters. Since massive individual differences were obtained, we must consider lines of argument by which these find-

---

[21] Four additional subjects were tested in the forced-choice condition *prior* to the free-paraphrasing condition to further check on the possibility that the production task might in some sense determine the recognition results. We found substantially the same error scores for the two tasks, and the same consistency over tasks under this condition.

ings could be explained away, leaving the theory of equal competence intact.

An important objection to any experiment of this kind concerns possible dialect distinctions among the populations tested. Is it possible that the educational groups represent different dialect groups? It will be recalled that the subjects were urban, white, mid-Atlantic monolingual speakers, and that there was no consistent dialect difference among them that we could observe. But there might be a subtler distinction. It is undeniable that the secretaries at least to some extent move in different social circles from the graduate students, read different novels, see different movies, and so on. The graduate students and the college graduates in these respects come from rather similar backgrounds, are exposed to similar professors, are made to read similar texts, pass similar examinations, and so forth.

If the population differences we have found are attributable in any large measure to dialect differences that arose in different social or intellectual climates, we should expect graduate students and college students to be much alike, and secretaries to be different. But this is not the result experimentally obtained. In fact, the similarity is much greater between the college and secretarial groups: there is virtually no overlap between the scores of members of these groups and members of the graduate group. Thus any explanation of the findings as artifact of intimate subdialect distinction is highly implausible.

But perhaps some subjects did not understand the instructions, and so were performing a different task. To be sure, the free-response and forced-choice situations produced the same result, but the instructions for both tasks were almost alike, so this point is inconclusive. However, we can rule out the interpretation of misunderstanding on several counts. The internal pattern of the results makes it certain that all subjects (barring those who were discarded) understood well enough to behave systematically: (1) for all subjects, over all stimulus items, fewer than one response in thirty fails to elicit the required syntactic format (a nominal or adjectival phrase); (2) for all subjects, the same stimulus types account for a similar proportion of error (i.e., there is no interaction between group membership and the difficulty of the various phrase categories). These findings suggest that subjects were responding to the same characteristics of the same stimuli.[22]

There is a further variant of this hypothesis: perhaps the situation was so artificial that only the "test-wise" individual could credit the kind of answer she was called upon to give. Perhaps it takes a sort of perverse sophistication to suppose that the right answer (to any question) could be *one who blackens house-birds.* The various subsidiary experiments do much to remove this possibility. In the forced-choice situation, the subject often has only a choice between eccentricities; the wrong answer, to the best of our ability to judge this, is in very many cases no more plausible than the right answer, and sometimes it is less plausible. The subjects did not choose haphazardly among the semantically implausible choices afforded them in the forced-choice situation. Furthermore (*see* note 4, p. 146), when subjects were effectively told which answers would be considered correct— and were paid for agreeing—we found that, even so, the response preferences of subjects were remarkably resistant to change. For the original stimulus list, a C-group population was successfully taught to choose the correct card, to choose as we would choose. Yet, asked to paraphrase the very same stimuli a week later, these subjects could not perform at anywhere near the level of the untrained A-group.

It would appear, then, that the results reflect genuine linguistic differences rather than extraneous features of the test situation. In a way, this is not too surprising. Individual differences in response to apparently linguistic tasks have been found before, at least where the tasks were not too simple (*see* Maclay

---

[22] Some curious hints about interpretation came out of interviews with subjects held after testing was complete. We asked subjects which of the tasks (free paraphrase or forced-choice) they had found easier to cope with. One C-group subject's response was particularly interesting. She claimed that the forced-choice situation was much easier for her because, she said, she had not noticed in the first hearing of the instructions (when given for the free-paraphrasing situation) our stricture to listen to stress ("yes, the *way* it is pronounced *is* important in deciding what it means"). When she heard the instructions again—for the forced-choice task—she did notice this aspect of the task requirement. "And so," she said, "this time I always knew the right answer; I just listened to the accent." Amazingly enough, comparison of her performance in the two tasks showed that she was consistent in her errors— despite her disclaimer, she made just about the same stress errors, as well as other errors, in both tasks!

and Sleator, 1960; Pfafflin, 1961; Stolz, 1967). An exception is the study by Livant who found no variation at all among the subjects he asked to paraphrase compound nouns. We can only conclude that Livant's three subjects were more linguistically sophisticated than our graduate students. If so, his study hardly constitutes a fair test of linguistic uniformity.

Of course there are few linguists who would not have granted performance inequities from the beginning. To most linguists the issue is not whether people differ in their performance, but whether such differences reflect any underlying differences in their linguistic competence. Necessarily, we have asked our subjects to "perform" because we could not ask them to "be competent." Their performances varied widely. We now examine the supposition that such enormous differences in performance are compatible with the hypothesis of equal competence.

Performance deficits might reflect some kind of statistical noise in the system: random errors due to lapses of attention, lowered motivation, and the like; or they could be attributed to a failure to attend to the salient syntactic features of the task. None of these factors adequately accounts for the failure of some of our subjects to cope with the task presented to them.

There is little evidence from the results that group C was less reliable or systematic in responses than group A. In the forced-choice situation, the less-educated subjects were very likely to choose a paraphrase if they had generated it earlier, whether that paraphrase was correct or incorrect. Thus they rarely made random errors. They chose systematically, if differently, from the A-group. Nor can group differences be accounted for by the sheer difference in the overall tendency to err. When we equate statistically for differing baselines for error, significant differences in the *kind* of error preferred by the various populations are not eliminated. It is thus difficult to argue that the group differences represent merely different aptitudes in responding stably in test situations.

It might be supposed that the less-educated subject is more likely to be misled by semantic features of the situation that are essentially extraneous to the syntactic problem. The instructions for both experiments ask the subjects to disregard semantic anomalies ("many of these compounds may seem odd or silly to you . . ."), but one might argue that not all of the subjects were able to oblige us by disregarding them. One might suppose that, while the same underlying grammatical organization holds for all subjects, some of them are more prone to semantic seduction than are others. To counter this, there is the evidence provided by the enormous effect of "unity," the tendency to perceive a semantically plausible sub-unit even if the stress feature of the compound is thereby rendered syntactically deviant. Here surely is an instance of semantic seduction. But it is no more apparent in one group than in another, once the overall differences in error rate are adjusted.

What other performance deficits could we claim for the C-group so as to guard their claim to equal competence? We know that the vocabulary was simple enough to be known even to first graders. We know that short-term memory was not unduly taxed: these subjects were quite reliable in repeating the compounds, and the errors they made in repetition were unrelated to stimulus complexity. Thus the hypothesis that the results were "input" errors, mishearing, or systematic failure to notice the stress or order of words must be rejected. The issue of familiarization with the task can also be excluded. Thoroughly familiarized C-group subjects, with nine runs through the stimuli with knowledge of result, failed to become functional graduate students (*see* note 4, p. 146). College students used to taking tests, used to being subjects in psychological experiments, similarly failed to be graduate students. On what grounds, then, can it be claimed that the obtained differences in performance are unrelated to differences in linguistic skills? Do we now want to assert that recognizing paraphrastic relations among sentences is not a linguistic skill? To do so would mean giving up what is surely at the intuitive heart of the theory. Somehow, abstract competence must be linked to concrete performance.

NOTES

1. All subjects provided nominal and adjectival phrase responses most of the time, which led us to believe that they all did understand the directions. Nevertheless, there must be some possibility of providing a correct paraphrase by chance and we wanted to exclude subjects who

might not be behaving systematically.

For example when the X-term was a noun and the stress pattern provided was *132*,

$$\text{an } N^2 \left\{ \begin{array}{l} \textit{for a} \\ \textit{that is} \\ \textit{that lives in a} \\ \textit{etc.} \end{array} \right\} N^1 \; N^3$$

was scored as a correct response, while the other five serial arrangements of the nouns were scored as errors. But the chance of correct responses cannot be assessed as easily as this example suggests. Since more than one kind of rule can generally be invoked in defense of other paraphrases, since the probabilities of chance correct responses are somewhat different for verb and adjective X-terms, since any word in any compound can be reassigned to another lexical class, and since, in fact, responses are occasionally sentences rather than relative clauses, it is impossible to provide any reasonable estimate of the probability of a chance correct response for stimuli in general.

After considering these various factors, we felt safe in assuming that any subject who gave correct responses over 25 percent of the time was surely not responding at random. Further, any subject who was reasonably rational in her responses to certain selected "easy" compounds could be assumed to be attempting to follow the instructions. (The easy items we selected were *black bird-house, bird wash-house, black-bird house, glass-house bird,* and *thin house-bird.* We expected subjects to answer at least three of these correctly.) Unless *both* of these two criteria were met, data for the subject were discarded.

On this basis, results for four of the eleven C-group subjects were excluded. It should be noted, however, that the excluded subjects did not seem to be qualitatively different in their response characteristics from those just ahead of them. All were sufficiently uniform in responding appropriately to the easy stimuli to conclude that they represented, so to speak, simply the bottom of the same curve. Nonetheless, we chopped off this bottom of the curve to ensure that population differences could not be interpreted as failure of some few subjects to understand the instructions effectively.

2. The error of format was generally accompanied by a stress or order error, as in *Wash the house-bird!* This seems to imply some disorganization in responses of this kind. Given our initial bewilderment about how to treat such responses, we tried at first a double scoring technique. It turned out that *in almost every case,* there was in fact another error in such responses, an error we could characterize as E_o, or E_s, and quite

often, E_{ch}. In practice, the results of the experiment pertaining to over-all error and also to error type are so massive that double scoring of this kind had a negligible effect. Thus, for simplicity, we stuck to a single scoring for every response: if E_s occurred in the context of E_t, the error was called E_t. This is comparable to the decision for E_{ch}, which we could similarly have scored as two errors, $E_o + E_s$.

Some further details of the scoring procedure should be noted. Given the particular nature of the instructions, we could have rejected other kinds of responses. For example, since we had told the subjects that the stimuli were compound nouns, we could have rejected responses in which what seemed to be a prenominal adjective was in fact treated as such by the subject. For example, subjects responded to *black bird-house* as *a bird-house that is black* (rule [viii]), but we could have in-sisted on responses like *a bird-house belonging to Negroes,* in which *black* is treated as a noun (rule [iv]). In practice, this requirement would not have distinguished among subjects; if this is an error, all subjects made it alike. In more general terms, our method of scoring only attempted to isolate cases in which the subject's response had no grammatical excuse at all. If the response reflected some grammatical relation that we had not intended, we disregarded that fact, provided that the relation reflected in the subject's response seemed to be a plausible one.

As another example, we accepted responses related to rule [x] which derives postnominal adjectival phrases (e.g., *as black as a bird-house* for *bird-house black*), although (as described in fn. 4, p. 107) we have pronounced relevant items in such a way that they should have been regarded instead as related to rule [iv] (e.g., *the paint used for bird-houses* for *bird-house black*). We accepted such responses because they were syntactically determined in conformance with the grammatical description of the language, and because in this particular case we found the phonological distinction between the two too small to result in complete reliability when pronounced without sentence context.

Of particular interest are responses that reflected a change in class membership. For example, in response to a stimulus like *bird-house thin,* a subject might respond *a diet-food for bird-houses,* which is cor-rect only insofar as adjectives may be reinterpreted as nouns. We are assuming that this kind of class extension is a "permissible" activity of the speaker; indeed, when we discuss the results of the experiment we will argue that this device is one of the underlying sources of crea-tivity in the use of language. Thus responses reflecting class extension were scored as correct paraphrases.

3. We have thus far commented only indirectly on the fact that the absolute number of errors was smaller in the forced-choice task than

in the free-paraphrase situation. The mean error per item in the paraphrasing experiment was .11 for the five subjects in the A-group and .56 for the eight subjects in the C-group. The corresponding figures for the forced-choice study are .05 and .40. What accounts for this increase in accuracy?

One might assume that, at least in part, the superiority of the forced-choice scores is a result of guessing. After all, even a monolingual speaker of Finnish should obtain an accuracy score of 50 percent. Given that the subject does know *something* (for even the worst of C-group subjects produces some acceptable paraphrases), obtained choice accuracy should be considerably higher. In fact, a guessing hypothesis of this sort turns out to be false, at least in part: C-group subjects uniformly perform *worse* than the guessing hypothesis would predict.

Consider the guessing model. Given N trials, what is a reasonable estimate of the total number of correct choices (T_{est}) for a given subject, assuming that the subject knows what she is doing on a certain number of these trials (M) and guesses randomly on the rest (N — M)? A reasonable estimate of M is the number of correct paraphrases previously produced by the subject herself. Given this figure, we can easily solve for T_{est}:

$$T_{est} = M + \frac{N - M}{2},$$

which can now be compared with the number of correct choices actually obtained (T_{obt}). We have already seen that choice accuracy is quite different depending on whether we are dealing with trials for which one choice alternative is a paraphrase previously endorsed by the subject or with trials for which neither of the alternatives is the subject's own. Accordingly, we present the comparisons of T_{est} and T_{obt} separately for these two conditions.

Figure 10 shows estimated and obtained choice accuracies plotted against each other for A-group and C-group subjects and for both kinds of trials. If the obtained choice accuracies were those predicted by the guessing model, the data points should fall on the diagonals. The upper panel of Figure 10 presents the results for trials on which the subject's own paraphrase (right or wrong) was available. We note that under these conditions the guessing model seriously *overestimates* the number of correct responses actually given by the C-group subjects (their data points fall below the diagonal). The estimated mean percent correct is 76, that actually obtained was 58 — a large and statistically very significant difference ($t = 7.2$, $df = 7$, $p. < .001$). The difference for graduate students goes in the same direction (97 percent vs. 95 percent) but is very small and insignificant ($p > .30$).

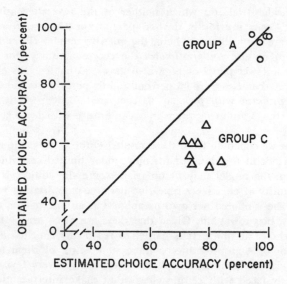

OWN PARAPHRASE AVAILABLE

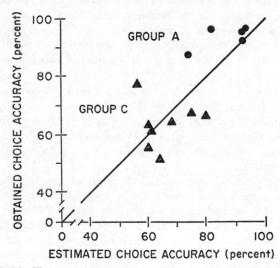

OWN PARAPHRASE NOT AVAILABLE

FIGURE 10. THE GUESSING MODEL: OBTAINED AND ESTIMATED CHOICE ACCURACIES. UPPER PANEL: TRIALS ON WHICH ONE ALTERNATIVE WAS SUB-JECT'S OWN PARAPHRASE. LOWER PANEL: NEITHER ALTERNATIVE WAS SUB-JECT'S OWN PARAPHRASE.

Next consider trials on which neither of the two alternatives was the subject's own previously devised paraphrase. Generally speaking, the results are very different: here, the guessing model either fits (for the C-group) or else *underestimates* the choice accuracy (for the A-group), as the lower panel of Figure 10 shows. Estimated and obtained mean choice accuracies were 66 percent and 62 percent for the C-group (quite insignificant with $p > .20$) as compared to 86 percent and 93 percent for the A-group (approaching significance with $t = 2.5$, $df = 4$, $p < .06$).

What can we conclude from these results? Quite clearly, the guessing model does not fit the data, or fits only under limited conditions. For the C-group, the model may fit on trials where the subject is denied the opportunity of effectively repeating her free-paraphrasing response. But where she is offered her own paraphrase as an alternative, the subject shows a bias toward it. Given that these are often errors, this bias depressed choice accuracy. It is harder to reach any conclusions about the behavior of A-group subjects; there were fewer of them to begin with, the trials in some of the phrase categories are very few, and we are obviously faced with ceiling effects that make interpretation difficult. It does appear that the guessing model underestimates the performance of these A-group subjects on items which offer two new choice alternatives: perhaps the subjects did better than guess at random, using partial information as an aid. After all, recognition tasks are usually easier than tasks which require production or recall. This is often attributed to the fact that partial knowledge aids recognition but not recall.

4. Subsidiary work is being done to explore these effects further. Particularly, we are studying paraphrasing in the context of learning and recall situations. This work has not progressed far enough for formal presentation. However, the preliminary findings from this further work do allow us to exclude certain trivializing explanations of the results described thus far.

Interesting practical and theoretical questions can be raised about whether the less-educated groups can be brought to the level of competence of the most-educated populations, that is, whether C-group subjects can learn to paraphrase. No simple familiarization and teaching technique that we have so far been able to devise has resulted in clear learning among subjects drawn from the C-group population.

We have, for example, trained four secretaries on the original stimulus list with immediate knowledge of result and payoff (five cents per correct choice). These subjects were first tested in the free-paraphrasing situation (mean percent error for the group was 64). In the first training session on forced-choice with knowledge of results, mean percent error was 38. After eight further sessions (on the same materials) mean percent error was 8. Following this procedure, the subjects were rerun on the free-paraphrasing task with the *identical* stimulus items. Even now, each subject still made more errors with this list than did any untrained graduate student. Percent error scores for the four subjects now were 24, 39, 40, and 49, while the most error-prone untrained A-group subject had erred on only 22 percent of the items.

Thus even when thoroughly familiarized with the task and its requirements, and although repeatedly and specifically informed of the correct paraphrases, these subjects still performed differently from those in the A-group. At this point the argument that some subjects may simply not have understood the instructions becomes altogether untenable. These subjects were further tested (for transfer) using *another* stimulus list syntactically identical to the first, in the free-paraphrasing situation. There was little or no discernible improvement in their performance.

Clearly the training procedure used here was far too crude to do more than provide a first step in studying the possibility of learning. We do not know whether paraphrasing skills can be taught fully, or even in part; and of course we do not know which methods would be effective, which not, and why. But at least it is clear that C-group subjects cannot readily be brought to the categorical level of competence displayed by the A-group through the use of simple techniques that familiarize them with the task, cue them to its requirements, and motivate them financially.

In some further pilot studies, we have begun to test the hypothesis that a difference in memory span or, perhaps, "computation space," may account for the obtained group differences (Gleitman and Bernheim, 1968). Subjects in all groups were asked simply to repeat the 144 stimuli a few seconds after hearing them on the tape; there was virtually zero error for A-group subjects, and only 10 percent error for C-group subjects. Errors were related to the "unity" factor, but were not related to the lexical and positional factors that determined so much of the error in the paraphrasing tasks. When the difficulty of the memory task was inflated by use of a paradigm similar to that used by Savin and Perchonock (1965), error in repetition was, of course, increased for all groups (here, the A-group subjects failed to repeat 4 percent of the stimuli correctly, and the C-group subjects failed in 22 percent of the cases). Again, however, errors did not correlate with the various syntactic features of the stimuli—as they did in the paraphrasing experiments. A significant effect of the "unity" factor was found but, for example, no effect of lexical class, of prenominal or post-nominal position of adjective or verb, and so forth, was found. Thus memorial problems do not appear to account for the various results reported here.

5

Some Remarks on
Paraphrasing

Consider how the subjects might have interpreted the bizarre
task we set for them. It would not have been altogether surprising if we could not get them to understand the instruction "Paraphrase arbitrary compound nouns!" by any amount of tutoring
or cajoling. At the very outset it is perhaps revealing that the
instructions were so simple to convey and that subjects' responses
were so orderly in terms of the linguistic abstraction. Our purpose here is to unravel some of the performance factors that
seemed to be involved in subjects' responses to the paraphrasing
tasks.

Transformational grammars as currently conceived of course
provide no actual apparatus for carrying out the various searches
and analyses that must be involved in producing and recognizing
paraphrases, but we can surmise something of how grammatical
organization is relevant to such tasks. Two different sentences are
said to have the same meaning even though their surface structures differ, provided that their deep-structure representations
are equivalent. If the relation between the relative clause and
the compound is strictly transformational, we might imagine the
paraphrasing task in these terms. Given the stimulus compound,
the subject imposes sufficient constituent analysis upon it to
allow computation of a deep structure and a surface structure,
and then computes an alternative surface structure from the
same basis. If the subject pursues such a course (by whatever

mechanism) she will come up with a pair of sentences that mean the same thing in terms of such concepts as subject-of, predicate-of, and the like. For the stimulus compounds and their relative clause paraphrases, the case is slightly different because—as we concluded in chapter 3—these constructions are not strictly in an equivalence relation. Nevertheless, it is clear that generative rules relate the bases underlying certain relative clauses to those underlying compounds. Presumably, once a basis for *black-house bird* is computed, the quasi-paraphrastic relation to *bird that lives in a black-house* is recognized by reference to the generative principles of chapter 3.[1]

To understand the subjects' success at paraphrasing compound nouns, we must grant considerable active appreciation of these linguistic relationships to all speakers. Without a generative model we could not understand the fact (a special case of a much more general fact) that compound nouns regularly elicit relative clauses when a meaningful alternative is asked for. Much less could we account by any other known device for the explicit expressions, heretofore never uttered, that are elicited by this technique. Thus the enormous effect of the structural properties of a phrase on the structure of the paraphrase it elicits is one more demonstration of the syntactic organization of linguistic behavior. In the unlikely event that further "evidence" for the generative view were necessary or in some new sense illuminating, there it is.

On the other hand, we have found some curious and unexpected modes of paraphrasing associated with particular phrase categories, and we have found massive population differences. Neither of these results follows in any obvious way from current linguistic theory. To understand the extreme difficulty of some phrase categories we will argue that some compound stimuli could not be directly matched to deep phrase markers, that they

---

[1] We have no knowledge of speech processing that will allow us to decide whether the strategies of understanding involve finding surface structures before deep structures, or the other way around, or even whether these two levels of analysis are really distinct in linguistic performance. Logically, it only seems necessary that the hearer provide some tentative bracketing and labelling of the input before a computation of deep structure takes place. Beyond this, we take no stand on what the actual strategies for imposing structural descriptions on inputs might be.

deviated in various ways from the rules the subjects "know." In particular, some compounds reflect a *core* system of great range and orderliness, while others reflect a *penumbra* of quasi-systematic relations in the language. To understand the population differences we obtained, we will assume that subjects differ in the compounds they regard as grammatical and that they differ in the strategies used for bringing deviant material back to grammaticalness.

Grammar: Core and Penumbra

Some phrases were more difficult to paraphrase than others. They elicited fewer identical paraphrases and often elicited responses that we rejected. This was so for all subjects. Although some subjects erred far more often than others, the same items were relatively more difficult for all. We know that the lexical class and the position of the X-terms—the structural properties of the various phrase categories—account for much of this variance. Phrases containing noun and prenominal adjective X-terms were overwhelmingly simpler to paraphrase than those containing verbs or postnominal adjectives.

One might suppose that "grammatical" compounds are easier to paraphrase than those which are "ungrammatical." If the hearer understands utterances partly by reference to his internalized generative grammar, there is good reason to expect him to falter when the utterance he hears is not in some sense reflected in this grammar. This is essentially the descriptive position we adopt: paraphrasability and grammaticalness are systematically related.[2] Subjects paraphrase correctly 73 percent of the time when rule [iv] (for subject-object compounds) is called for and

---

[2] It hardly needs pointing out that paraphrasability cannot be the criterion of grammaticalness. Obviously such an assumption would beg the question, but aside from that it would fail to account for the fact that some ungrammatical sentences can be paraphrased readily (*Anybody isn't sleeping = Nobody is sleeping*) and that some grammatical sentences defy paraphrase (*The glass that the maid that the agency hired dropped broke on the floor*). Grammaticalness and paraphrasability are by no means equivalent.

72 percent of the time when rules [viii] and [ix] (for prenominal adjectives) are called for. On the contrary, they paraphrase correctly only 58 percent of the time when rules [v], [vi], and [vii] (for compounds containing verbs) are involved, and 41 percent of the time when rule [x] (for postnominal adjectives) is involved. (These figures exclude "mixed" lexical items.) One might consider revising the grammatical description of chapter 3 to reflect these differences. Perhaps the "difficult" rules should be removed from the grammar.

Leaving aside the unpleasantly *ad hoc* character of this proposal, it fails to account both for facts about the language (there are clearly nondeviant expressions, even novel ones, that are based on the tentatively excluded rules) and facts about the experimental outcome (the most educated population paraphrases correctly most of the time, even for the difficult types). We can cope with these facts only by conceding that these rules express significant generalizations about the structure of English.

As an example of the problem here, consider the very "easy" phrase category involving a prenominal adjective (rule [viii]):

bright bird-house

and the very "difficult" phrase category involving a postnominal adjective (rule [x]):

bird-house bright.

The former is an instance of a grammatical type that occurs enormously more often in everyday use than the latter. But the postnominal does not appear to be syntactically deviant. There are numerous attested cases (*dirt poor, knee deep, dog tired, pea-soup green, wafer thin*) and the advertising people grace us with new instances every day (*Arid dry, country fresh, baby smooth, caffeine free, fawn brown*). To account for this host of phrases, continually and regularly coming into the language, we must include compound adjectives in a grammar of English. The same is apparently true for compounds formed with verbs, where again there are attested cases (*chimney-sweep, door-stop, push-cart, draw-bridge*) and obvious productivity (*car-wash, push-button, guess-work, work-day, drive-in bank, pick-up sticks, go-go girl*). Thus neither *bird-house bright* nor *house-bird wash* can categorically be termed ungrammatical, for both exemplify vital on-going processes in the language.

On the other hand, it cannot be denied that there are status differences among these constructions. The prenominal (modifier) use of adjectives is almost totally productive in English, but the postnominal use is obscurely limited to ill-defined adjective subcategories. For color adjectives and some others, usage is widespread and productive. Yet many other hypothetical examples sound deviant indeed (*fox sly, ball round, professor absent-minded*), even though these surely meet the semantic requirement of an intimate bond between the elements. (It is not as though *cow sly* or *ball square* were the excluded cases.) Similarly, the restrictions on compounds with verbal elements seem eccentric. We cannot characterize the affixes that occur naturally on various nominalized instances (e.g., *chimney-sweep* and not *chimney-sweeper*, but *book-keeper* and not *book-keep*, both *bar-keeper* and *bar-keep*), though these are often understandable in a historical context. No more can we characterize the set of verbs that sound natural with zero suffixation (e.g., the stimuli with *eat* seem distinctly less natural than those with *kill*).

In short, rule [iv] for nominal compounds and rules [viii] and [ix] for prenominal adjectives reflect very general patterns in current English. The other rules reflect partial and restricted systems that even grammarians are hard put to explicate. Such differences of status among constructions are widely acknowledged. We will use the term *core* to refer to central aspects of the grammatical system and *penumbra* for the more peripheral features. The latter term indicates that though this distinction is clear for extreme cases, no easy line can be drawn. The grammatical facts are that compound adjectives and compounds with verbal components are only partially productive and highly restricted in range. The experimental fact is that speakers are less facile with novel instances of these penumbral language features: all subject populations paraphrase core constructions more capably and more regularly than penumbral constructions (*see* tables 7 and 8 for some examples of subjects' responses to compounds involving core and penumbral features. Additional examples appear in the appendix).

TABLE 7. RESPONSES TO A CORE CONSTRUCTION (RULE [VIII]) AND A PENUMBRAL CONSTRUCTION (RULE [X]). Responses we scored as errors are followed by a parenthetical note containing first the error type, and second our reconstruction of a stimulus for which the subject's response would have been correct. As always, E_o stands for error of order, E_s for error of stress, E_{ch} for error of chaos, and E_f for error of format. The examples given here and in table 8 were chosen to avoid the complicating factor of "unity." Each subject's response appears in a fixed position in the tables of this chapter and in the appendix, so that something of the response styles of individuals can be seen.

(a) Responses to *black house-bird (A C-C)*

A-group
a house-bird that's black
a black domesticated bird
a house-bird that's black
a house-bird that has black feathers
birds which are kept in houses and are the color black
a house-bird that has black plumage
a bird found around houses that's black in color

B-group
a house-bird that is black in color
a black bird that lives in the house
a house-bird which is black in color
a bird that lives in a house and is black
a house-bird which is black
a bird which is kept in a home and its color is black
a house-bird that's black

C-group
a house-bird that's black
a house-bird who is black in color
a black bird who lives in a house
a black house-pet
a home painted black for birds (E_o—black bird-house)
house-bird the color black
a bird that lives in a black house (E_s—black-house bird)

(b) Responses to *house-bird black (C-C A)*

A-group
blackness characteristic of a house-bird
a new name for a color of women's dresses
bird-black for house-birds (E_s—house-bird bird-black)
black paint for smearing on house-birds
a man who blackens house-birds, or as black as a house-bird

as black as a house-bird
paint as black as a house-bird

B-group
  the black color that you see on certain bird-houses (E_o—bird-house
    black)
  black stuff that comes from house-birds
  blackening for house-birds
  a bird that lives in a house and cleans shoes (?)
  a house-bird that has been painted black (E_o—black house-bird)
  a bird that lives in a house as a pet and his color is black (E_o—black
    house-bird)
  a black house-bird (E_o—black house-bird)

C-group
  the color of the house-bird—black house-bird
  your pet is dark in color, is black (E_f—the house-bird is black)
  a house-bird that is black (E_o—black house-bird)
  home that's black (E_{ch}—black (bird)-house)
  black paint for a bird's house (E_o—bird-house black)
  a house-bird that's black and dirty (E_o—black house-bird)
  a house-bird that is black (E_o—black house-bird)

The *difference* in paraphrasing performance, over groups, is quite similar for core and penumbral constructions. For both, C-group subjects err roughly five times as often as A-group subjects. Specifically, the A-group paraphrases inappropriately 7 percent of the time for core constructions and 17 percent of the time for penumbral constructions. The C-group paraphrases inappropriately 41 percent of the time for core constructions and 77 percent of the time for penumbral constructions. Some secretaries *never* devised a correct paraphrase on the difficult models.[3]

[3] This is particularly surprising because by and large the lexical items that appear in the stimulus compounds do fall within what is known of the domain of these rules. For example, the three adjectives *thin, bright,* and *black* do occur in attested compound adjectives such as *paper thin, wafer thin, star bright, shining bright, onyx black, coal black.* Two of the three verbs we used (*kill* and *wash,* though not *eat*) do commonly serve as nominals without suffixation. Still, the average subject could not cope with novel instances of these words (in this situation, in these constructions, with these instructions).

It should be noted that some ceiling and basement effects make it difficult to determine whether group differences were really the same for core and penumbral features. Since A-group subjects were almost perfect in paraphrasing core constructions, they could do no better; thus we may be underestimating differences for the sample phrase categories. Similarly, since the

TABLE 8. RESPONSES TO A CORE CONSTRUCTION (RULE [IV]) AND A PENUMBRAL CONSTRUCTION (RULE [V]). Error types are given in parentheses along with our reconstruction of the phrase for which the obtained response would have been correct. The symbol + indicates that a class-changing suffix on the X-term was assumed to be involved in the subject's response. Though we have granted the subjects some dubiously zero-able suffixes, errors are still very frequent for stimulus items containing verbs.

(a) Responses to *house-bird boot* (C-C N)

A-group
    a boot for house-birds
    galoshes worn by a parakeet
    a boot for house-birds
    a boot for house-birds
    a covering made for house-birds to wear called boots
    a boot worn by house-birds
    a boot designed by birds to be worn in houses (E_s—house bird-boot; possibly E_o—bird-house boot)

B-group
    the boots belonging to a house-bird
    a boot from a bird that lives in a house
    boot for a house-bird
    a kind of shoe which belongs to a parakeet
    a shoe belonging to a house-bird
    a type of shoe a person could wear but it is shaped rare because it is the shape of a house-bird, bird-house (?!)
    kind of boot known as a house-bird boot

C-group
    the boot of the house-bird
    the boot, the shoe, the house-boot of the bird (E_{ch}—bird house-boot)
    a boot that is in the house (E_{ch}—house-boot)
    a type of boot
    boot, shoe covering for canaries or any house-birds
    a boot belonging to a house-bird
    a boot that belongs to the house-bird

(b) Responses to *house-bird wash* (C-C V)

A-group
    a washing of the house-bird
    the laundry done by canaries
    laundry for house-birds
    soap for domestic birds
    an apparatus for washing house-birds

to wash as if one were washing house-birds (?)
the time you wash your house-birds

B-group
the washing of the house-bird
a bird-house with a wash outside (E_{ch}—wash bird-house)
a bird-bath for house-birds
a house washed by a bird (E_{ch}—bird-wash+ed house)
a house-bird which has been washed (E_o—wash+ed house-bird)
a domesticated bird who needs to be washed (E_o—wash+able house-bird)
a kind of wash that's called a house-bird wash

C-group
the wash from the house-birds—they do their weekly wash
like a bird-bath that is something like a home where the birds come (E_s—house bird-wash)
a bird that washed the house (E_{ch}—house-wash bird)
a sort of bird-house—the birds do their cleaning, their wash (E_{ch}—wash bird-house)
a place to wash house-birds, pet birds
a house where birds do the wash (E_{ch}—bird wash-house or bird-wash house)
a house-bird that washes (E_o—wash+ing house-bird)

The drop in performance for the latter constructions (for all groups) reflects the intuitive and systematic suggestion that there is a difference in grammatical status among our stimuli. But the level of performance of C-group subjects for penumbral features is so low as to raise questions about their "competence" in these instances.

We adopt the view that paraphrasing performance reveals an important aspect of linguistic competence, an aspect that is of particular centrality in the transformational approach. If this is so, then 77 percent error in this task is distinctly more than we should expect. If the C-group subjects' performance for core features had been equally poor, our inclination would have been

C-group was so close to zero performance for penumbral constructions, they could hardly do worse, and again population differences may be partially masked. On the other hand, simpler test items—for example, two word compounds involving core features—might have revealed a level of grammatical organization at which the populations do not differ. Harder items might have revealed stratification within the A-group. Thus the constant ratio of errors over all phrase categories may be a simple consequence of the narrowness of the range of stimuli, along the relevant dimensions.

to write off the whole procedure as irrelevant to their linguistic capacities. But since C-group subjects' performance with core features does reflect some competence with these types, and competence with the task requirements, it seems that their near-zero performance with penumbral features must be interpreted as near-zero competence for such entities. If the subject can almost never paraphrase correctly, why grant her a "rule" whose underlying purpose is to explicate her ability to recognize this relation? To overlook occasional errors by invoking performance factors seems reasonable. To ignore uniform performance (here, uniform error) seems excessive.

We might then conclude that penumbral rules are simply additional rules of grammar, restricted though they are in range and frequency of use. Elite speakers "have" them and others do not. Perhaps only the most talented speakers will fully assimilate these peripheral relations. Our grab bag of nonliterary graduate students only partially represents this linguistic elite—hence their occasional errors. If this view is adopted, the claim is that speakers differ in their knowledge of the "fully grammatical" constructions in the language. We lean toward this interpretation. On the other hand, we have already noted some obscure restrictions on the penumbral rules that provide some motivation for distinguishing them from rules of grammar, and we cannot deny that all subjects in our A-group population had increased difficulty with these types, though in general they could cope with them. If these quasi-systematic penumbral relations are too narrow to bear novel use, then perhaps all subjects must treat them by use of an ancillary device, *a semigrammar* (of which more below).

It seems undeniable that there is a level of grammatical organization common to all speakers of a dialect. It may well be that significant differences do not creep in until recursiveness is involved (thus always raising the possibility that constraints on "computation space" may account for the result) or until the entities tested move suspiciously close to the semigrammatical range. But note that if we grant that all populations are equal in grammatical matters, excepting only the ability to deal with recursiveness (particularly where embedding is involved) and semigrammaticalness, we have simultaneously given up some interesting claims about the abilities of normal populations. A system which is nonrecursive and which does not allow analogic extension will lack much of the unlimited quality described in grammars. Unlimited innovation in such a system would be restricted to the duller, formally quite distinct, iterative processes such as coordinating conjunction.

Neither our knowledge of the grammatical facts here nor the limited results of our experimental probes permit resolution of these questions; hence the term *penumbra*. A further task in interpretation is independent of this problem: whatever the systematic status of the various phrase categories, there are striking and consistent differences in style of response by the various subject populations. We will attempt to characterize these differences in terms of approaches to perceived deviance.

Semigrammar

We now turn to the question of deviant sequences. What if the compound (structurally organized by the subject using whatever mechanism we wish to imbue her with) does not fall within the grammatical system? Suppose no structural description for this word sequence exists in the subject's grammar. Given the equivocal grammatical status of penumbral expressions and the semantic oddity of some compounds in all phrase categories, it seems plausible that these were often perceived as deviating in some way from well-formedness. Question arises as to how we ought to expect the subject to behave in response to perceived deviance.

Perhaps one should now expect a kind of *tilt*-response. The subject might balk altogether when confronted with an anomalous compound. Such is the paradigmatic response of various extant parsing machines. But this is not what people do—certainly not in ordinary linguistic exchange—classification not being the usual purpose of discourse. Only on the rarest of occasions was there even a whisper of reproach from our subjects. Only grammarians under very special circumstances can stand back and contemplate sentences as objects for classification. The ordinary speaker apparently rejects an utterance just in the limiting case in which the sequence has no semblance of structure (this being the instance from which arises the belief that people other than grammarians can be induced to provide classificatory judgments directly). Typically, the listener will assume that whatever is said has meaning. If he cannot understand an utterance as uttered, he tries to understand it as it ought to have been uttered. In short, he takes such utterances to be *semigrammatical* and tries to find his way back to the grammar. Often he does not perceive deviance in any conscious way, and we have to infer his knowledge of deviance from aspects of his understanding.

In order to interpret the experimental results in some finer detail, we must assume that subjects were on many occasions responding to entities that they perceived as deviant. Unfortunately, linguistic theory currently offers no useful framework for interpreting responses to deviance. It deals directly only with well-formed sentences. It will be helpful, however, to state informally what we mean by deviance and to describe some proposals of the linguists toward a theory of semigrammaticalness.

We have seen that part of understanding involves apprehension of underlying structure. For grammatical sentences, the speaker-hearer is said to have a built-in schema (a grammar) to which he refers, by whatever means, in assigning this structure to inputs. But an ungrammatical sentence is one the internalized generative grammar does not describe. Then, to put things simply, an ungrammatical utterance ought not to be comprehended directly by this means. But this situation is not altogether black and white. Very many sequences fail to be grammatical only by a little and are readily comprehensible. For example, *I think anybody isn't listening* is a deviant but understandable paraphrase of *I think nobody is listening* or *I don't think anybody is listening*. *The magician vanished the rabbit* slightly garbles *The magician made the rabbit vanish*. There is no end to the number or variety of such examples.

Since semigrammatical sentences are intuitively related to grammatical sentences, it seems reasonable that any theory that describes them must take off from the grammar proper. It must assume that comprehensible deviant sentences are systematic deformations of well-formed sentences. The description must at the same time be separate from the grammar, for by including the description of these entities in the grammar itself, we lose the mechanism that accounts naturally for their perceived deviance. Notice that any successful theory would have to distinguish among *degrees of grammaticalness*, for not all sequences are as transparent as the examples above, for example, *The vanish rabbit magician made the.* While the earlier examples appear to be anomalies that might occur in informal or poetic discourse, this last expression is thoroughly disordered (Katz, 1964, provides the terms *semisentence* and *nonsentence* to distinguish between these cases).

Chomsky (1964*b*) has proposed a method for assigning degrees of grammaticalness to strings by reference to a finite hierarchy of categories that are related to sentences at various levels of representation. Each utterance referred to the grammatical mechanism is said to be projected as a string of formatives at each of these levels. Thus, for example, the famous sentence *Golf plays John* has a grammatical representation at the level of analysis we can call a lexical-category sequence, that is, it is an instance of *noun-verb-noun*, a permissible sequence. But this same sentence fails to be represented at a more refined level in the hierarchy where the noun class is further dissected into animate and inanimate nouns and the verb class subcategorized into verbs that can select inanimate subjects and verbs that cannot. At this level the sequence *noun* $_{inanimate}$ *-verb* $_{animate}$ *-noun* $_{animate}$ has no representation. The category level at which the sentence fails to be represented is taken to be the degree to which it is ungrammatical. In plain terms, *Golf plays John* is said to be constructionally nondeviant to the extent that it is a recognizable case of subject-verb-object. But it is constructionally deviant to the extent that its verb seems to require an animate subject.

As Katz (1964) has shown, there are difficulties with this approach because the various levels in Chomsky's proposed hierarchy do not necessarily bear a one-to-one correspondence to degrees of perceived deviance. Whatever the facts here, a successful theory of semigrammaticalness will have to provide a method for isolating the place and manner of deviation. But such a theory will have to be more ambitious than Chomsky's, for the listener does more than perceive anomaly. He somehow understands.

To understand the understanding of deviant utterances, Ziff (1964) proposed that, in addition to the rules of grammar, the language user be equipped with a small set of devices that will enable him to "find his way back" by some optimal route from a semigrammatical utterance to a sentence described in the grammar. The length or tortuousness of the route back would then be conceived as the measure of deviance. Suppose that Chomsky's model in some revised form would enable the listener to isolate the source and manner of the deviation. A further model would still be necessary to get back to the grammar. Ziff suggests that these semirules will involve the elementary manipulations of the grammar proper: serial reordering, deletion, class extension, and the like. The assumption is that the speaker uses the same formal devices to deal with semigrammaticalness that he uses in understanding grammatical sentences. This proposal plausibly suggests that the "semigrammar" will consist of a few very general and simple operations. (We would hardly wish to impute a highly specific apparatus—alongside the grammar—to the already overburdened normal speaker.) Yet the simplicity of this proposal is also its undoing; the linguistic machinery Ziff provides can produce utter chaos (again, *see* Katz, 1964, for an illuminating discussion). To understand this point, consider one of the rules Ziff proposes:

Addition/Deletion: . . . A . . . → . . . A . . . B . . .
. . . A . . . B . . . → . . . A . . .

Armed with this rule alone, the hearer could endlessly exchange classes, change phrase boundaries, invert, and so on, by successive additions and deletions, arbitrarily interpreting any utterance as anything whatsoever. If, like Alice's caterpillar, people felt free to follow this kind of caprice, they would never be able to understand each other.

Katz (1964) seems to offer an alternative. He proposes that in addition to the rules of grammar the speaker has a set of *transfer rules* to cope with deviance, and a set of *traffic rules* that set limits on tolerable deviation. The transfer rules are to be closely analogous to the phrase structure and transformation rules of the grammar proper. They differ by relaxing some of the specifications for those rules. For example, a semi-Passive rule, unlike the Passive rule, might relax the requirement that the verb be transitive. Thus we would derive such semi-Passive expressions as *Two pounds were weighed by the chicken,* and *Home was remained by the children.* Similarly, a phrase-structure rule that develops nouns might relax the specification animate/inanimate, thus eventually permitting *Golf plays John, The spooky forest frightens the potatoes,* and so on. But Katz acknowledges that the rules of a semigrammar must be more general than this. Otherwise we would need more transfer rules than transformational rules.[4] He suggests that the semigrammar rules might be written so as to apply to classes of grammar rules and that the proposed traffic rules would set needed limits on their applicability in a single derivation. Since we have no way of classifying rules of grammar, we can hardly judge the success this enterprise might have. At best, Katz's proposal suggests that semigrammar rules will have to be more closely related to grammar rules than are Ziff's. But at worst, when we attempt to generalize these rules, they will suffer from excessive power, that is, they will be Ziff's rules.

In sum, these linguists have commented on the fact that deviant sentences are often comprehensible and that they are analogous in certain ways to well-formed sentences. Most of the informal "semirules" proposed are designed to deal with relaxations of selectional restrictions. They are class-extension devices. But no one has commented usefully on just what these rules are

---

4 This follows because, for example, one can conceive various violations of the Passive rule. In the semisentence *The house down was brought by the orator* an appropriate transitive verb *(bring-down)* appears. What is wrong here, apparently, is that the passive was formed on a phrase marker underlying *The orator brought the house down* rather than on a phrase marker underlying its transformational equivalent *The orator brought down the house.* In other words, the error here is in the ordering of the rules. A wholly different violation appears in *The consul killed by Brutus,* again a comprehensible semi-Passive, in which the error is omission of a form of *be* when the construction is not embedded in a matrix *(He buried the consul killed by Brutus).* We would not want to account for all these cases by assuming, in addition to the Passive rule, three semi-Passive rules, especially as these troubles will proliferate endlessly, *The consul was killed Brutus, The consul were killed by Brutus,* and so on.

to be, how to write them, and particularly how to limit them. Therefore, we have to conclude that no one has developed a theory to account for the comprehensibility of deviant sentences. All that we have firmly in hand is the original intuition. Semigrammatical sentences are systematic deformations of grammatical sentences and somehow the speaker-listener knows how to undo these deformations in very many instances.

In the discussion that follows, we will try to point to the routes our subjects seem to have taken in getting back to the grammar. One or another of the descriptions we have sketched above sometimes seems to reflect rather neatly what was done. Hopefully such empirical findings can eventually provide clues toward an appropriate theoretical formulation, but we will propose no theory. At any rate, an explanation of semigrammaticalness seems to resist discovery through those acts of contemplation (by linguists) that have yielded up such fruitful theories of well-formedness.

THE SEMIGRAMMAR AND CORRECT RESPONSES

We have claimed that conformance to the rules of chapter 3 was the criterion for scoring a response correct. But the scoring procedure can be truly mechanical only if each word, as used in each compound, can be assigned to a fixed lexical-class category. This is no easy task—obviously, this scoring problem is one reason why we later performed the forced-choice experiment. For the free-paraphrasing experiment, a response was scored correct if it reflected a grammatically determined response, even if this involved lexical-class extension. We scored a response as incorrect only when it involved some further manipulations of the input, such as those that Ziff's system would (at worst) allow. Many questions arise, however, as to whether class extension is a grammatical or a semigrammatical operation. Question also arises as to the sense in which meaning is preserved (or even known) when class extension is involved in the performances we called paraphrasing.

Consider the compound *house-bird thin.* This compound has a penumbral reading through rule [x] and can be paraphrased *as thin as a house-bird.* Clearly this is a correct response. But suppose the subject says *a product used to slim obese house-birds,* that is, she takes *thin* to be a noun and invokes rule [iv]. Is this wrong? After all, Webster II does not list *thin* as a noun (excepting the idiomatic *thick and thin*). Do we assume, then, that the subject here perceived the stimulus as deviant, that *thin* was not perceived as a noun until after some "semigrammatical" class-extension operation? Much more interestingly, given that this response was a response to perceived deviance in a nondeviant expression (our definition of "wrong"), is it not in some way creative ("especially good") rather than merely ordinary ("grammatically determined") or unperceptive ("especially dense")? We take up these points separately below, though there is certainly some question of whether they are separate issues: (1) how can one tell when a semigrammar rule has been invoked? (2) when is the use of a semigrammar rule a "good" use of English?

When is the Semigrammar Used?   Everyone who has written on the subject of semigrammaticalness agrees that some deviant expressions represent violations of selectional rules and must be described in terms of a class-extension operation. But class extension is not always extragrammatical. For example, the various affixing rules of the grammar (*Noun* → *Verb* + *tion*) add new members to lexical classes. Compounding itself is another such process. For other cases, it is unclear whether class extension refers to a grammatical or semigrammatical process in the language. For example, is semigrammaticalness involved in the decision to treat *thin* as a noun?

When Ziff discussed class extension, he was thinking of instances such as Dylan Thomas' expression, *a grief ago*. For this case, it is plain that a step has been taken beyond the normal selectional regularities in the language. *Grief* is surely not (or not until the moment Thomas wrote it) a temporal noun like *week, month, decade,* and the special force of the poetic line derives in part from the supposition that this word was "added" to the class of temporal nouns, while maintaining its basic sense of *sadness* and *loss*. Here there is no doubt that the extension is perceived by reader and writer as linguistically deviant (obviously not in any pejorative sense, obviously quite the reverse of that). Similarly, in the test situation, a person who says that *bird-house eat* is *a picnic in a bird-house* is extending the word *eat* beyond its established bounds. (There is a difference we are not competent to discuss. When we hear *a grief ago* we derive aesthetic pleasure, while *bird-house eat* is merely queer.)

Very different from the cases of *eat* and *grief* in this context is the instance with which we began: *house-bird thin, a product used to slim obese house-birds.* Here we are not altogether convinced that the compound was really deviant. Does this extension of class membership depend upon an *extra*grammatical mechanism? After all, as mentioned in chapter 3, many simple English words move comfortably among the noun, adjective, and verb classes (*That is a yellow page; Yellow is my favorite color; Pages yellow with age*). Thus the move *Noun → thin* is perhaps best described as an instance of a regular process of English word-formation, zero suffixation, and not as a semigrammatical process at all. While Webster does not list *thin* as noun, neither does he list *apples* as plural, but adding *-s* to a new word is in no sense deviant. If zero suffixation were a fully productive process, there would be nothing anomalous in doing this for the first time with some word. The problem of decision arises because suffixation is not uniform in English, and so one is pressed in judging the legitimacy of any novel form. *-Ing* can be added to every verb, *-tion* is somewhat more restricted, *-wise* is imperiously added to a growing number of nouns, *-ship* is sinking, perhaps no longer productive at all (*courtship, lordship,* but not *wooship, babyship*). Though zero suffixation is clearly productive, intuitively there appear to be limits. There is something anomalous (odd, clever, humorous) about saying that *house-bird thin,* on the analogy of *wheat-thin,* is *a cracker made out of ground-up house-birds.*

In sum, for an individual example it is difficult to say whether the subject was using the rules of English word-formation or the rules of semigrammar. On these grounds alone, there is justice as well as necessity in scoring all responses involving class extension as correct. But there is a problem beyond this practical difficulty.

When is the Semigrammar Used Successfully?   Sometimes the decision to score the response correct when it involved extension seemed just right, as when *house-bright bird* was said to be *a bird who brightens houses.* Sometimes the scoring decision seemed hopelessly wrongheaded as when we accepted *the dead bird in the house* or *the bird in the house who is very kill* in re-

sponse to *house kill-bird*. Sometimes we thought the subject ought to get double credit as when she said that *a house-bird kill* was *an annual hunt to cut down the population of parakeets*. Surely if this last reflects a response to deviance, it has an entirely different quality from the alternative response *Kill your house-bird!* It appears to be an integral manipulation of language structure, the kind of analogic extension that—like recursiveness—adds to the language some of its creative or unlimited quality. It is not a failure to see through to the structure of the phrase. Class extension, in this sense, predominates in the most-educated population. (*See* tables 9 and 10, as well as further data in the appendix, as examples of this.)

For reasons we have been at pains to describe, it is not possible to give quantitative evidence about this difference in response style among the populations. Yet we notice an abstract quality in the approach of the most-educated population, an approach which is on occasion more like that of the grammarian than like that of a mere user of language. These subjects occasionally complain of deviance ("but *eat* is a verb—!"), they frequently note ambiguities, provide alternative responses, and become attached to their own reconstructions. On the contrary, the C-group subjects tend to avoid the process of extension and are straight-faced when they claim that *bird-house black* is a *black bird-house*. Even when a derived lexical classification is readily available, the less-educated subjects rarely make use of it, thus artificially inflating the difficulty of many stimulus items. For example, the "basic" use of *glass* is probably prenominal when it is used in the sense of a material like brick or wood (*the glass table*). But in this (material) sense it can also be used in head-noun position (*that green stained-glass*). And it is surely also a simple noun in contexts like *The baby drinks from a glass*. Yet the less-educated subjects often interpret *bird-house glass* as *glass bird-house, a bird-house made of glass* (*see* table 11). Why not *glass used to make a bird-house* or *the glass used in the bird-house?* No one can deny that each subject knows what a glass is. But even in the forced-choice situation, when both options were displayed, these subjects preferred the inversion still. They seemed to be in the tyrannical grip of basic lexical classification, and we could not break this "set," if set it was. In sum, there is a striking qualitative difference in the paraphrasing styles of subject populations: the most-

TABLE 9. INSTANCES OF CLASS EXTENSION. Both here and in table 10 responses scored as errors are followed by the symbol of the error type and our reconstruction of a stimulus for which the subject's response would have been correct. Correct responses are followed by the rule assumed to be relevant. When class extension seems to be involved, the nature of that extension is indicated.

Responses to *house-bird bright (C-C A)*

A-group
  brightness that's characteristic of a house-bird ([x], bright+ness, Noun → bright)
  the smartest birds that live in houses (E_o—bright house-bird)
  as bright as a house-bird ([x])
  something for brightening house-birds ([v], bright+en+er, Verb → bright)
  a color as bright as color found on some house-birds ([x], Noun → bright)
  as bright as a house-bird ([x])
  as bright as a bird around the house usually is ([x])

B-group
  a star that's named for house-brights (?!, E_{ch})
  a house-bird that is bright (E_o—bright house-bird)
  the brightener that was used for birds in the house ([v], bright+en+er, Verb → bright)
  a house as bright as a bird (E_{ch}—bird-bright house)
  a house-bird which is multicolored (E_o—bright house-bird)
  a house pet that's intelligent (E_o—bright house-bird)
  a house-bird that's bright (E_o—bright house-bird)

C-group
  a bright in color house-bird (E_o—bright house-bird)
  the house of a pet (E_{ch}—(bright) house-bird (bird)-house)
  a bird that lives in a house and is very intelligent (E_o—bright house-bird)
  a description of brightness ([x], bright+ness, Noun → bright)
  a gaily colored bird (E_o—bright (house)-bird)
  a house-bird that's bright and colorful (E_o—bright house-bird)
  a house-bird that's bright (E_o—bright house-bird)

TABLE 10. FURTHER INSTANCES OF CLASS EXTENSION. This stimulus resulted in more error for A-group subjects than any other single stimulus, presumably because in addition to the difficulty of the phrase category, the verb *eat* resists class reassignment by zero suffixation. The interpretation of *eat* as *food* is fairly frequent, and this appears in some dialects of American English. The scoring problems are most intractable for this stimulus, and thus it is a good example of why "right" and "wrong" are not simple matters to determine in the free-paraphrasing situation. Answers are called correct when we could conceive some zero affix (no matter how improbable) that would account for the subject's response. What is of importance here is not our judgment of relative correctness, but the profound difference in response style among the groups. Class extensions are common in A-group responses (even for errors) but rare in C-group responses. Note further that "semantic ingenuity" can hardly be denied to the C-group.

Responses to *eat house-bird* (*V C-C*)

A-group
 a house-bird named after George Eat ([viii], Noun → eat)
 a house-bird which eats ([vii])
 a house-bird that's very eat ([viii], Adjective → eat)
 house-bird food (E_o—house-bird eat, Noun → eat)
 food shaped in the form of a house-bird (E_o—house-bird eat, Noun → eat)
 the eating of birds that live in houses (E_o—house-bird eat, Noun → eat)
 a species of house-bird which is eaten ([viii], ed+ible house-bird, Adjective → eat)

B-group
 a command saying everyone should eat house-birds (E_t—Eat house-birds!)
 Eat a house-bird! (E_t—Eat a house-bird!)
 the birds that eat the house (E_{ch}—house-eat bird)
 the bird who lives in the house and they make food out of him ([viii], ed+ible house-bird, Adjective → eat)
 a house-bird which is eating ([vii])
 a house-bird which can be consumed ([viii], ed+ible house-bird, Adjective → eat)
 a command to eat a house-bird (E_t—Eat a house-bird!)

C-group
 where they killed the poor house-bird and they ate it (E_o—house-bird eat, Noun → eat)
 telling the house-bird to eat (E_t—Eat, house-bird!)
 You just told your pet to eat its food (E_t—Eat, house-bird!)

a house-bird which eats house-hold tea leaves (?!)
Eat a pet bird (E_r—Eat a house-bird!)
Eat the house-bird (E_r—Eat the house-bird!)
a house-bird which eats ([vii])

---

educated group often responds to deviance by enlarging the scope of word-class extension operations, while the least-educated group does this only rarely.

Occasionally the complaint has been made that these differences among our groups may be "merely" differences in the ability or inclination to play with linguistic structure. This interpretation cannot account for the inability of some subjects to deal with penumbral features (which require no play) nor for their differing choices among semigrammar rules, which we will discuss next. Still, some of the outcome of the experiments can be understood as a difference in the ability or inclination to manipulate linguistic entities consciously and systematically. But this distinction cannot fruitfully be called "mere." (Differences between Nabokov and the rest of us cannot so lightly be shrugged aside.) Whatever it is, it is hardly extralinguistic.

THE SEMIGRAMMAR OF THE LAST RESORT

There are limits to the speaker's semantic ingenuity and limits to the sense that can be wrung out of a deviant phrase by extending the classificatory capacity of its words. Some speakers may understand *Golf plays John* by stretching the verb (*Golf obsesses John*), but for many this sentence will resist interpretation. Nevertheless, the possibility of providing something very like a passive paraphrase is readily available: *John is played by golf.* Without understanding *Wednesday is perpendicular to my brother,* one can regard it as equivalent in intent to *Wednesday and my brother are perpendicular to each other.* Apparently the utterance is here represented at some intermediate category level where it is not deviant (much as Chomsky supposes). A further step is now taken. The domain of a transformation is (also semigrammatically) redefined in terms of that intermediate level; a "relaxed" version of the transformation, in Katz' sense, is relevant to the paraphrase. The point becomes clearer when the main

TABLE 11. Responses to the "mixed" item *house-bird glass (C-C NA)*. Notation describing error is the same as in previous tables in this chapter. *Glass* is often interpreted as a modifier even though an interpretation as head noun is easy to provide and is the only interpretation that takes the surface order of the elements into account. Note that incorrect responses often reflect some dim awareness that the stimulus was not *glass house-bird*—the linking verb *made-from* is often avoided and other (hard to fathom) relations are suggested. Even with our compassionate scoring here, we must conclude that few subjects outside the A-group were correct.

A-group
 glass for making house-birds
 a very small drinking cup used by a canary
 glass for house-birds
 glass for house-birds
 a way of describing thickness of glass—glass as thick as (or in the
  shape of) glass of a bird-house (E_o—bird-house glass)
 glass that protects house-birds
 the glass that is produced by birds around the house

B-group
 the glass which is used for reconstruction of house-birds
 a house-bird which drinks from a glass (E_o—glass+ophile house-bird)
 glass which is used for house-birds
 glass taken out of a bird's home (E_o—bird-house glass)
 a house-bird on a glass (E_o—glass+perching house-bird)
 decoration used in the home—in the shape of a bird and made of
  glass (E_s—house bird-glass)
 a glass bird that's in a house (E_o—glass house-bird

C-group
 a glass house-bird (E_o—glass house-bird)
 house-bird that's in a glass (E_o—glass + dwelling house-bird)
 a drinking glass or a cup made out of glass of a bird in a house
 a bird that is made of glass (E_o—glass (house)-bird)
 a special glass to use in a bird's house (E_o—bird-house glass)
 a house-bird made from glass (E_o—glass house-bird)

---

terms are nonsense syllables. *A zup was hepped by the ruf* is probably a paraphrase of *The ruf hepped a zup,* assuming only that *zup* and *ruf* are nominals and *hep* is a transitive verb. Dumpty (as reported in Carroll, 1865) has given adequate demonstration of how far such skills can be pushed. Presumably, they come into play only in response to perceived deviance. Note, however, that one who provides "paraphrases" at this level is to some extent playing with syntactic fire. If $ruf = pig$, $hep = cost$, and $zup = dime$, the passive will be stranger than anticipated.

There is some indication that the most-educated group of subjects occasionally manipulated the compounds in this way, bypassing the question of meaningfulness in both stimulus and "paraphrase." Consider the following A-group responses:

> *boot bird-house* = *a bird-house that's gotten boot*
> *house-bright bird* = *a bird of house-bright*
> *kill bird-house* = *a bird-house that's very kill.*

The subject who responds in this way is apt to look defiant or even triumphant and we have no way to thwart her with our feeble operational techniques. If we ask, "What could that mean?" we do not know how to evaluate the explanation she will (promptly) provide.

Whether we call such responses correct or incorrect is of very little moment (actually, we accepted them), but it is of some interest to know when they crop up. Clearly no quantitative statement is possible, for reasons we have implied: for an individual case we have no way of ascertaining the extent to which the subject finds her response a meaningful one (perhaps she does know what it means for a bird-house to get boot). But in general we have no doubt that the aura of meaninglessness for such responses was quite deliberate. The subject traded semantic penetrability for syntactic appropriateness. Such responses are restricted to A-group subjects and occur only on occasions when the stimulus compound was singularly opaque for all subjects. *Kill bird-house* defies interpretation. It is close to impossible to compute a deep structure for this phrase that will be compatible with the surface structure that we gave. Yet the words *kill* and *bird-house* can surely be used in some meaningful, if whimsical, context, that is, as an order to kill the bird-house. Perhaps the C-group subject who makes this leap to meaningfulness will—like the A-group subject—now note a horrendous incompatibility between the surface structure of *kill bird-house* and the surface structure of *Kill the bird-house!* But she will apparently tolerate this discrepancy as preferable to meaninglessness. This tolerance is what we call "error." No doubt the A-group subject goes as doggedly for the meaning of each stimulus and is willing to put up with some radical classificatory distortions to get at it. But on occasion such stratagems will fail, and then the A-group subject may prefer an abstract and meaningless manipulation to an incompatibility between deep and surface structure.

If the A-group subject sometimes operates by semigrammatical and uninterpretable manipulations at surface levels, she is surely not approaching the stimulus by the everyday techniques involved in understanding discourse. To the extent that such procedures were somehow used by A-group subjects, the performances we measured were not always typical paraphrasing performances. Thus some differences among the subject populations may be differences that lie outside the sphere of competence that a grammar ought to describe. But the game these subjects played is a linguistic game nonetheless, in fact a game of syntax, and its rules must be granted to the most-educated group. Activities of this sort may well be components in the understanding of playful and poetic discourse, and in the understanding of grammarians. The uncritical habit of calling everything that a grammar does not describe a "performance factor" may have the unfortunate consequence of lumping together such extragrammatical linguistic skills with a variety of extralinguistic matters.

THE SEMIGRAMMAR AND INCORRECT PARAPHRASES

All of the subjects gave some responses that we scored as errors. Here there was no difficulty in evaluation. Though often it was difficult to say what was correct about the correct responses (*see* tables 9 and 10), it was patently clear that there was something radically wrong with the wrong responses. It could be asserted, perhaps, that when subjects provided these false responses they had "failed to paraphrase," but this account is in some ways misleading. It is not as though they occasionally disregarded the instructions or failed to know what it means to "say it in your own words." Presented with compounds based on core features, all subjects paraphrased with fair consistency. We will therefore suppose that even when the subject erred, she still in some sense paraphrased successfully. The error lay in paraphrasing a phrase other than the one we had provided. This assumption is specifically embodied in the technique used for scoring error type. It may be helpful to summarize this technique again.

First we asked whether the subject's paraphrase was predictable in terms of the grammatical rules; if so, we scored it as correct. If the subject's response could not be derived by the rules of grammar, we assumed that she had paraphrased some phrase other than the one we thought we had presented to her. Thus the response *a house for skinny birds* is surely not a paraphrase of *bird-thin house* but it is an adequate paraphrase of *thin-bird house*. It was now assumed, not that the subject had paraphrased *bird-thin house* wrong, but rather that she had paraphrased *thin-bird house* right. (Whether this assumption is more than a metaphor is debatable. The subjects certainly acted "as if" they were pursuing such a course, but whether this description literally reflects the underlying mechanism, we cannot tell from these experiments alone.) The final step was to compare the two presumed stimulus items: the one on the tape and the one the subject somehow decided to "hear." [5] If the two differed, the response was called an error. For the example just given the real (*bird-thin house*) and hypothetical (*thin-bird house*) compounds differ in that one is an inversion of the other, an "error of order." Thus we are interpreting these strange responses much in the terms of Ziff's account: a deviant utterance was reordered (E_o), or its phrase boundaries changed (E_s), or both of these at once (E_{ch}), or constant terms and intonational markers reassigned to it in such a way that its whole constructional status was altered (E_t). In effect, subjects who erred acted as though what they heard on the tape was a mixed-up version of something else,

---

[5] To reiterate a point we have made before, it is clear that "input" errors occur only very rarely. Of course the subject actually hears the words with stress and position as they are presented. Whether the compound is still available to the subject after she gives a false paraphrase is another matter. There are instances of spontaneous postparaphrase repetition on the tapes in which the subject gives the wrong paraphrase but repeats the right stimulus. There are also many cases in which the spontaneous "repetition" is an error consonant with the paraphrasing error. A preliminary check on this point would be to ask subjects to repeat the stimulus after giving each paraphrase, but so far we have no data on this question.

something meaningful. Where in the processing strategy this determination was made, we cannot know.[6]

In general, then, we assume that the subject produced a grammatically determined paraphrase compatible with the surface structure implied in the stimulus whenever she could do so. In the case of the less-educated subjects, this typically meant whenever a core rule was relevant to deciphering the stimulus compounds. For the most-educated subjects, it typically meant when the stimulus could be seen as involving either core or penumbra (many provisos to these "typical" cases will be added as we go along). In our terms, the subject had three options when she could not relate the stimulus compound to a rule of grammar that she knew and a meaning she could believe in. She could balk (the *tilt*-response), she could operate through a "relaxed" interpretation of grammaticalness (a "Katz-like semigrammar"), or she could reevaluate what she had heard and then paraphrase that new object (a "Ziff-like semigrammar"). The subject almost invariably took one of the latter courses. In only about half a dozen instances (out of 3,024) did she refuse to respond.

Speaking generally, the strength of the association between phrase category and error type establishes the fact that subjects behaved systematically even when the stimulus was perceived as grammatically deviant. Thus to some extent, speakers are competent not only with new instances of known constructions but with constructional novelties as well. When subjects erred, the choice of error (or route back) depended heavily on the phrase category of the stimulus. Errors of order were typically associated with postnominal adjectives and prenominal verbs, errors of stress with nouns, and errors of format with verbs, particularly in first serial position.[7]

[6] Again this account is neutral with respect to the order in which the hearer computes deep and surface structure. If deep structure is found first, then the subject who errs is said to disregard some discrepancy, say of serial order, between the surface structure derived from the obtained base and the surface structure implied by the compound as given. If surface structure is determined first but no match can be found with a deep structure, the account is that some juggling of the surface elements (e.g., of their order) takes place until a match can be found with some basis.

[7] The association between errors of stress and nouns may be partly an artifact. It is not that nouns are more likely to lead to errors of stress, but that they are less likely to lead to errors of order, format, or chaos. Neither order

These obtained associations between error type and phrase category support little interpretation. To some extent, the facts are self-explanatory. If the subject sees her central task as determining the meaning of each compound, we need only note that most subjects do not understand postnominal adjectives in this context while they do understand prenominal adjectives. An inversion is hardly surprising under these circumstances. If the subject assigns deep-structure relations to *thin* (modifier-of) and *bird-house* (head-noun) she becomes on occasion indifferent to the discrepancy between the surface structure implied for these relations (*thin bird-house*) and the utterance she has heard (*bird-house thin*). (If this is the interpretation, we have no difficulty understanding that a subject who blithely paraphrases both *thin bird-house* and *bird-house thin* as *a narrow bird house* will never utter the sentence *Look at that bird-house thin!* as a stylistic variant of *Look at that thin bird-house!*) Similarly, while the subject may not understand that verbs are used in compounds, she certainly knows that they are used in imperative sentences. The paths people follow are understandable if we assume that they know how to paraphrase and that they see their task as finding a meaningful and grammatical object on which to exercise this skill. If the A-group subject knows more of the grammar and has more freedom to reclassify, she has less occasion for this kind of error.

Beyond these very general remarks we cannot speculate on how or why people choose routes as they do. To say that the paths chosen are understandable is not to say that alternative paths are not. In this sense, the experimental results throw no new light on the question of what the structure of a semigrammar mechanism should look like. In terms of Ziff's programmatic statement, many alternative paths are possible, and there is no obvious way to determine the shortest ("optimal") route. No counterproposal that we know of avoids this difficulty. The presumed paths followed by subjects in the experimental situation

---

nor format changes can so easily affect the grammatical status of three-noun compounds, so boundary changes predominate for this category. The use of E_s is dependent upon semantic features of the phrases that operate whatever the lexical classification of the test word. These are discussed in the next section.

do not suggest ways to constrain the too-powerful theoretical account. If the subject could not paraphrase *house-bird thin,* she paraphrased *thin house-bird* (an inversion). But why did she not paraphrase *house-bird* (deleting *thin*), or *thin bird-house* (two inversions), or *thin-house bird* (inversion and boundary change)? We cannot say whether the routes most commonly traveled by our subjects were optimal. To say that they were understandable suggests at most that a system exists waiting to be described.

The differences in choice of error among the population groups are even more puzzling. Whatever the quantitative difference, the A-group subjects did use the "Ziff-like semigrammar" on some occasions. But when they did so, they were disproportionally prone to errors of order (60 percent of all scorable errors for this group, compared to 42 percent and 35 percent for the B-group and C-group respectively). The less-educated groups contributed almost all the errors of chaos and format. Again, it is as though the C-group is willing to tolerate more extreme discrepancies between deep structures and their surface manifestations. Whatever the reasons, the finding is that the groups differ significantly in their style of repairing deviance.

SEMANTIC FACTORS

The discussion so far might suggest that there should be no errors in the paraphrasing tasks when all three terms of the compound are nouns. Here the relevant rule ([iv]) is in the core grammar. Although it is true enough that this condition led to fewer errors than did the others, at 27 percent the error rate was still far from negligible. Similarly, some of the errors for prenominal uses of adjectives (rules [viii] and [ix]) cannot be explained on syntactic grounds.

The overall premise we adopt to explain error in these cases is the same as taken previously: a wrong paraphrase is a paraphrase of a phrase other than the one we gave the subject. Preceding sections dealt with substitutions that repaired perceived syntactic flaws (e.g., paraphrasing *black house-bird* instead of *house-bird black*) that interfered with meaningful interpretation. For the examples to be discussed now, the grounds for substitution seem to be semantic. As before, the task is to characterize the phrase that the subject, as it were, substituted for the stimulus.[8]

It is plain that not all compounds are equally acceptable on semantic grounds. Though almost all of the phrases can be assumed to be previously unheard, some are more immediately plausible than others on pragmatic grounds (whether houses can have feet, whether bird-houses can be thin or black, whether house-birds can be judged for intelligence, and so on). Further, as already mentioned in the discussion of the "appropriate verb" and the naming operation [ix], compounds imply some kind of intimate relationship among the elements that comprise them. If a compound cannot be so interpreted, it sounds unnatural. If this is so, it is hardly surprising that *house-bird* is semantically "easier" even though no more familiar than *house-foot*. What continuing bond is implied by *house-foot?* For some generalized foot, it is difficult to imagine why it should be related to a house. Is it perhaps the foot one always puts in the house first? Or the stay-at-home foot? A measure used only when measuring houses? Improbable. How about *boot-bird?* Is this perhaps a bird who brings you your boots? Far-fetched.

Put another way, while it is easy enough to transform a two-noun compound into a relative clause, the problem of finding an appropriate linking verb is often far from negligible, for the bond formed must be both plausible and intimate. Subjects sometimes solved the problem by treating the modifier simply as a name, in which case the relation is generic and the base meaning of the modifier need have no sensible relation to the head: thus a *house-foot* is *a foot called House:* a *boot-bird* is *a species of bird.* On other occasions, the subject evidently failed to find

8 The semantic factors discussed here affected responses to penumbral stimuli as well as to the core compounds that are used as examples in this discussion. In such cases, however, the effects of semantic rectification were partially masked by various effects of syntactic rectification. Thus for ease of explication, we limit this discussion to the instances where no difficult rule was involved. Note, however, that the effects of dual difficulty are readily apparent in the experimental results since they frequently lead to dual error. Thus, for example, *bird house-bright* can be repaired semantically by a stress shift to become *bird-house bright;* and it can then be moved from penumbra to core by an inversion, now yielding *bright bird-house.* Thus phrase categories of this sort (*C-A C, C C-A*) are associated with errors of chaos.

the link. In this case, she apparently paraphrased another compound, one for which the integral relation could be established.

The data show clear evidence of the effect of this kind of semantic factor. It is best illustrated by what we have called "the unity effect" (*see* chap. 4). Two-thirds of the stimulus items include the sequences *bird/house* or *house/bird* (specifically, whenever the X-term is in first or third serial position). When these sequences are embedded in the item in such a way that they are intonationally unified into a subcompound, subjects have little trouble in finding legitimate paraphrases (all other matters of population and construction being held equal). Thus for example, *bird-house foot* and *house-bird foot* are relatively easy to paraphrase. On the other hand, when these sequences are embedded in such a way as to be intonationally disunified, so that they really do not form a sub-unit at all, the resulting three-word sequence is extremely difficult to paraphrase. Thus *house bird-foot* and *bird house-foot* lead to many more errors. This effect is even more pronounced when the X-term is an adjective in first serial position: *bright bird-house* is absurdly simple, *bright-bird house* absurdly hard (*see* table 12 and the additional examples in the appendix). Confronted with the disunified items, the subjects tend to interpret them as if they were unified. Asked to paraphrase *bird house-foot* they paraphrase *bird-house foot* instead. Reflecting our syntactic bias, we call this systematic reinterpretation of constituent boundaries an error, specifically an error of stress. Errors with compounds in which *bird* and *house* were disunified in this sense occurred nearly twice as often as they did for unified compounds. It is worth noting that this ratio was about equal for the three groups.[9]

To interpret this effect, consider the task of a subject given a three-noun compound, say (N_1-N_2) (N_3). She must find two relative clauses, each with its appropriate link; for nouns, the "appropriate verb." First she must decide what links N_1 and N_2, and then she must repeat this process for N_3 and the unit N_1-N_2.

[9] Note that not all errors with core items were errors attributable to the unity effect. Although other errors with core constructions are very rare for the A-group, C-group subjects do commit some order and chaos errors with unified core constructions, though these may also be attributable to semantic oddity. *Foot bird-house* and *house-bird boot* are not exactly transparent in meaning even though no unity problem is involved.

TABLE 12. Responses to the "unified" compound *bright bird-house* and the "nonunified" compound *bright-bird house*. Errors for unified compounds involving core rules are rare (for the example here, *bright bird-house,* no errors occur, but occasional errors do occur in this phrase category, e.g., table 7a). Errors are frequent for the nonunified instance, *bright-bird house.* The errors are almost always errors of stress, that is, the nonunified item is unified by the subject.

(a) Responses to *bright bird-house* (*A C-C*)

A-group
a bird-house that's bright
a sunny house that birds live in
a really smart bird-house
a gaily colored bird-house
a bird-house which is bright in color
a bird-house with big windows
a house in which birds live which is bright

B-group
a very bright house for birds
a bird-house that is bright in color
a house for birds which is bright
a bird's home which is lit up
a bird-house which is very bright
a bird-house painted bright colors and looks cheerful
a bright house for birds

C-group
a bright colored bird-house
the sunny, gaily painted home for birds
a bird-house that looks cheerful and is a very happy house
a bright, brightly colored bird-house
a bright bird-house
a light and colorful bird-house
a bird-house that is bright

(b) Responses to *bright-bird house* (*A-C C*)

A-group
a house for a bird that's especially bright
a shiny house where birds live (E_s—a bright bird-house)
a house for bright-birds
a bird-house that's bright (E_s—bright bird-house)
a house in which lives a particular kind of bird, known as bright-birds
a house for brightly colored birds
a house which will accommodate only very intelligent birds

B-group
a house for intelligent birds, bright-birds

a bright house for a bird (E_s—bright bird-house)
a house for bright and shiny birds
a bird's home which is lit up (E_s—bright bird-house)
a lively colored bird in a house (E_o—house bright-bird)
a bird-house which has been painted and decorated in lively colors
   (E_s—bright bird-house)
a bird-house for bright-birds

C-group
a brightly colored, where sun can come into the bird-house (E_s—bright
   bird-house)
a gaily painted dwelling for birds (E_s—bright bird-house)
a cheerful bird-house (E_s—bright bird-house)
a bright bird-house (E_s—bright bird-house)
a light, airy house for birds (E_s—bright bird-house)
a bright house where birds live (E_s—bright bird-house)
a house for bright-birds

If finding the appropriate link is not a trivial task, the situation is obviously much simpler if one of these relations has already been established. This is why the unified compounds are easier to paraphrase, in general, than the others. For both *house-bird* and *bird-house,* the linking verb *live* is plausible and appropriate. Little wonder that when these words occur contiguously, but are disunified, the subject "changes" or "disregards" the constituent boundaries (commits an error of stress) and paraphrases the unified compound instead.[10]

A SUMMARY OF GROUP DIFFERENCES

We have argued that speakers can paraphrase systematically when the phrase provided is *for them* well-formed and meaningful. We have shown that certain constructional types (the penumbra) are less likely to be seen as well-formed, and that

[10] If the subject's difficulty with nonunified pairs was, as we say, difficulty in finding the link, one might question why this effect was obtained in the forced-choice experiment, and for that matter even in the repetition situation. Here the link between the elements of the compound is provided on the response card. But to say that a link is suggested to the subject does not imply that she will find it plausible and appropriate. It appears that, on the contrary, she still prefers to disregard the constituent boundaries of the compound in the interest of unifying the constant terms, thus choosing an error of stress over the correct paraphrase.

certain sequences (those that are disunified) are less likely to be seen as meaningful. In these difficult cases, all subjects are less likely to paraphrase in accordance with the "rules" we proposed in chapter 3. The error rate of the most-educated groups rises for both syntactic and semantic anomalies, but the consistency of these subjects with these difficult phrase categories is still impressive. We cannot explain this consistency except by conceding that these subjects' responses reflected some perceived grammatical regularity. On the contrary, for penumbral and disunified compounds, the C-group subjects' performance plummets so catastrophically that it becomes unrealistic to grant them knowledge of the linguistic regularities that underlie A-group responses. In general, then, our claim is that grammaticalness for each speaker and grammaticalness in the language cannot be wholly the same thing. There are differences in the extent to which various individuals approach aspects of the abstraction. Obviously the differences show up primarily with more difficult entities; there is undoubtedly a core grammar that speakers have in common. So long as we do not argue from an equalitarian and nativist position, these population differences will create no special descriptive problem. On the contrary, we have some basis for describing the intuitively obvious fact that there are large and pervasive differences in the grammatical sophistication of speakers.

We have argued further that the strategies of the subject populations for computing deep structures from inputs may well vary. Where the phrase is deviant, the A-group subject tends to reclassify. Where this method does not avail, she will sometimes resort to surface-level manipulations. All subjects attempt to find a meaningful interpretation of the compound, but A-group subjects are more bound to the restriction that deep and surface interpretations be compatible. The C-group subject tolerates more, and more extreme, discrepancies between deep and surface representations of the presumed compound. These distinctions in approach are so large and consistent as to suggest that very different descriptions of the notion *semigrammar* may be required to explain the behavior of various speaker populations.

Concluding that population differences occur for semigrammar as well as grammar, we again depart from the view of many transformational linguists. Katz (1964) writes that "semisentences are comprehensible to each speaker according only to his linguistic abilities," and these abilities are asserted to be the same for all speakers of the same dialect. This hypothesis cannot be maintained in the light of our findings. Speakers vary enormously in their approach both to grammar and semigrammar, and although of course the various approaches may be equally "good," it is hopeless to maintain that they are all equal. There is, in short, no interesting interpretation of the hypothesis of equal competence.

Classifying and Paraphrasing

While people classify rather poorly, they paraphrase rather well. Try getting even a "good" speaker to classify. He will twist and turn to evade doing what you ask. If you give him sentences that are patently deformed monstrosities, he will respond "poetic," or "I wouldn't say it, but it is fine for other people," or "perfectly good in the fourteenth century." If, to avoid all this, you insist on a simple yes or no, he will give responses that cannot sensibly be related to his knowledge of language (three times out of every twenty-one, apparently, he will *label break to be calmed about and*). From such frustrating encounters with empirical reality derive the more Byzantine interpretations of the performance-competence distinction, the belief that the relations between speaker and language are abstract and inaccessible, and the unshakable faith that failure to classify has nothing to do with the speaker's linguistic organization (his *competence*) but is uniformly attributable to some confluence of linguistically external psychological variables (his *performance*). It seems to us that limitations on the speaker's capacity have to be viewed in the light of his aims as a language user. Apparent incompatibilities between speaker and system need not summarily be relegated to hypothetical extralinguistic spheres; rather, the speaker must be asked a question he can understand.

The experiments we have reported are based on the view that

the nature of what the speaker constructs from what he hears (be it right or wrong by some systematic criteria) is partly discernible from the paraphrase he reports. Thus paraphasing failures, unlike classifying failures, seem to be understandable in terms of linguistic organization. However small the substantive step toward this goal taken in our work, we believe it likely that an understanding of the speaker's working competence has to come from considering his knowledge of sentential relations, from paraphrase. That is the name of the transformational game, and it is the informant's undoubted knowledge of these relations that primarily and centrally leads to the concept of deep structure. If this is so, there is very little reason to be intimidated by the speaker's mulish disinclination to classify, to distinguish between syntactic anomaly and truth value, and the like. In some sense he is obviously competent to do these things, and it is a symptom of his competence that these skills do not reveal themselves "operationally" in the tasks often used to test them.

The act of classifying runs against the linguistic grain; paraphrasing runs with it. When stumped, the average speaker tends to restructure and rehear what has been said, to grant it meaning. We submit that this is not the usual meaning-is-all, structure-is-nothing, kind of argument, which is surely vacuous for natural language. Semistructured entities are recrafted in the service both of syntax and of meaning. In this process, the underlying classificatory act—on which the act of building a structure is surely contingent—is masked. It is a curiosity that empiricists and transformationalists, though they differ so radically in their view of the speaker, have sometimes both assumed that much of what the individual knew could be leached out by asking him whether a sentence was or was not "in" his language; that classification could be made overt. This assumes that the speaker (though neither linguist nor psychologist) could take an "objective" look at surface features of the utterance without regard to the logical structure he imposes upon it. We have seen that elite speakers can occasionally operate in this way, manipulating surface forms with airy disregard for deep structure. But the ordinary speaker can hardly do this unless he is a trained grammarian, just as an ordinary introspector is unable to avoid the "stimulus error" unless trained in E. B. Tichener's laboratory.

It is in this sense that the theoretical issues raised here are rather reminiscent of the debates between functionalist and structuralist psychologies at the turn of the century, the opposition between Act and Content.

One final point. The empiricist movement in linguistics failed in part because of a doctrinaire belief that the grammar had to be saddled with the speaker, thus building into the language description every false start, cough, slip of the tongue, cut-corner of verbal behavior. The result was a failure to reveal the system that lay below. But the recent attempt of transformational linguists to saddle the speaker with the grammar is no less problematical, especially when coupled with a sweeping claim for equal competence. Granting every speaker's subtle and creative skills with language, we are still left with some interesting differences among individuals, and with some apparently stringent limitations on the capacity to cope with complex instances. Experimentally, we find that people have trouble even with three-word compounds. In fact, the palpable existence, in bronze, of our prize compound noun *Volume Feeding Management Success Formula Award* now seems rather embarrassing.

Consider a hypothetical situation. One advertising executive says to the other, "Let's give an award for succeeding in finding a formula for managing the feeding of people in large volumes. What shall we call it?" "Obviously," retorts the other advertising executive, "a volume feeding management success formula award." This ranks high among implausible retorts. It takes no experiment to discover that few individuals could on a single occasion match this phrase and paraphrase.

The compound itself is, no doubt, the monument of a long entrepreneurial history in which the establishment of the journal *Volume Feeding Management* was an epochal event. The phrase is an accretion, built of time and experience. Unlimited creativity is there in the Language, but it is not "there" and there to the same degree, in each individual. If we try to equate the speaker's underlying competence with the laws of Language itself, we erase the distinction between speaker and system as surely as did those linguists and those psychologists who denied the distinction between language and speech.

Appendix

I. Stimulus Lists and Sample Responses

A. SAMPLE RESPONSES OF REPRESENTATIVE SUBJECTS TO ALL STIMULI IN THE FREE-RESPONSE TASK

Below are listed all responses for the median subject in each of the population groups. Stimuli are organized by phrase category. Subjects' wrong responses are scored by error type (O = order, S = stress, Ch = chaos, F = format).

PHRASE CATEGORY *N C-C*

foot bird-house
  A: a bird-house that's foot
  B: a bird-house for feet
  C: the end of a bird-house, the bottom of a bird-house   (O)

boot bird-house
  A: a bird-house that's gotten boot
  B: a bird-house for boots
  C: shoes for bird-houses   (O)

foot house-bird
  A: a house-bird that's "foot" . . . which is like being "camp"
  B: a bird known as a foot-house bird   (S)
  C: the foot of the house-bird   (O)

boot house-bird
  A: a house-bird that's "boot" . . . like "camp"
  B: a house-bird that's known as a boot-house bird   (S)
  C: a shoe of a house-bird   (O)

PHRASE CATEGORY *N-C C*

foot-bird house
  A: a house for foot-birds
  B: a house for birds to put their feet in   (O)
  C: a house for foot-birds

boot-bird house
  A: a house where boot-birds are kept
  B: a bird-house for boots   (S)
  C: a house where the birds have their boots   (O)

foot-house bird
  A: a bird that lives in foot-houses, which are like keepers' lodges
  B: a kind of bird called a foot-house bird
  C: a special type of bird, like a foot-house, we'll invent a new
      species of birds

boot-house bird
  A: a bird that lives in a house in which boots are stored
  B: a kind of bird called a boot-house bird
  C: birds who live in boot-houses, a boot-house may be a small
      house

PHRASE CATEGORY *C N-C*

bird boot-house
  A: a house where boots for birds are kept
  B: a boot-house for birds
  C: a house where the birds keep their boots

house foot-bird
  A: a name of a house or a foot-bird that's kept in a house
  B: a foot-bird that lives in a house
  C: a different species, called foot-bird, in a house

house boot-bird
  A: a kind of bird, boot-bird, who is kept in a house
  B: a bird called a house-boot bird   (S)
  C: a house-boot meaning house-shoes for birds   (Ch)

bird foot-house
  A: a foot-house which is maybe a very small house for birds
  B: a foot-house for birds
  C: a type of house, a foot-house for birds

PHRASE CATEGORY *C-N C*

house-foot bird
  A: a bird that lives in the foot of a house, maybe that means in the cellar
  B: a type of bird called a house-foot bird
  C: a house-bird that's under your feet   (S)

bird-foot house
  A: a house in which bird-feet are stored
  B: a house for birds' feet
  C: the foot or a leg of a bird in a house   (O)

bird-boot house
  A: a house for storing bird-boots
  B: a boot-house for birds   (S)
  C: a bird-house for shoes   (S)

house-boot bird
  A: a bird that looks like bedroom slippers
  B: a kind of bird known as a house-boot bird
  C: a bird that wears house-boots

PHRASE CATEGORY *C-C N*

bird-house boot
  A: a boot (like a cover on a convertible) which is used for covering bird-houses
  B: a bird-house in a boot   (O)
  C: a boot which belonged to a bird-house as in the olden days, etc.

bird-house foot
  A: like foot-and-mouth disease for birds that are kept in houses   (O)
  B: a foot for bird-houses
  C: the foot of a bird-house

house-bird foot
  A: a disease of the foot which house-birds get
  B: a kind of foot called a house-bird foot
  C: the foot of a house-bird

house-bird boot
  A: a boot for house-birds

B: a kind of a boot known as a house-bird boot
C: the boot of the house-bird

PHRASE CATEGORY C C-N

bird house-foot
A: a disease like scrubwoman's knee that birds get
B: a foot for bird-houses   (S)
C: a foot-house for birds   (O)

bird house-boot
A: a boot to be worn around the house . . . for birds
B: a boot known as a bird-house boot   (S)
C: house-boots for birds

house bird-foot
A: a disease birds get from being in the house
B: a foot for house-birds   (S)
C: a leg of a house-bird   (S)

house bird-boot
A: a boot for birds for wearing in the house
B: a boot that's known as a house-bird boot   (S)
C: birds' boots, birds' shoes

PHRASE CATEGORY A C-C

thin bird-house
A: a very thin bird-house
B: a bird-house that's thin
C: a narrow bird-house

bright bird-house
A: a gaily colored bird-house
B: a bright-house for birds
C: a bright-colored bird-house

thin house-bird
A: a domesticated bird that's gotten thin
B: a house-bird that's thin
C: a thin and undernourished house-bird

bright house-bird
A: a brightly colored bird that's kept in a house
B: a house-bird that's very bright
C: an intelligent house-bird

black bird-house
  A: a house for birds which has been painted black
  B: a bird-house that's black
  C: a bird-house and the color of it is black

black house-bird
  A: a house-bird that has black feathers
  B: a house-bird that's black
  C: a house-bird that's black

PHRASE CATEGORY *A-C C*

black-house bird
  A: a bird that lives in black-houses, which are houses that
      Negroes live in
  B: a kind of bird, a black-house bird
  C: a house, that would be black, with a bird in it   (O)

thin-bird house
  A: a house for thin-birds
  B: a bird-house that's thin   (S)
  C: a thin, narrow bird-house   (S)

bright-bird house
  A: a bird-house that's bright   (S)
  B: a bird-house for bright birds
  C: a bright colored, where the sun can come into the bird-house   (S)

thin-house bird
  A: a very small bird that can be kept in a thin house
  B: a house-bird that's thin   (S)
  C: an underfed house-bird   (S)

bright-house bird
  A: a kind of bird that lives in bright houses, which is like the
      kind of place you keep plants in
  B: a house-bird that's bright   (S)
  C: an intelligent house-bird   (S)

black-bird house
  A: a house for keeping black-birds in
  B: a house for black-birds
  C: a dark colored bird in a house   (O)

PHRASE CATEGORY *C A-C*

house thin-bird
  A: a domesticated thin-bird
  B: a house for thin-birds   (O)
  C: a house for thin birds, underfed birds   (O)

house bright-bird
  A: a bright bird, like a parakeet, that lives in a house
  B: a bright bird in a house
  C: a bright house in color, for birds   (Ch)

bird thin-house
  A: a thin-house for birds
  B: a thin-house for birds
  C: a narrow house for birds

bird bright-house
  A: a cleaning product birds should use to keep their
      house clean   (O)
  B: a bright-house for birds
  C: the nice bright-colored house for birds

house black-bird
  A: a black-bird that can be kept in the house
  B: a black-bird that's kept in a house
  C: a type of bird like a black-bird or sparrow

bird black-house
  A: a black-house for birds
  B: a black-house for birds
  C: a black-house for birds

PHRASE CATEGORY *C-A C*

bird-bright house
  A: the name of a house
  B: a house for bright birds   (O)
  C: a cheerful house, a cheerful bird-house   (S)

house-black bird
  A: a bird whose feathers are used for making stuff to blacken
      houses
  B: a type of bird, a house-black bird
  C: a black-bird in the house   (S)

bird-black house
- A: a house where bird-black, or bird shoe polish, is used . . . is stored
- B: (misheard stimulus—not scored)
- C: a black home for birds   (S)

house-thin bird
- A: a bird that's become thin from living in a house
- B: a bird that lives in a house and is thin   (S)
- C: a house, a narrow house, a small house for birds   (Ch)

house-bright bird
- A: a bird as bright as a house . . . a bird that's bright from living in a house
- B: a bird that's house-bright
- C: a bright house, bright and colored for birds   (Ch)

bird-thin house
- A: a house for thinning birds, for keeping them while they're thinning
- B: a house that's bird-thin
- C: an underfed bird in a house   (Ch)

PHRASE CATEGORY *C-C A*

house-bird black
- A: black paint for smearing on house-birds
- B: a black house-bird   (O)
- C: the color of the house-bird, black house-bird

bird-house thin
- A: a kind of paint, or something, for using on bird-houses
- B: a bird-house that's thin   (O)
- C: a thin, a narrow small bird-house   (O)

bird-house bright
- A: a cleaner for bird-houses
- B: a bird-house that's bright   (O)
- C: a bright house for birds   (O)

house-bird thin
- A: something—as thin as a housebird
- B: a house-bird that's thin   (O)
- C: a thin and underfed house-bird   (O)

bird-house black
- A: like shoe-black or shoe polish for bird-houses

B: a black bird-house (O)
C: the color of a bird-house, a black and dark house-bird

house-bird bright
A: something for brightening housebirds
B: a house-bird that's bright (O)
C: a bright, bright in color, house-bird (O)

PHRASE CATEGORY *C C-A*

bird house-bright
A: something birds can use to keep their houses bright
B: a house-bird that's very bright (Ch)
C: a birdhouse where a lot of air came in and it would be
   bright in there (O)

bird house-thin
A: house-thin for birds
B: a bird-house that's thin (O)
C: a house for thin birds (Ch)

bird house-black
A: a brand name of enamel used to blacken a house
B: a bird that's a house-black
C: a dark colored house for birds (O)

house bird-thin
A: bird-thin that is to be used in the house rather than outside
B: a thin house-bird (O)
C: a thin house-bird (O)

house bird-bright
A: the name of a camp cabin at a boys' camp (O)
B: a house-bird that's bright (O)
C: a bright and intelligent bird in a house (O)

house bird-black
A: a product used for dyeing birds black that can be used safely
   in the house
B: a house for black birds (Ch)
C: a house for black birds (Ch)

PHRASE CATEGORY *V C-C*

eat house-bird
A: house-bird food (O)

B: a command to eat a house-bird   (F)
C: where they kill the poor house-bird and they ate it   (O)

kill bird-house
  A: the name of a bird-house in which birds are killed
  B: a house for kill-birds   (S)
  C: a house where they kill birds

wash bird-house
  A: a label—*wash*—then parenthesis bird-house, telling you the
        specific use of this specific kind of wash   (F)
  B: a bird-house that's washed
  C: a clean bird-house

kill house-bird
  A: the name of a euthanasia solution   (O)
  B: a house-bird that kills
  C: take the life of a house-bird   (F)

wash house-bird
  A: a kind of cleaning product . . . it's really house-bird
        wash   (O)
  B: a bird that's known as the wash-house bird   (S)
  C: clean the bird-house!   (F)

eat bird-house
  A: an edible bird-house
  B: a bird-house where the birds eat
  C: a bird-house where the birds eat, where they have their meals

PHRASE CATEGORY *V-C C*

kill-house bird
  A: a bird that lives in that place in prison where guys are waiting
        to be executed: death-house bird
  B: a command to kill the house-bird   (F)
  C: taking the life of a house-bird   (F)

wash-bird house
  A: a house where wash-birds are kept
  B: a house for wash-birds
  C: a place where they wash the birds   (O)

wash-house bird
  A: a bird that lives in wash-houses, or laundries

B: a bird that's called a wash-house bird
C: a wash-house for the birds   (O)

eat-bird house
A: a house for an eat-bird, eat-bird is a species of bird
B: a house for birds to eat   (O)
C: a house where they eat birds   (O)

eat-house bird
A: a bird kept in eat-houses, which are like roadside diners
B: a bird known as an eat-house bird
C: a place where the birds eat, dining room   (O)

kill-bird house
A: a house named for kill-birds which are like hawks
B: a house that's known as a kill-bird house
C: a dead bird in a house   (O)

PHRASE CATEGORY *C V-C*

bird eat-house
A: a roadside stand for birds
B: an eating house for birds
C: a place where the birds eat, where they would get their feed

house kill-bird
A: a kill-bird that is a domestic animal kept in a house
B: a kill-bird that lives in a house
C: a house where they kill birds   (Ch)

house wash-bird
A: a wash-bird that lives in a house
B: a bird that washes houses   (S)
C: a bird that was just washed

bird kill-house
A: a house in which you keep the birds who are to be killed
B: a killing house for birds
C: a place where they kill birds

bird wash-house
A: a wash-house for birds, where birds are washed
B: a wash-house for birds
C: a place where birds would go to be washed

house eat-bird
A: an eat-bird that can be kept in the house

B: a house where they eat birds　(Ch)
C: in the twilight hour the house eats the bird　(F)

PHRASE CATEGORY *C-V C*

house-wash bird
    A: a bird that excretes some product that can be used in a household cleaning agent
    B: a name of a type of bird, a house wash-bird　(S)
    C: a bird of a different species, say a sparrow bird, in this case

bird-kill house
    A: a house where birds are killed, or a house that kills birds
    B: a killing house for birds where they kill birds
    C: a house where they kill birds

bird-wash house
    A: a house in which birds are washed, a house in which bird-wash is stored
    B: a wash-house for birds
    C: similar to a bird-bath, a place where the birds could wash

house-eat bird
    A: the name of a kind of bird
    B: a bird that eats houses
    C: an eating house for birds　(Ch)

bird-eat house
    A: a house for bird-eat . . . food for birds
    B: an eating house for birds
    C: a house where birds eat, where they have their meals

house-kill bird
    A: a bird that house-kills
    B: a kind of bird that's house kill-bird　(S)
    C: a bird goes into a house, a house-kill　(F)

PHRASE CATEGORY *C-C V*

house-bird kill
    A: a euthanasia solution for house-birds
    B: a kill that's a house-bird kill
    C: the murder of house-birds, like a big kill, a house-bird kill

house-bird wash
    A: a soap for domestic birds

B: a kind of wash that's called a house-bird wash
C: the wash from the house-birds, they do their weekly wash

bird-house eat
    A: (stimulus not presented)
    B: a bird-house that eats   (O)
    C: the food they have for the birds in the bird-house

house-bird eat
    A: food for house-birds
    B: a house-bird that eats   (O)
    C: the house-bird is eating, taking food   (F)

bird-house kill
    A: something for destroying bird-houses
    B: a house-kill for birds where birds are killed   (S)
    C: a kill like you killed a lot of birds and brought them into
        the bird-house

bird-house wash
    A: a cleansing product for bird-houses
    B: a kind of wash called a bird-house wash
    C: wash or clean the bird-house   (F)

PHRASE CATEGORY *C C-V*

house bird-eat
    A: bird-eat that can be used in houses rather than in
        industrial places
    B: a command to tell the house-bird to eat   (F)
    C: food for house-birds   (S)

bird house-kill
    A: like "Raid" or "Realkill" for birds
    B: a house-kill, it's for birds
    C: a bird-house where they killed birds   (Ch)

bird house-wash
    A: a cleaning product used for birds that live in a house
    B: a house-wash for birds
    C: a detergent for cleaning houses, a house-wash

house bird-kill
    A: something you can use for killing birds when they're in
        the house
    B: a bird-kill that's done in a house
    C: killing birds, taking the life of birds in a house

bird house-eat
- A: house-eat is a kind of snack for birds (F)
- B: an eating house for birds (O)
- C: where the birds would get their food (O)

house bird-wash
- A: bird-wash is like soap . . . used on birds . . .
  used in the house
- B: a bird-wash that takes place in a house
- C: the birds wash the house (F)

PHRASE CATEGORY *NA C-C*

glass house-bird
- A: a house-bird that's been modeled out of glass
- B: a glass bird they have in houses used for ornament
- C: birds who live in glass houses (S)

stone bird-house
- A: a bird-house that's made of stone
- B: a bird-house made of stones
- C: the material which the bird-house is built of, stone as
  opposed to cinder block (O)

stone house-bird
- A: stone model of the breed house-bird
- B: a house-bird made out of stone
- C: a structure built of stone to house house-birds (O)

glass bird-house
- A: a bird-house made out of glass
- B: a bird-house that's made out of glass
- C: a glass transparent where you could look into a bird-house (O)

PHRASE CATEGORY *NA-C C*

glass-bird house
- A: a house which is lived in by glass-birds
- B: a bird-house that's made out of glass (S)
- C: a house made of glass for birds (S)

glass-house bird
- A: a bird that lives in a glass house
- B: a bird that lives in a glass house
- C: birds that live in glass houses

stone-bird house

    A: a house in which stone models of birds are on display

    B: a bird-house made out of stones   (S)

    C: a bird-house built of stone   (S)

stone-house bird

    A: a bird that lives in a stone-house

    B: a bird that lives in a stone-house

    C: a type of house-bird   (S)

PHRASE CATEGORY *C-NA C*

bird-stone house

    A: a house made out of bird-stone

    B: a bird-house made out of stone   (S)

    C: a building built of bird-stone

house-glass bird

    A: that's a bird to house-glass with

    B: a bird known as a house-glass bird

    C: a glass-bird in a house   (S)

bird-glass house

    A: a house made out of bird-glass

    B: a glass house for birds   (S)

    C: a transparent house for birds   (S)

house-stone bird

    A: the name of a kind of bird

    B: a bird that's known as a house-stone bird

    C: a stone house built of stone for birds   (Ch)

PHRASE CATEGORY *C-C NA*

house-bird stone

    A: stone or gravel or something for house-birds

    B: a stone for house-birds

    C: the stone of the house-bird

bird-house glass

    A: glass to be used in a bird-house

    B: a glass bird-house   (O)

    C: a glass-house for birds   (O)

house-bird glass

    A: glass for house-birds

B: a glass bird that's in a house   (O)
C: a glass house-bird   (O)

bird-house stone
    A: the kind of stone you put in bird-houses
    B: a stone known as a bird-house stone
    C: a stone structure, stone bird-house, a bird-house that's
        built of stone   (O)

PHRASE CATEGORY *C C-NA*

bird house-stone
    A: a house-stone is maybe something you wipe your feet on
        . . . a doormat or mudscraper, and this one is for
        birds to use
    B: a stone bird-house   (O)
    C: a bird-house that is built of stone   (O)

house bird-glass
    A: a mirror or a window for birds that live in houses (S)
    B: a kind of bird-glass they keep in the house
    C: bird-glass is a new type of glass they have for putting
        in houses

house bird-stone
    A: a bird-stone for using in the house
    B: a house for bird-stones   (O)
    C: a bird made of stone in a house   (O)

bird house-glass
    A: house-glass, as opposed to automobile glass, that birds use
    B: a bird-house made out of glass   (O)
    C: a glass-house for birds   (O)

PHRASE CATEGORY *AV C-C*

shut bird-house
    A: a closed bird-house—an airtight bird-house
    B: a bird-house that's shut
    C: close the bird-house   (F)

shut house-bird
    A: a house-bird that's been isolated
    B: a house-bird that's shut in
    C: close the house-bird   (F)

dry bird-house
- A: a bird-house that's dry
- B: a bird-house that's dry
- C: a dry, meaning not wet, a dry bird-house

dry house-bird
- A: a house-bird that's dry
- B: a house-bird that's dry
- C: a dry, warm, not wet house-bird

PHRASE CATEGORY *AV-C C*

dry-bird house
- A: a house for dry-birds
- B: a bird-house that's dry   (S)
- C: a dry warm house as opposed to a wet bird-house   (S)

dry-house bird
- A: a bird that lives in dry-houses—a place where clothes are put to dry
- B: a house-bird that's dry   (S)
- C: a house-bird that's dry   (S)

shut-bird house
- A: a house for shut-birds
- B: a shut bird-house   (S)
- C: close the bird-house, or a closed bird-house   (S)

shut-house bird
- A: a bird that lives in a shut-house
- B: a bird that's shut in a house   (O)
- C: a closed house, a shut house, a closed house for birds (O)

PHRASE CATEGORY *C AV-C*

house shut-bird
- A: something for keeping birds shut up suitable for use in a house   (O)
- B: a bird-house that is shut   (Ch)
- C: (misheard stimulus)

bird dry-house
- A: a drying-out house for birds, or a dehumidified place for birds
- B: a house where birds dry, where they can dry out
- C: a warm, unwet house for birds

bird shut-house
  A: a shut-house for birds
  B: a house that's shut to birds
  C: a closed house for birds

house dry-bird
  A: a towel used for drying birds that live in a house   (Ch)
  B: a bird that's always house-dry   (S)
  C: a house that's not wet for birds   (Ch)

PHRASE CATEGORY *C-AV C*

house-dry bird
  A: a bird who's been toilet-trained
  B: a kind of bird called a house dry-bird   (S)
  C: a house where they put the birds that are dry   (Ch)

house-shut bird
  A: a bird, that is being confined to a house—like bed-ridden
  B: the bird that's kept shut in a house
  C: a shut, closed house for birds   (Ch)

bird-dry house
  A: a house that's as dry as a bird
  B: a house where birds dry out
  C: a dry bird rather than a wet bird in a house   (Ch)

bird-shut house
  A: a house shut up tight as a bird when he's bending down,
      sleeping
  B: a house that's kept shut by the birds
  C: a closed house for birds   (S)

PHRASE CATEGORY *C-C AV*

bird-house dry
  A: something for keeping bird-houses dry
  B: a bird-house that's dry   (O)
  C: a dry bird-house   (O)

bird-house shut
  A: a peculiar name for a door on a bird-house, or a mechanism
      to close a birdhouse
  B: a bird-house that's shut   (O)
  C: a closed bird-house   (O)

house-bird dry
 A: like "kitty-litter," shavings, you put in the cages of house-birds
 B: a dry house-bird   (O)
 C: a dry house-bird   (O)

house-bird shut
 A: something for shutting house-birds
 B: a house-bird that's shut in   (O)
 C: a closed house-bird   (O)

PHRASE CATEGORY C C-AV

house bird-dry
 A: kind of "kitty-litter" for birds that are kept in houses (S)
 B: a game where birds dry in a house
 C: a building where they keep dry birds   (Ch)

house bird-shut
 A: something for keeping birds quiet that's used in the house,
   like the black thing you pull over parrots
 B: a house that the birds shut   (O)
 C: a closed-in bird-house   (Ch)

bird house-dry
 A: a kind of house-dry for birds
 B: it's where all birds get together and have a house-dry
 C: the bird-house is dry, it's not wet   (F)

bird house-shut
 A: a bird that's been shut in the house   (O)
 B: a bird-house that's shut   (O)
 C: a closed house, locked house for birds   (O)

B. RESPONSES FOR ALL SUBJECTS FOR REPRESENTATIVE STIMULI IN THE FREE-RESPONSE TASK

PHRASE CATEGORY N C-C

foot bird-house

A-Group:
a bird-house for a foot

a ground floor apartment for birds
a bird-house for feet
a bird-house that's foot
a bird-house in the shape of a foot
a bird-house for feet
a house for birds which is at the bottom of a house which is for
   birds

B-Group:
a bird-house that takes care of the bird's feet
a foot-shaped bird-house
a bird-house that is used for feet
a bird's home which is made of a foot
a small bird-house in which birds walk with only their feet
   touching
a house for birds and it's built in the shape of a boot
a bird-house for feet

C-Group:
the end of a bird-house, the bottom of a bird-house   (O)
a home for birds where the foot comes in
a bird that has feet that lives in the house   (Ch)
a bird cage with the purpose of healing birds' feet
a house for birds' feet
(inaudible)
a house for a foot-bird   (S)

PHRASE CATEGORY *N-C C*

boot-bird house

A-Group:
a house for boot-birds
the home of a kind of bird that has large feet
a house for boot-birds
a house where boot-birds are kept
a house for a boot-bird, called that because of its color
a house for birds that are partial to boots
a bird-house for boot-birds

B-Group:
a place where they keep the boots for birds, a house where they
   keep the boots for birds   (O)
a bird-house made of boot   (S)
a house for boot-birds
a bird's home which is made out of a boot   (S)

a type of house for a type of bird
a house for birds which someone wants to get rid of, in other
    words to boot something   (S)
a bird-house for boots   (S)

C-Group:
a house where the birds have their boots   (O)
a bird-house made to the shape of a boot   (S)
the man who makes the boot bird-houses   (Ch)
a type of bird-house   (S)
a bird-house, a boot used for a bird-house   (S)
a house where boot-birds are kept
a house for boot-birds

PHRASE CATEGORY *C N-C*

house foot-bird

A-Group:
a kind of a bird who lives in a house
a domesticated bird that sits at your feet
a foot-bird that lives in a house
the name of a house or a foot-bird that's kept in a house
a type of bird which lives in the home
a bird with feet who lives in a house
the foot-bird who lives in the house

B-Group:
a house whose name is foot-bird   (O)
a bird that stays at your feet and lives in a house
a foot-bird coming from a house
a bird who's a servant in a home
a house belonging to a bird known as a foot-bird   (O)
a type of bird that lives in a house and is called a foot-bird
a foot-bird that lives in a house

C-Group:
a different species, called foot-bird, in a house
a dwelling, a home for a bird that would walk more than he
    would fly   (O)
a bird-house made from feet   (Ch)
a bird that walks around the house   (S)
a bird of the feet, a bird in the house for feet
a foot-bird in a house
a foot-bird that lives in a house

PHRASE CATEGORY *C-N C*

bird-foot house

A-Group:
a house for birds' feet
a building where they gather specimens of birds' feet
a foot-house for birds (S)
a house in which bird-feet are stored
a house in the shape of a bird's foot
a house where bird-feet are kept
a house in the shape of a foot of a bird

B-Group:
the house for the feet of the birds, in other words, shoes
a house for bird-feet
a house for bird's feet
a home that's made out of the foot of a cardinal
a house with a bird whose foot is oversized (O)
a house in which people live and was built in the shape of
    a bird's foot
a house for birds' feet

C-Group:
the foot or a leg of a bird in a house (O)
a dwelling for a bird's foot
a bird-house that is shaped like a foot (S)
a bird-cage in which they treated birds' feet
a place for birds' feet
a bird whose feet live in a house (Ch)
a foot-house where a bird lives (S)

PHRASE CATEGORY *C-C N*

bird-house foot

A-Group:
a foot that's used in a bird-house
a scaly disease of feet
a foot that belongs to a bird-house
like foot-and-mouth disease for birds that are kept in houses (O)
a measuring unit used to measure capacity of bird-houses
a foot shaped like a bird-house
the foot or bottom of a bird-house

B-Group:
(inaudible)
the foot of a bird-house
the foot of a bird-house
a foot which is made out of the home of a bird
the base of a bird-house
the bird-house in the shape of a foot   (O)
a foot for bird-houses

C-Group:
the foot of a bird-house
the leg or stand on which the bird-house stands
a bird-house that has a foot on the outside   (O)
a type of foot disease
the feet on a bird's house
a foot on a bird-house
a foot that's on a bird-house, the foot of a bird-house

PHRASE CATEGORY *C C-N*

bird house-boot

A-Group:
a boot that a bird wears in a house
slippers for birds to wear in a house
a house-boot for birds
a boot to be worn around the house . . . for birds
garments made for birds made to wear in houses, house-boots
    for birds
boots that a bird wears in the house
a boot made to be worn by houses, designed by birds

B-Group:
the boots that birds wear in their new house, a slipper
a boot that contains a bird-house   (S)
house-boots that are used by birds
a bedroom slipper belonging to a bird
the boot of a house-bird   (Ch)
a house for birds which is built in the shape of a boot   (O)
a boot known as a bird-house boot   (S)

C-Group:
house-boots for birds
like a slipper a bird would use in the house
a bird that plays with a house-boot   (O)
a type of boot worn in a house

a shoe for a pet bird (Ch)
a boot in a bird-house (S)
a boot that belongs to a bird-house (S)

PHRASE CATEGORY *A C-C*

bright bird-house

A-Group:
a bird-house that's bright
a sunny house that birds live in
a really smart bird-house
a gaily colored bird-house
a bird-house which is bright in color
a bird-house with big windows
a house in which birds live which is bright

B-Group:
a very bright house for birds
a bird-house that is bright in color
a house for birds which is bright
a bird's home which is lit up
a bird-house which is very bright
a bird-house painted bright colors and looks cheerful
a bright house for birds

C-Group:
a bright-colored bird-house
the sunny, gaily colored home for birds
a bird-house that looks cheerful and is a very happy house
a bright, brightly colored bird-house
a bright bird-house
a light and colorful bird-house
a bird-house that is bright

PHRASE CATEGORY *A-C C*

bright-house bird

A-Group:
a bird who lives in bright houses
a bird attending the university
a house-bird that's very smart
a kind of bird that lives in bright houses, which is like
    the kind of place you keep plants in (S)

a certain kind of bird that lives in a house known for its
  brightness
a bird that lives in a solarium
a bird which is found in a house which is bright

B-Group:
(inaudible)
a house-bird who is bright   (S)
the bird that comes from the bright and shiny house
a smart bird who lives in a house   (S)
a bird in a bright house
a bird which people keep as a pet . . . which is intelligent,
  smart, bright   (S)
a house-bird that's bright   (S)

C-Group:
an intelligent house-bird   (S)
an intelligent pet   (S)
a bird that is an intelligent bird   (S)
a brightly colored bird   (S)
a gaily colored domesticated bird   (S)
a bright house-bird   (S)
a bird from a bright house

PHRASE CATEGORY *C A-C*

house black-bird

A-Group:
a black-bird that lives in a house
tame black-birds which live in a house
a black-bird for houses
a black-bird that can be kept in the house
a black-bird which lives in a house
a black-bird that lives in a house
a black-colored bird that lives in a house

B-Group:
a black-bird that lives in a house
a black-bird that lives in a house
(misheard stimulus)
a black-bird which lives in a house
the house of a bird which is black in color, a black-bird   (O)
a black-bird which lives in a house
a black-bird that's kept in a house

C-Group:
a type of bird like a black-bird or a sparrow
the home of a black-bird   (O)
a black-bird that lives in a house
a type of bird, found in the house, which is usually black
a pet black-bird in a house
a house for a black-bird   (O)
a black-bird that lives in a house

PHRASE CATEGORY *C-A C*

bird-black house

A-Group:
a house that's the color called bird-black, like a black bird's eye
a house which is as dirty as birds
a house covered with bird-black
a house where bird-black, or bird shoe polish, is used
. . . is stored
the house of someone who blackens birds
a house for keeping material for blackening a bird
a house which has become black by the birds

B-Group:
a house made of bird-black
a house for black-birds   (O)
a house that . . . darken birds
the house of a bird which is black, a bird's house which is black   (S)
a house of the color bird-black
a house for birds which has been painted black   (S)
(misheard stimulus)

C-Group:
a black home for birds   (S)
a home for birds that would be black in color   (O)
a bird that has a black-house   (Ch)
a type of bird-cage or bird-house   (S)
a black-colored house for a bird   (S)
a black-bird in a house   (Ch)
a black-house for birds   (S)

PHRASE CATEGORY *C-C A*

bird-house thin

A-Group:
thinness characteristic of a bird-house

someone who's lost so much weight they're as thin as a bird-house
as thin as a bird-house
a kind of paint, or something, for using on bird-houses
material used to make bird-houses thin
as thin as a bird-house
one who is as thin as a bird-house

B-Group:
a thin cracker that's made of bird-houses
a thin bird-house   (O)
(misheard stimulus)
a wafer that's made in the home of a bird
a thin bird-house   (O)
a bird-house which was built thin rather than wide   (O)
a bird-house that's thin   (O)

C-Group:
a thin, a narrow small bird-house   (O)
a very narrow or small dwelling for birds   (O)
a bird-house that is very thin   (O)
a small bird-house   (O)
a not thick nest for a bird   (O)
a long, thin bird-house   (O)
a thin bird-house   (O)

PHRASE CATEGORY *C C-A*

bird house-thin

A-Group:
a bird that's called house-thin   (O)
someone who is as thin as a bird kept in a house   (Ch)
a house-thin for birds
a house-thin for birds
diet food sold for birds that are too plump, to thin them, and
    it is called house-thin because it will thin birds kept in houses
a bird that is thin enough to be in a house   (O)
one who is as thin as a bird-house   (S)

B-Group:
part of a thin bird-house, a bird that lives in a house-thin and
    that's its name because it's a thin house   (Ch)
the thin bird that lives in the house   (Ch)
a house for thinning birds   (Ch)
a bird which is as thin as some houses   (O)

a bird in a narrow house (Ch)
a bird-house which when built was not built wide but rather
  long and thin (O)
a bird-house that's thin (O)

C-Group:
a house for thin birds (Ch)
a narrow dwelling for birds (O)
a bird-house that's kind of thin (O)
a too thin bird-house (O)
a narrow house for a bird (O)
a bird is in the house (F)
a bird-house that is thin (O)

PHRASE CATEGORY *V C-C*

wash bird-house

A-Group:
a load of wash that's called bird-house (O)
a bird-house painted by a technique know as *wash*
a bird-house that's very wash
a label—*wash*—then parenthesis bird-house, telling you the
  specific use of this specific kind of wash (F)
a bird-house having the purpose of permitting the washing
  of birds
a bird-house for washing, in which laundry is done
a product for cleaning bird-houses (O)

B-Group:
a bird-house in which birds do their washing
to wash a bird's house (F)
the bird-house used for washing
a bird-house which is white-washed
a bird-house which is being washed
a type of house for birds . . . and the name of it is called
  the wash bird-house
a bird-house that's washed

C-Group:
a clean bird-house
someone's telling a bird-house to do some wash (F)
a girl who helps to wash a bird-house (O)
clean the bird-house (F)
clean a nest (F)
wash the bird-house (F)
a bird-house for washing

PHRASE CATEGORY *V-C C*

wash-house bird

A-Group:
a bird having something to do with a wash-house
a kind of bird that lives near wash-houses
a bird that lives in the wash-house
a bird that lives in wash-houses, or laundries
a bird that lives near wash-houses
a bird who lives around a wash-house
a bird that hangs around wash-houses

B-Group:
a bird that flies around wash-houses and bothers all the people
    trying to do their washing
a bird that lives in a wash-house
a bird from the wash-house
a bird which is found in places where they wash things
a bird in a wash-house
a place where birds could go to be washed   (O)
a bird that's called a wash-house bird

C-Group:
a wash-house for the birds   (O)
you're giving your pet a bath   (F)
the children want to give a bird a bath   (F)
a clean house-bird   (S)
a bird that has a laundry
a washed house-bird when it's clean   (S)
a bird that lives in a wash-house

PHRASE CATEGORY *C V-C*

bird kill-house

A-Group:
a house that birds use to kill
a place where they murder birds
a kill-house for birds
a house in which you keep the birds who are to be killed
slaughtering centers for birds who are used for food
a place of execution for birds
a slaughter house for birds

B-Group:
a house where they slaughter birds
a bird that killed a house   (Ch)
the killing house used for birds
a place where they put birds to death
a dead bird in a house   (Ch)
some type of house a bird could live in and it's called a kill-house
a killing house for birds

C-Group:
a place where they kill birds
somebody's telling a bird to attack its home   (F)
a bird that lives in a jailhouse and is going to be killed   (O)
a type of house where birds can't survive
a place to kill birds
a slaughtering house for birds
the bird that lives in a kill-house   (O)

PHRASE CATEGORY *C-V C*

house-kill bird

A-Group:
a bird that kills houses
a bird which kills houses
a bird that's good for house-kills
a bird that house-kills
a bird which is dangerous in the home because of its tendency to
     attack others
a bird that kills by incarcerating victims in a house
a bird known for the fact that he kills houses

B-Group:
a bird that destroys houses
a bird was killing a house   (F)
birds killed in houses
birds that are killed by houses
a bird which has been killed in a house
a species of birds called house-kill birds
a kind of bird that's house kill-bird   (S)

C-Group:
a bird goes into a house, a house-kill   (F)
the house has just done away with its birds   (F)
a bird that gets killed in his house
a bird used to kill household insects

a dead bird
a house where birds are killed   (Ch)
a kill-bird that lives in a house   (S)

PHRASE CATEGORY *C-C V*

bird-house wash

A-Group:
wash that comes from a bird-house
the laundry that's hanging out behind the bird-house
the laundry from a bird-house
a cleansing product for bird-houses
products to clean bird-houses, or laundry of the bird-house
a material for washing bird-houses
the act or product that cleans bird-houses

B-Group:
the time of year when everybody washes their bird-houses
the wash that is hung out in front of bird-houses
a method of cleaning bird-houses
a cleaning that a bird gives to a house   (S)
a bird-house which is being washed   (O)
a cleansing agent to clean the bird-house
a kind of wash called a bird-house wash

C-Group:
wash or clean the bird-house   (F)
a detergent used to clean the bird's home
a bird that washes his house   (Ch)
a type of bath
a laundry for washing birds   (O)
a bird-house that's being washed   (O)
the wash from a bird-house

PHRASE CATEGORY *C C-V*

house bird-wash

A-Group:
a place in a house for washing birds
where a lot of birds come into the house to wash
a bird-wash that occurs in a house
bird-wash is like soap . . . used on birds . . . used in
    the house

a product made for washing birds sold in small enough quantity
  to be used in houses
the bird's domestic laundry
a place for washing birds, found in a house

B-Group:
a time when houses go around washing all the birds
a house for washing the birds   (O)
a bird-bath which is inside the house
a house that is cleaned by a cardinal   (O)
(inaudible)
a type of cleansing agent used to clean birds with . . .
  manufactured by a company called *House*
a bird-wash that takes place in a house

C-Group:
the birds wash the house   (F)
some kind of soapy substance for a pet to clean him   (S)
a bird that takes a bath in his house   (Ch)
a type of bird-washing done in the house
a pet, a place to wash a pet bird   (S)
(inaudible)
a house-bird that washes   (Ch)

C. STIMULUS LIST 2

The following compounds were presented to subjects in the familiarization tasks.

1. old [1] mouse [3] school [2]
2. hat [1] school [3] mouse [2]
3. school [2] hat [1] tell [3]
4. mouse [1] hat [3] push [2]
5. green [2] hat [1] mouse [3]
6. school [2] clean [1] mouse [3]
7. push [1] school [3] hat [2]
8. school [2] hat [1] mouse [3]
9. mouse [2] school [1] clean [3]
10. tell [2] mouse [1] hat [3]
11. hat [1] old [3] mouse [2]
12. hat [2] school [1] green [2]
13. mouse [2] green [1] hat [3]
14. school [2] tell [1] mouse [3]
15. hat [1] school [3] clean [2]
16. school [1] hat [3] old [2]
17. hat [1] push [3] mouse [2]
18. hat [1] mouse [3] school [2]
19. clean [1] mouse [3] hat [2]
20. hat [2] mouse [1] school [3]
21. school [1] old [3] mouse [2]
22. hat [2] push [1] mouse [3]
23. green [2] school [1] hat [3]
24. mouse [1] school [3] tell [2]
25. tell [1] mouse [3] school [2]
26. mouse [1] hat [3] school [2]
27. push [2] mouse [1] hat [3]
28. school [1] clean [3] hat [2]
29. school [2] mouse [1] old [3]
30. hat [2] mouse [1] green [3]
31. school [2] green [1] mouse [3]
32. mouse [1] tell [3] school [2]
33. old [2] mouse [1] hat [3]
34. mouse [1] school [3] hat [2]

35. clean [1] hat [3] mouse [2]
36. school [2] push [1] hat [3]
37. mouse [1] hat [3] clean [2]
38. school [1] mouse [3] hat [2]
39. hat [2] old [1] mouse [3]
40. push [2] school [1] mouse [3]
41. mouse [1] school [3] green [2]
42. tell [1] hat [3] school [2]
43. old [2] mouse [1] school [3]
44. hat [2] school [1] mouse [3]
45. hat [2] mouse [1] push [3]
46. green [1] mouse [3] hat [2]
47. school [1] mouse [3] tell [2]
48. clean [1] school [3] hat [2]
49. mouse [1] tell [3] hat [2]
50. green [1] school [3] mouse [2]
51. school [1] hat [3] mouse [2]
52. hat [2] school [1] clean [3]
53. mouse [2] push [1] school [3]

54. school [2] hat [1] old [3]
55. mouse [2] school [1] hat [3]
56. hat [1] mouse [3] push [2]
57. green [1] school [3] hat [2]
58. hat [2] old [1] school [3]
59. mouse [2] school [1] tell [3]
60. clean [2] school [1] mouse [3]
61. hat [1] school [3] green [2]
62. tell [2] hat [1] mouse [3]
63. school [2] mouse [1] hat [3]
64. school [1] mouse [3] old [2]
65. push [1] mouse [3] school [2]
66. school [2] clean [1] hat [3]
67. push [1] hat [3] mouse [2]
68. mouse [2] hat [1] school [3]
69. school [1] green [3] mouse [2]
70. clean [2] mouse [1] school [3]
71. old [1] school [3] hat [2]
72. mouse [2] tell [1] hat [3]

II. Mean Error by Phrase Category, Error Type, and Group in the Free-Response Experiment

Table A. Mean Error by Group, Phrase Category, and Error Type (× 1000)

Phrase Category	Errors of Order			Errors of Stress			Errors of Chaos			Errors of Format		
	A	B	C	A	B	C	A	B	C	A	B	C
N C-C	36	0	144	0	143	143	0	36	71	0	36	143
N-C C	36	36	108	0	286	143	0	36	36	0	0	36
C N-C	0	178	108	0	36	36	0	143	107	0	0	0
C-N C	0	71	108	71	143	357	0	71	71	0	0	0
C-C N	0	107	72	36	0	36	0	36	36	0	0	0
C C-N	144	214	216	0	321	428	0	143	36	0	0	0
A C-C	24	0	48	0	0	143	0	0	24	0	24	24
A-C C	0	95	48	167	452	690	0	0	0	0	0	0
C A-C	72	214	144	24	95	24	24	71	95	0	0	0
C-A C	24	167	96	0	214	524	0	119	333	0	0	24
C-C A	24	595	816	24	0	0	0	71	48	0	0	24
C C-A	360	500	696	71	0	24	95	238	190	0	24	71
V C-C	336	142	360	0	71	167	0	48	24	95	95	262
V-C C	96	190	192	48	238	95	24	167	286	0	48	262

Phrase Category	Errors of Order			Errors of Stress			Errors of Chaos			Errors of Format		
	A	B	C	A	B	C	A	B	C	A	B	C
C V-C	72	48	72	24	24	48	24	286	214	0	48	143
C-V C	0	0	0	0	48	167	0	167	238	0	48	119
C-C V	24	238	216	48	71	286	0	143	143	0	24	167
C C-V	48	333	240	24	71	0	24	95	286	24	24	48

Table B. Mean Error by Group and Phrase Category (× 1000)

Phrase Category	A	B	C
N C-C	36	216	504
N-C C	36	360	324
C N-C	0	360	252
C-N C	72	288	540
C-C N	36	144	144
C C-N	144	684	684
A C-C	24	24	240
A-C C	168	552	744
C A-C	120	384	264
C-A C	24	504	984
C-C A	48	672	888
C C-A	528	768	984
V C-C	432	360	816
V-C C	168	648	840
C V-C	120	408	480
C-V C	0	264	504
C-C V	72	480	552
C C-V	120	528	864

III. Right (R) and Wrong (W) Response Alternatives Presented to Subjects in the Forced-Choice Task

(Stimuli are in the order of presentation)

1. foot [1] bird [3] house [2]
   R: a house for a kind of bird called a foot-bird
   W: a bird-house with feet

2. house ^{2} shut ^{1} bird ^{3}
   R: a shut-bird who lives in the house
   W: a bird that is shut up in the house

3. black ^{1} house ^{3} bird ^{2}
   R: a bird who lives in a black house
   W: a black bird who lives in a house

4. bird ^{1} stone ^{3} house ^{2}
   R: a house made out of bird-stone
   W: a stone house for birds

5. house ^{1} wash ^{3} bird ^{2}
   R: a bird who is around the house-wash
   W: a house in which a bird gets washed

6. bird ^{1} house ^{3} boot ^{2}
   R: a boot to wear in a house for birds
   W: a house for birds that is shaped like a boot

7. glass ^{2} house ^{1} bird ^{3}
   R: a house-bird that is made of glass
   W: a bird who lives in a glass house

8. house ^{2} bird ^{1} eat ^{3}
   R: a meal for a bird and it takes place in a house
   W: food for house-birds

9. house ^{1} bird ^{3} kill ^{2}
   R: poison for the bird that lives in the house
   W: a bird being killed in a house

10. bird ^{2} house ^{1} bright ^{3}
    R: something birds can use to keep their houses bright
    W: a cheerful bird-house

11. thin ^{2} bird ^{1} house ^{3}
    R: a house for birds that is thin
    W: a house for thin birds

12. bird ^{2} dry ^{1} house ^{3}
    R: a dry house for birds
    W: a bird which lives in a dry house

13. kill ^{1} house ^{3} bird ^{2}
    R: a bird found around slaughter-houses
    W: to take the life of a house-bird

14. bird ² boot ¹ house ³
    R: a boot-house for a bird
    W: a bird that lives in a boot-house

15. house ² glass ¹ bird ³
    R: a bird made of glass in the house
    W: a structure that contains birds that are glass

16. house ² bird ¹ dry ³
    R: a drying of birds that's done in the house
    W: a place to dry pet birds

17. bird ¹ house ³ foot ²
    R: a foot that's used in a bird-house
    W: a bird-house that has a foot

18. house ¹ bird ³ stone ²
    R: a stone that is used by house-birds
    W: a stone that has been placed in a bird-house

19. wash ¹ bird ³ house ²
    R: a house for a wash-bird
    W: to clean a bird's house

20. shut ² bird ¹ house ³
    R: a bird-house that is closed up
    W: close up the bird-house

21. eat ² house ¹ bird ³
    R: a bird in the house who eats
    W: a command to eat a pet bird

22. bird ¹ bright ³ house ²
    R: a house that is as bright as a bird
    W: a bright and cheerful house for birds

23. house ¹ black ³ bird ²
    R: a bird that blackens houses
    W: a black-bird who lives in the house

24. bird ² house ¹ thin ³
    R: house-thin for birds
    W: a bird-house that is thin

25. house ² thin ¹ bird ³
    R: a thin type of bird that lives in the house
    W: a house containing thin birds

26. bird ² eat ¹ house ³
    R: a restaurant for birds
    W: a bird that would eat its own house

27. wash ¹ house ³ bird ²
    R: a bird who lives near wash-houses
    W: you're giving your pet a bath

28. shut ² house ¹ bird ³
    R: a house-bird who is shut in
    W: a bird who is shut in the house

29. bird ¹ house ³ dry ²
    R: as dry as a bird's house
    W: a bird's house that isn't wet

30. house ¹ bird ³ black ²
    R: black paint for smearing on pet birds
    W: a house-bird that is black

31. house ¹ foot ³ bird ²
    R: a bird that lives at the bottom of houses
    W: a foot-bird that lives in the house

32. bird ² house ¹ stone ³
    R: a stone in the shape of a house and the stone is used by birds
    W: the kind of stone used for building bird-houses

33. bird ¹ kill ³ house ²
    R: a house in which birds are killed
    W: a bird that kills a house

34. bright ² bird ¹ house ³
    R: a house for birds that is very bright
    W: a house for birds who are very bright

35. house ² bird ¹ glass ³
    R: glass for birds that is used in the house
    W: glass that is used to make house-birds

36. boot ¹ bird ³ house ²
    R: a house for birds who wear boots
    W: a house for birds which is made out of a boot

37. stone ² bird ¹ house ³
    R: a stone house for a bird
    W: a house for a stone bird

38. dry [1] bird [3] house [2]
    R: a house for a dry bird
    W: a bird-house that is dry

39. house [2] bird [1] shut [3]
    R: an attempt to rid houses of birds
    W: a pet bird that's closed up in the house

40. house [1] bird [3] wash [2]
    R: the laundry done by pet birds
    W: a house where birds do their wash

41. foot [1] house [3] bird [2]
    R: a bird who lives in a foot-house
    W: birds that have feet as big as a house

42. house [1] boot [3] bird [2]
    R: a bird who lives in a boot that's found in a house
    W: a bird who lives in a house that has a boot in it

43. house [2] bright [1] bird [3]
    R: the intelligent bird who lives in the house
    W: house that contains intelligent birds

44. bird [1] black [3] house [2]
    R: a house which is as black as birds
    W: a black-colored house for birds

45. bird [2] glass [1] house [3]
    R: a glass house for birds
    W: a bird who lives in a glass house

46. bird [2] house [1] kill [3]
    R: a gathering of birds to destroy a house
    W: a slaughter-house for birds

47. thin [2] house [1] bird [3]
    R: a bird that's kept in a house and is thin
    W: a house for thin birds

48. bird [1] house [3] eat [2]
    R: a meal that takes place in a bird-house
    W: eat the bird-house

49. eat [1] bird [3] house [2]
    R: home for the species named eat-birds
    W: a place where the birds eat

50. house ² stone ¹ bird ³
   R: a bird made of stone and kept in a house
   W: a stone house in the shape of a bird

51. boot ¹ house ³ bird ²
   R: a bird who lives in a house made out of a boot
   W: kick the house-bird

52. bright ² house ¹ bird ³
   R: a cheerful bird who lives in a house
   W: a bird who lives in a cheerful house

53. kill ² bird ¹ house ³
   R: a bird-house that is used for killing
   W: to destroy a bird-house

54. bird ¹ wash ³ house ²
   R: a house where birds are washed
   W: a bird who cleans his home

55. bird ² shut ¹ house ³
   R: a shut house for birds
   W: shut up the house with the birds in it

56. house ¹ bird ³ foot ²
   R: the foot of a house-bird
   W: a house that is shaped like a bird's foot

57. house ¹ dry ³ bird ²
   R: a bird who is as dry as a house
   W: a dry bird who lives in a house

58. bird ² house ¹ black ³
   R: a bird who paints houses black
   W: a house painted black for a bird

59. house ² bird ¹ thin ³
   R: a thinning out of birds that takes place in the house
   W: a thin bird in a house

60. bird ¹ house ³ glass ²
   R: glass to be used in the bird-house
   W: a bird-house that's made of glass

61. bird ² thin ¹ house ³
   R: a narrow house for a bird to live in
   W: a skinny bird who lives in a house

62. bird ² house ¹ wash ³
R: a gathering of birds to wash their houses
W: a type of bird who washes his house

63. glass ¹ bird ³ house ²
R: a house where birds made of glass live
W: a house made of glass for birds

64. stone ² house ¹ bird ³
R: a bird made of stone and kept in a house
W: a bird living in a stone house

65. bird ¹ foot ³ house ²
R: a house for the foot or leg of a bird
W: a bird-house that is shaped like a foot

66. bird ¹ house ³ shut ²
R: the closing of the bird-house
W: a closed bird-house

67. house ¹ eat ³ bird ²
R: a bird who eats up his house
W: a house where birds are eaten

68. black ² bird ¹ house ³
R: a black house for birds
W: a house for black-birds

69. house ¹ bird ³ boot ²
R: a boot for house-birds
W: the kind of boot worn in the house by birds

70. dry ¹ house ³ bird ²
R: a bird who lives in a dry house
W: a dry bird who lives in a house

71. house ² kill ¹ bird ³
R: a bird who kills who lives in a house
W: a house where birds are killed

72. house ² bird ¹ bright ³
R: material for brightening birds that's kept in the house
W: a brightly colored bird who lives in the house

73. house ¹ bird ³ dry ²
R: as dry as a pet bird
W: a pet bird that is not wet

74. shut [1] bird [3] house [2]
    R: a house for shut-birds
    W: a bird-house that is closed

75. bird [2] bright [1] house [3]
    R: a bright-colored house for birds
    W: a bird that lives in a bright house

76. bird [2] house [1] foot [3]
    R: the foot which birds keep in the house
    W: the foot of a bird-house

77. bird [1] boot [3] house [2]
    R: a house where birds keep their boots
    W: a bird-house that is shaped like a boot

78. wash [2] bird [1] house [3]
    R: a bird-house where birds do their washing
    W: clean the bird-house

79. house [2] black [1] bird [3]
    R: a black-bird who lives in a house
    W: a house for a black-bird

80. kill [2] house [1] bird [3]
    R: a pet bird that destroys
    W: to destroy the pet bird

81. bird [1] house [3] thin [2]
    R: as narrow as a bird-house
    W: a narrow bird-house

82. house [2] bird [1] stone [3]
    R: a stone for birds that is kept in the house
    W: a bird made of stone in a house

83. house [1] glass [3] bird [2]
    R: a bird which is made of house-glass
    W: a glass statue of a bird that is in the house

84. eat [1] house [3] bird [2]
    R: a bird who is kept in the eat-house
    W: eat the bird in the house

85. house [1] shut [3] bird [2]
    R: a bird that is shut up in the house
    W: a closed house for birds

86. black [2] house [1] bird [3]
R: a pet bird that is black in color
W: a bird who lives in a black house

87. bird [2] house [1] boot [3]
R: a boot that a bird wears in the house
W: the boot found in bird-houses

88. glass [1] house [3] bird [2]
R: a bird who lives in a glass house
W: a glass statue of a house-bird

89. house [2] wash [1] bird [3]
R: the bird who washes who lives in the house
W: a bird cleaning its house

90. bird [2] stone [1] house [3]
R: a stone dwelling for birds
W: a dwelling for stone birds

91. house [2] bird [1] kill [3]
R: the killing of birds that takes place in the house
W: a pet bird that would kill

92. bird [1] house [3] bright [2]
R: a cleaner for bird-houses
W: a gaily colored bird-house

93. thin [1] bird [3] house [2]
R: a house for a thin bird
W: a narrow bird-house

94. house [1] bird [3] eat [2]
R: food for a pet bird
W: a pet bird who eats

95. bird [1] dry [3] house [2]
R: a house as dry as birds
W: a dry house for birds

96. foot [2] bird [1] house [3]
R: a bird-house for feet
W: the bottom of a bird-house

97. house [2] foot [1] bird [3]
R: the foot-bird that lives in the house
W: a bird-house that is made from feet

98. bird [1] eat [3] house [2]
    R: a house where birds eat
    W: a bird eating his house

99. house [1] bird [3] glass [2]
    R: glass for birds who live in the house
    W: a pet bird made of glass

100. shut [1] house [3] bird [2]
    R: a bird who lives in closed houses
    W: a closed house for a bird

101. house [1] thin [3] bird [2]
    R: a bird who is thin from being in the house
    W: a skinny pet bird

102. boot [2] bird [1] house [3]
    R: a bird-house in the shape of a boot
    W: a boot in a bird-house

103. wash [2] house [1] bird [3]
    R: a housebird who likes to wash
    W: giving a housebird a bath

104. bird [2] house [1] dry [3]
    R: material for drying houses, used by birds
    W: a house for birds that isn't wet

105. bird [1] house [3] stone [2]
    R: a stone for a bird's house
    W: a bird's house made of stone

106. bird [2] kill [1] house [3]
    R: a killing house for birds
    W: a bird that lives in a kill-house

107. bright [1] bird [3] house [2]
    R: a house for bright birds
    W: a bird-house that is bright

108. house [2] bird [1] black [3]
    R: material for blackening birds that is kept in the house
    W: a pet bird that is black in color

109. foot [2] house [1] bird [3]
    R: a house-bird which is known for its foot
    W: a bird who lives in a foot-house

110. house ² boot ¹ bird ³
R: a boot-bird that lives in a house
W: a bird who wears house-boots

111. house ¹ bird ³ shut ²
R: a lock that shuts house-birds
W: a closed-in house-bird

112. bird ¹ house ³ kill ²
R: the destruction of bird-houses
W: destroy bird-houses

113. thin ¹ house ³ bird ²
R: a bird who lives in a skinny house
W: a skinny pet bird

114. stone ¹ bird ³ house ²
R: a house for birds who are made of stone
W: house for birds which is made of stone

115. bird ² black ¹ house ³
R: a black house for birds
W: a house for black-birds

116. bird ² house ¹ eat ³
R: a meal in the house, for birds
W: a bird that eats in the house

117. dry ² bird ¹ house ³
R: a house for birds that is dry
W: a house for birds who are dry

118. bird ¹ glass ³ house ²
R: a house made of bird-glass
W: a glass house for birds

119. house ² bird ¹ wash ³
R: a place in the house for washing birds
W: a place to wash a pet bird

120. house ¹ bright ³ bird ²
R: a bird who brightens houses
W: a bright bird that lives in a house

121. house ¹ bird ³ thin ²
R: as thin as a house-bird
W: a skinny house-bird

122. bird ² house ¹ glass ³
    R: a glass used by birds in a house
    W: a glass house for birds

123. house ¹ stone ³ bird ²
    R: a bird made of stone called house-stone
    W: a stone statue of a bird kept in the house

124. eat ² bird ¹ house ³
    R: a bird-house that can eat
    W: eat the bird-house

125. bird ¹ shut ³ house ²
    R: a house that's closed against birds
    W: a closed bird-house

126. boot ² house ¹ bird ³
    R: a house-bird who wears boots
    W: a bird who lives in the boot-house

127. bird ¹ house ³ black ²
    R: blackening used on bird-houses
    W: bird-house that is painted black

128. bird ² wash ¹ house ³
    R: a wash-house for birds
    W: a bird that washes his house

129. house ² bird ¹ foot ³
    R: the bird's foot that's kept in the house
    W: the foot of the bird who lives in the house

130. kill ¹ bird ³ house ²
    R: a house belonging to a kill-bird
    W: to destroy a bird's house

131. house ² dry ¹ bird ³
    R: the dry bird who lives in the house
    W: a bird who dries houses

132. bright ¹ house ³ bird ²
    R: a bird who lives in a gaily colored house
    W: a gaily colored pet bird

133. bird ¹ house ³ wash ²
    R: laundry from a bird-house
    W: a bird-house that is washed

134. glass [2] bird [1] house [3]
   R: a bird-house made of glass
   W: glass used in bird-houses

135. house [1] kill [3] bird [2]
   R: a bird that kills houses
   W: the house kills its birds

136. house [2] bird [1] boot [3]
   R: the boot of a bird worn in a house
   W: the boot of a pet bird

137. bird [1] thin [3] house [2]
   R: a house for thinning birds
   W: a narrow bird-house

138. dry [2] house [1] bird [3]
   R: a house-bird who is dry
   W: a bird who lives in a dry house

139. house [1] bird [3] bright [2]
   R: as bright as a house-bird
   W: a bright house-bird

140. bird [2] house [1] shut [3]
   R: something a bird uses to close his house
   W: a closed bird-house

141. black [1] bird [3] house [2]
   R: the house of a black-bird
   W: a bird's house that is black

142. bird [2] foot [1] house [3]
   R: a foot-house for birds
   W: a bird who lives in a foot-house

143. house [2] eat [1] bird [3]
   R: an eat-bird that lives in a house
   W: a house that devours birds

144. stone [1] house [3] bird [2]
   R: a bird who lives in a house made of stone
   W: a pet bird made of stone

A somewhat revised list of alternatives was used in the studies of learning, because certain response types (e.g., *as X as a Y*) never were the modal *error* but often were the modal *correct* response. Thus the subjects in a learning task in which they received knowledge of result could well learn such trivial facts (always choose *as X as Y* if it occurs) instead of what we wanted them to learn. Some two dozen changes were made in the list of alternatives to mitigate this problem.

IV. Instructions to Subjects

A. FREE-RESPONSE EXPERIMENT

This is an experiment on English compound nouns. Examples of English compound nouns are *milkman* and *money-back-guarantee*.

I will play some compound nouns on this tape recorder. When you hear one of these compounds, I would like you to give me a phrase that means about the same thing. For example, if I say *milkman*, you would say *a man who brings the milk*, or something like that. If I say *money-back-guarantee*, you would say, *a guarantee that you'll get your money back*. I do not want you to just use the same words in another sentence. For example, the sentence *Milk falls on the man* contains the words *milk* and *man*, but it does not mean the same thing as *milkman*. *A man who brings the milk* does mean about the same thing as *milkman*. *A guarantee that you'll get your money back* does mean about the same thing as *money-back-guarantee*.

All the compounds you will hear will be three-words long. To make sure you have no problems about hearing them, here is a list of the words that will appear in various combinations of three. [Subject is here given a typed list of all the words.] No other words will ever be used.

Some of the compounds you hear may be familiar to you, and you may know what they mean. Others may never even have been said before by anyone. Try to think what they might mean if they were ever used. Sometimes this may be something that strikes you as silly or even impossible. For example, I am sure you have never heard the words *duck* [1] *food* [3] *man*.[2] Try to think what it might mean if it were used. I guess it would be *a man who makes duck food,* or *a man who brings food for ducks.* Is this clear?

You will hear about 150 of these. Each time you will give me a sentence or phrase that means about the same thing as the compound you hear. If you want me to repeat one of them for any reason, just ask. Take as long as you like to answer.

Sometimes people ask me whether they should pay attention to the way we *say* the compound. The answer is yes, because the way we say it may affect the meaning. If you become tired, tell me, and we will take a break. We will take a break after each fifty anyway.

Remember: I want you to give me a phrase or sentence that means about the same thing as the compound noun you will hear. I will remind you of this automatically after each twelve, so don't think that my reminding you indicates that you have been doing anything wrong.

> After the instructions are given, the experimenter plays the first stimulus. Now the subject invariably asks a question of this general form: "Now? Is this what? Now I'm supposed to say what that means?" The experimenter says, "Yes." Now the subject gives a response, and then usually asks: "Is that right? Is that what you want me to do?"
>
> The experimenter answers (regardless of whether the subject got the right answer or the wrong answer):
>
> "Yes, if that is a sentence or phrase that means about the same thing to you. I'm supposed to keep a straight face here, and not show whether or not I agree with your answer, so don't think your answers are wrong because I don't nod or say yes or anything like that."
>
> The following portion of the instructions is repeated after every twelve stimuli, unless or until the subject gets annoyed and says she understands perfectly well and is bored with the repetition of instructions:
>
> "I am now repeating part of the instructions, as I told you I would. Remember: I want you to give me a phrase or sentence that means about the same thing as the compound noun you will hear."

B. FORCED-CHOICE EXPERIMENT

I'm sure you remember the work we did the last time with English compound nouns. Today I am going to give you just about the same thing, but in a new way.

I am going to play the stimuli one after another, just as I did the other time, and again you should ask me to repeat any of them if you want, and you should take as much time as you wish to give your answer.

The difference is only this: today I am going to use these two packs of cards. Each card has on it an answer to one of the stimuli. Look at the first card of each pack [show]. Both of these are answers to a stimulus. One of them will be the right answer and one of them will be the wrong answer. You are to point to the one you think is best. Don't forget—we want you to choose as the best answer the one that means most nearly the same thing as the stimulus you hear. For instance, if you heard *milkman,* which of these two cards would you choose? Take your time, and ask for repetitions whenever you want them. If you get tired, tell me and we will take a break. We will take a break after each fifty anyway.

Once again, as it was the other time, it is important to listen to the way the compound is said, because that can affect the meaning.

Also: sometimes two words in these answers will have a hyphen or dash between them. That means that the two words are pronounced together, treated more or less like one word. This using of a hyphen *can* change the meaning of the words. For instance, these two cards have the same words on them, *green* and *house,* but on one card there is a hyphen between the two words. We would pronounce these two answers differently, and the meanings would be different. How would you pronounce them? What do they mean?

By the way, sometimes you will hear a stimulus, and the answer you may think of might be different from what it says on either of the cards. Your idea may be a correct one—you know there is often more than one right answer on this test. Today we are not interested in *your* answer—we got that last time. Now we are just interested in which of *these* two answers you think is better. Similarly, if the two answers you are offered seem to be equally correct, please choose one anyway.

Any questions?

Bibliography

Bellugi, U. 1965. The Development of Interrogative Structures in Children's Speech. In *The Development of Language Functions*, ed. K. F. Riegal. Development of Language Functions, rpt. no. 8. Mimeo. Ann Arbor, Mich.: U. of Mich.

Bem, D. J., and S. L. Bem. 1968. Nativism Revisited. *J. exp. Anal. Behav.* 11:497–501.

Berko, J. 1961. The Child's Learning of English Morphology. In *Psycholinguistics*, ed. S. Saporta, pp. 359–75. New York: H. R. & W.

Bever, T. G., J. A. Fodor, and W. Weksel. 1965. The Acquisition of Syntax: A Critique of "Contextual Generalization." *Psychol. Rev.* 72:467–82.

Bever, T. G., J. A. Fodor, M. Garrett, and J. Mehler. n.d. Unpublished experiment cited in J. A. Fodor and M. Garrett, 1966, p. 151.

Bever, T. G., J. R. Lackner, and R. Kirk. 1969. The Underlying Structures of Sentences Are the Primary Units of Immediate Speech Processing. *Perception and Psychophysics* 5:225–34.

Bloomfield, L. 1933. *Language*. New York: Henry Holt & Co.

Blumenthal, A. L. 1966. Observations with Self-Embedded Sentences. *Psychonom. Sci.* 6:453–54.

———. 1967. Promoted Recall of Sentences. *J. verb. Learn. verb. Behav.* 6:203–6.

Bolinger, D. L. 1958. A Theory of Pitch Accent in English. *Word* 14:109–49.

———. 1961. Contrastive Accent and Contrastive Stress. *Language* 37:83–96.

———. 1968. Personal communication.

Bolinger, D. L., and L. J. Gerstman. 1957. Disjuncture as a Cue to Constructs. *J. Acoust. Soc. Am.* 29:778.

Braine, M. D. S. 1963. The Ontogeny of English Phrase-Structure: The First Phase. *Language* 39:1–13.

———. The Acquisition of Language in Infant and Child. In *The Learning of Language*, ed. C. Reed. Champaign, Ill.: Natl. Council of Teachers of English, forthcoming.

Brodbeck, A. J., and O. C. Irwin. 1946. The Speech Behavior of Infants without Families. *Child Develpm.* 17:145–56.

Brown, R. 1958. *Words and Things*. Glencoe, Ill.: Free Pr.

Brown, R., and U. Bellugi. 1964. Three Processes in the Child's Acquisition of Syntax. In *New Directions in the Study of Language,* ed. E. H. Lenneberg, pp. 131–61. Cambridge, Mass.: M.I.T. Press.

Brown, R., and C. Hanlon. 1968. Derivational Complexity and Order of Acquisition in Child Speech. 1968 Carnegie-Mellon Symposium on Cognitive Psychology, at Harvard U. Mimeo.

Carmichael, L. 1926. The Development of Behavior in Vertebrates Experimentally Removed from the Influence of External Stimulation. *Psychol. Rev.* 33:51–58.

Chomsky, N. 1957. *Syntactic Structures.* The Hague: Mouton.

———. 1959. Review of *Verbal Behavior* by B. F. Skinner. *Language* 35:26–58.

———. 1961. On the Notion "Rule of Grammar." In *Proceedings of Symposia in Applied Mathematics.* Vol. 12. Structure of Language and Its Mathematical Aspects, ed. R. Jakobson, pp. 6–24. Providence, R.I.: Am. Math.

———. 1964a. Current Issues in Linguistic Theory. In *The Structure of Language,* eds. J. A. Fodor and J. J. Katz, pp. 50–118. Englewood Cliffs, N.J.: P.-H.

———. 1964b. Degrees of Grammaticalness. In *The Structure of Language,* eds. J. A. Fodor and J. J. Katz, pp. 386–87. Englewood Cliffs, N.J.: P.-H.

———. 1965. *Aspects of the Theory of Syntax.* Cambridge, Mass.: M.I.T. Press.

Chomsky, N., and M. Halle. 1968. *The Sound Pattern of English.* New York: Har.-Row.

Davis, K. 1947. Final Note on a Case of Extreme Social Isolation. *Amer. J. Sociol.* 52:432–37.

Dennis, W. 1940. The Effect of Cradling Practices upon the Onset of Walking in Hopi Children. *J. genet. Psychol.* 56:77–86.

Dumpty, H. n.d. Reported in L. Carroll, *Alice's Adventures in Wonderland,* 1865.

Fillmore, C. J. 1968. The Case for Case. In *Universals in Linguistic Theory,* eds. E. Bach and R. T. Harms, pp. 1–88. New York: H. R. & W.

Fodor, J. A., and T. G. Bever. 1965. The Psychological Reality of Linguistic Segments. *J. verb. Learn. verb. Behav.* 4:414–20.

Fodor, J. A., and M. Garrett. 1966. Some Reflections on Competence and Performance. In *Psycholinguistics Papers,* eds. J. Lyons and R. J. Wales, pp. 135–54. Edinburgh: Edin. U. P.

Fodor, J. A., J. Jenkins, and S. Saporta. n.d. Unpublished manuscript cited in J. A. Fodor and M. Garrett, 1966, p. 150.

Gardner, B. T., and R. A. Gardner. 1968. Development of Behavior in a Young Chimpanzee. Mimeo. Reno, Nev.: U. of Nev.

Gleitman, L. R. 1965. Coordinating Conjunctions in English. *Language* 41:260–93.

———. 1967. Compound Nouns and English Speakers. Ph.D. thesis, U. of Pa.

Gleitman, L. R., and R. Bernheim. 1968. The Recall of Compound Nouns. *Technical Rpt.,* no. 12. Mimeo. Philadelphia: Ea. Pa. Psychiat. Inst.

Gough, P. 1965. Grammatical Transformations and Speed of Understanding. *J. verb. Learn. verb. Behav.* 4:107–11.

Greenberg, J. H. 1966. Some Universals of Grammar with Particular Reference to the Order of Meaningful Elements. In *Universals of Language,* 2nd ed., ed. J. H. Greenberg, pp. 58–90. Cambridge, Mass.: M.I.T. Press.

Greenough, J. B., and G. L. Kittredge. 1962. *Words and Their Ways in English Speech.* Boston: Beacon Pr.

Harris, Z. S. 1957. Co-occurrence and Transformation in Linguistic Structure. *Language* 33:293–340.

––––––. 1963. Lectures on transformational linguistics, U. of Pa.

Hayes, C. 1951. *The Ape in Our House.* New York: Harper.

Hill, A. A. 1961. Grammaticality. *Word* 17:1–10.

Hirsh, I. J. 1966. Teaching the Deaf Child to Speak. In *The Genesis of Language,* eds. F. Smith and G. A. Miller, pp. 207–16. Cambridge, Mass.: M.I.T. Press.

Hockett, C. F. 1966. The Problem of Universals in Language. In *Universals of Language,* 2nd ed., ed. J. H. Greenberg, pp. 1–22. Cambridge, Mass.: M.I.T. Press.

Hymes, D., ed. 1964. *Language in Culture and Society.* New York: Har.-Row.

Jacobs, R. A., and P. S. Rosenbaum. 1968. *English Transformational Grammar.* Waltham, Mass.: Blaisdell.

Jespersen, O. 1955. *Growth and Structure of the English Language.* 9th ed. Garden City, N.Y.: Doubleday.

––––––. 1961. *A Modern English Grammar.* Vol. 1, Part II, Syntax. London: Allen & U.

Johnson, N. F. 1965. The Psychological Reality of Phrase-Structure Rules. *J. verb. Learn. verb. Behav.* 4:469–75.

Joos, M., ed. 1958. *Readings in Linguistics.* 2nd ed. Baltimore: American Council of Learned Societies, Art Litho.

Katz, J. J. 1964. Semi-Sentences. In *The Structure of Language,* eds. J. A. Fodor and J. J. Katz, pp. 400–416. Englewood Cliffs, N.J.: P.-H.

Katz, J. J., and P. M. Postal. 1964. *An Integrated Theory of Linguistic Descriptions.* Cambridge, Mass.: M.I.T. Press.

Kellogg, W. N., and L. A. Kellogg. 1933. *The Ape and the Child.* New York: McGraw.

Labov, W., and P. Cohen. 1967. *Systematic Relations of Standard and Non-Standard Rules in the Grammars of Negro Speakers.* Project Literacy Reports, no. 8. Mimeo. Ithaca, N.Y.: Cornell U.

Lees, R. B. 1960. *The Grammar of English Nominalizations.* The Hague: Mouton.

Lenneberg, E. H. 1964a. A Biological Perspective of Language. In *New Directions in the Study of Language,* ed. E. H. Lenneberg, pp. 65–88. Cambridge, Mass.: M.I.T. Press.

––––––. 1964b. Speech as a Motor Skill with Special Reference to Non-Aphasic Disorders. *Monogr. Soc. Res. Child Develpm.* 29:115–26.

––––––. 1967. *Biological Foundations of Language.* New York: Wiley.

Lenneberg, E. H., I. A. Nichols, and E. F. Rosenberger. 1964. Primitive

Stages of Language Development in Mongolism. *Proc. Assoc. Res. nerv. ment. Disease* 42:119–37. Cited in Lenneberg, 1967.

Livant, W. H. 1961. Productive Grammatical Operations: I: The Noun-Compounding of 5-year-olds. *Lg. Lrning* 12:15–26.

McCarthy, D. 1954. Language Development in Children. In *Manual of Child Psychology*, 2nd ed., ed. L. Carmichael, pp. 492–630. New York: Wiley.

McCawley, J. 1968. The Role of Semantics in a Grammar. In *Universals in Linguistic Theory*, eds. E. Bach and R. T. Harms, pp. 125–69. New York: H. R. & W.

Maclay, H., and M. Sleator. 1960. Responses to Language: Judgments of Grammaticalness. *IJAL* 26:275–82.

McMahon, L. E. 1963. Grammatical Analysis as a Part of Understanding a Sentence. Ph.D. thesis, Harvard U. Cited in G. A. Miller, 1964.

McNeill, D. 1966a. Developmental Psycholinguistics. In *The Genesis of Language*, eds. F. Smith and G. A. Miller, pp. 15–84. Cambridge, Mass.: M.I.T. Press.

———. 1966b. The Creation of Language by Children. In *Psycholinguistics Papers*, eds. J. Lyons and R. J. Wales, pp. 99–115. Edinburgh: Edin. U. P.

Marchand, H. 1966. *The Categories and Types of Present-Day English Word-Formation*. University, Ala.: U. of Ala. Pr.

Marks, L., and G. A. Miller. 1964. The Role of Semantic and Syntactic Constraints in the Memorization of English Sentences. *J. verb. Learn. verb. Behav.* 3:1–5.

Mehler, J. 1963. Some Effects of Grammatical Transformations on the Recall of English Sentences. *J. verb. Learn. verb. Behav.* 2:346–51.

Mehler, J., and P. Carey. 1967. Role of Surface and Base Structure in the Perception of Sentences. *J. verb. Learn. verb. Behav.* 6:335–38.

Menyuk, P. 1969. *Sentences Children Use*. Cambridge, Mass.: M.I.T. Press.

Miller, G. A. 1962. Some Psychological Studies of Grammar. *Amer. Psychologist* 17:748–62.

———. 1964. Language and Psychology. In *New Directions in the Study of Language*, ed. E. H. Lenneberg, pp. 89–107. Cambridge, Mass.: M.I.T. Press.

Miller, G. A., K. McKean, and D. Slobin. n.d. Experiment cited in G. A. Miller, 1962, pp. 757–59.

Miller, G. A., and S. Isard. 1963. Some Perceptual Consequences of Linguistic Rules. *J. verb. Learn. verb. Behav.* 2:217–28.

Miller, G. A., and K. McKean. 1964. A Chronometric Study of Some Relations Between Sentences. *quart. J. exp. Psychol.* 16:297–300.

Miller, W., and S. Ervin. 1964. The Development of Grammar in Child Language. *Monogr. Soc. Res. Child Develpm.* 29:9–34.

Nida, E. A. 1949. *Morphology: The Descriptive Analysis of Words*. 2nd ed. Ann Arbor, Mich.: U. of Mich. Pr.

Osgood, C. E. 1966. Language Universals and Psycholinguistics. In *Universals of Language*, 2nd ed., ed. J. H. Greenberg, pp. 236–54. Cambridge, Mass.: M.I.T. Press.

Pfafflin, S. M. 1961. Grammatical Judgments of Computer-Generated Word Sequences. Mimeo. Murray Hill, N.J.: Bell Telephone Laboratories.

Postal, P. M. 1968. Epilogue to *English Transformational Grammar*, by R. A. Jacobs and P. S. Rosenbaum. Waltham, Mass.: Blaisdell.

Putnám, H. 1961. Some Issues in the Theory of Grammar. In *Proceedings of Symposia in Applied Mathematics*. Vol. 12. Structure of Language and Its Mathematical Aspects, ed. R. Jakobson, pp. 25–42. Providence, R.I.: Am. Math.

Savin, H. B., and E. Perchonock. 1965. Grammatical Structure and the Immediate Recall of English Sentences. *J. verb. Learn. verb. Behav.* 4:348–53.

Shipley, E. F., C. S. Smith, and L. R. Gleitman. 1969. A Study in the Acquisition of Language: Free Responses to Commands. *Language* 45:322–42.

Skinner, B. F. 1957. *Verbal Behavior.* New York: Appleton.

Sperry, R. W. 1968. Hemisphere Deconnection and Unity in Conscious Awareness. *Amer. Psychologist* 23:723–33.

Stolz, W. S. 1967. A Study of the Ability to Decode Grammatically Novel Sentences. *J. verb. Learn. verb. Behav.* 6:867–73.

Sutherland, N. S. 1966. Discussion of J. Fodor and M. Garrett, Some Reflections on Competence and Performance. In *Psycholinguistics Papers*, eds. J. Lyons and R. J. Wales, pp. 154–62. Edinburgh: Edin. U. P.

Wason, P. C. 1961. Response to Affirmative and Negative Binary Statements. *Brit. J. Psychol.* 52:133–42.

Webster's New International Dictionary of the English Language. 2nd ed., unabridged. 1960. Eds. W. A. Neilson, T. A. Knott, and P. W. Carhart. Springfield, Mass.: Merriam.

Whorf, B. L. 1956. *Language, Thought, and Reality: Selected Writings of Benjamin Lee Whorf.* Ed. J. B. Carroll. Cambridge, Mass.: M.I.T. Press.

Yngve, V. H. 1960. A Model and an Hypothesis for Language Structure. *Proc. Amer. Phil. Soc.* 104:444–66.

Ziff, P. 1964. On Understanding "Understanding Utterances." In *The Structure of Language*, eds. J. A. Fodor and J. Katz, pp. 390–400. Englewood Cliffs, N.J.: P.-H.

Index